Courting

in

Alabama

*When Lawyers Take Over
a State's Politics*

by
Winthrop E. Johnson

Prescott Press, Inc.

Prescott Press, Inc.
P.O. Box 53788
Lafayette, Louisiana 70505

Library of Congress Card Catalog Number 98-67877
ISBN 0-933451-41-5

Contents

Acknowledgments

Many people deserve thanks in the making of this book. First, I am thankful that it was such an interesting historical event. I thank God for opening the eyes of the Alabama electorate during the election of 1994 and its aftermath. I want to thank Perry Hooper, Sr. for stepping out of semi-retirement and stepping up to the plate to do something that no one thought could be done. I am thankful for his years of public service to the State of Alabama, and I am glad he has finally received the recognition he richly deserves for changing Alabama politics forever. I am thankful to those Hooper called his "Patrick Henry" lawyers, who opposed the "trial lawyer" juggernaut. That team, Bert Jordan, Glenn Murdock, Al Agricola, and Rusty Johnston, as well as all the associates and partners who assisted them during their many hours of work, worked many "all-nighters" responding to the legal machinations of the trial lawyers. I want to thank the main players in the Hooper campaign team, Jack Campbell, Sam Duvall, and Scott Whiteley, whose hard work and commitment helped Hooper to overcome incredible odds. I want to thank my wife, who endured much during this organized chaos called a political campaign and the litigation that followed. Finally, I want to thank Sonny Hornsby and the trial lawyers for being so stubborn. Without them, there would be no story. I am glad that the people of Alabama have now been educated in a marvelous and dramatic way about the legal world, the judiciary, and elections. I hope and pray that they always guard their right to vote.

Introduction

On 17 November 1994, I sat in a courtroom in Montgomery, Alabama, and watched as a judge changed the rules of counting votes—after the election had already occurred! The counting of illegitimate, absentee ballots had always been notorious in Alabama, but it was normally done under cover of night. I watched as it was done openly and unashamedly. I knew it was not out of principled objection to the law as it existed before the election. The purpose of the court action was specifically to insure the election of one man who had lost the chief justice seat of the Alabama Supreme Court by less than 300 votes. The court action occurred on the day that the secretary of state planned to count the votes. A "legal" coup occurred before my very eyes.

This book tells the story of the election that lead up to that court action and the events that followed, as both sides sought to use the courts to uphold or overturn the judge's decision. I followed the matter very closely because I had helped with the Republican chief justice candidate's campaign. He was the challenger whose victory was being stolen by the Democratic incumbent.

Veteran political analysts at the time called the Alabama Supreme Court chief justice election of 1994 the dirtiest political campaign they had ever seen. If they exaggerated, they had good reason. This was not a normal political race for the legislature or the governorship. It was a race for the office of chief justice of the Alabama Supreme Court, the highest judicial office in the state, the administrative head of the state court system. For many, judicial campaigns were not supposed to be so rancorous. They were supposed to be staid, noncontroversial, low budget races between two candidates who essentially held the same position on most issues. The two candidates were supposed to remain "dignified."

One veteran reporter wrote in an editorial about the "good ole days," when the judicial candidate simply showed up at rallies and passed out cards and spent, at most, $10,000 on his campaign. Such a scenario made it sound as if whoever wanted to be a judge was able to become one, no matter what his principles or character. All he had to do was obtain the endorsement of the establishment of the Alabama Democratic party. The "good ole days" never existed, except within the confines of the one-party system to which Alabama had become accustomed since the days of Reconstruction. It was a time when a few lawyers in the Democratic party chose who would be a justice on an appellate court. Once that nominee had the backing of the Democratic party, it was unquestionable that person would be elected. The Republican party had not won a seat on a state appellate court in Alabama for over 100 years.

I agree that judges should be above some of the partisan rancor that occurs in many other types of elections. However, in a society divided by a variety of viewpoints, religions, and opinions, eliminating partisanship means eliminating the viewpoint of a large bloc of voters in a particular jurisdiction. Perhaps, at one time, the philosophical distinction between judicial candidates would have been minuscule. But that was before the days of "judicial activism" and the big money that could be gained from enormous punitive damage awards. Judicial activism was best known in the federal courts. Gigantic punitive damage awards were common in Alabama. Remember the BMW case, in which a jury awarded a doctor in Birmingham four million dollars for his purchase of a new BMW that had a touched-up paint job. Yale Law School Professor George Priest studied Alabama's punitive damage system and concluded: "It used to be that a million dollar verdict distinguished a plaintiff lawyer. Now in Alabama that's considered a defense verdict."

The self-appointed autonomy of federal judges led to a philosophical liberal activism. The self-appointed autonomy of Alabama judges led to a tendency toward chaos in Alabama's tort law. The Alabama courts were consistent on one subject—using the Alabama Constitution to strike down tort reform. While federal judges followed what they thought were the best liberal judgments for the so-called "good" of society, Alabama judges seemed to follow the money—the money that lawyers earned from huge judgments, that is. I'm not saying that all the judges personally profited from the judgments. It was simply the way things were done for members of the club, the bar association. Everyone on the bar profited. As long as no one made a fuss about tort reform, that profitable business of lawsuits and judgments would continue. Until the political campaigns of 1994 and 1995, an accusation of selfish interest, even corruption, against the lawyers in the system seemed like speculative vitriol. After November 1994, such an accusation seemed to be proven on a daily basis before the eyes of everyone in the state of Alabama. Ironically, in Alabama's 1994 chief justice election, the federal courts had to come to the rescue of the winning candidate.

Another example of the problem in Alabama's judiciary was forum shopping. There was an incredible disparity in punitive damage awards within the state. Plaintiff lawyers knew the hot spots and would target business for tort actions in those counties. A jury in one county might throw out a tort case, while a jury in another county might award a multi-million dollar judgment in the very same type of case. The latter type of jury inhabited the poorest rural counties of Alabama, and there were many theories as to why they awarded amazing judgments. No matter the reason, it angered the business community for lawyers to take advantage of certain juries to make millions for their clients and themselves. The legal advice to a company that was sued in such a county was almost always "settle"; it did not matter how meritorious the company's defense.

State court system statistics showed that from 1992 to 1996 civil suits actually dropped in number in Alabama. Some counties, however, did not follow that trend; their filings increased: Barbour-150%, Bullock-140%, Greene-117%, Lowndes-91%, Pickens-81%, Chambers-77%, Fayette-70%, and Sumter-54%. In Barbour County, juries had awarded over

100 million dollars in civil suits since 1990. In a December 4, 1995 Montgomery Advertiser article, David Nix, the Barbour County circuit clerk, said, "When one person heard about someone else getting a lot of money in a suit, they started thinking maybe they could get some, too." In the latter part of 1996, the Alabama State Bar initiated the unprecedented action of investigating the juries in Barbour County. Not long after that investigation began, the Barbour County Circuit Judge announced that he would resign at the end of the year. In his court Alabama's best known plaintiff trial lawyer, Jere Beasley, had obtained some of his largest damage verdicts.

The most influential lawyers in the state of Alabama may have chosen the Democratic candidate for an appellate court election. (Or perhaps the ones with the most to gain from making sure the "right" candidate ran for that judicial office did the choosing.) However, with the big-money verdicts handed down in Alabama, it appeared as if the judge became the protector of the financial interest of one segment of society—the lawyers. That is how much of the electorate in Alabama came to see it, at any rate. Sometimes that financial interest took precedence over the interests of the rest of the state. That financial interest was always veiled in arguments about the constitution and the fundamental rights of the "victim," but as time went by, and judgments got higher, that argument became more and more difficult to sell. The lawyers did not want to give up the playground that they had controlled for so long. They claimed to know better than the public what was in the best interest of the public. So what if these big judgments helped line their pockets? They were preserving "justice," pursuing the bad guys (meaning insurance companies and "big" business). Today, asking a lawyer for his opinion on tort reform is like asking a drug dealer for his opinion on the war on drugs. His financial interest may be too prominent in his mind for him to give an objective response.

So, were the judges in Alabama liberals? Most lawyers in Alabama would tell you they were far from liberal in their political views. Yet many used the so-called "victim" of corporate greed to fleece corporations and insurance companies out of millions of dollars in questionable lawsuits. It was socialism by judicial decree. For the lawyers, preserving the award for the "victim" was the preeminent concern of the appellate judge. This was not judicial activism because Alabama, they claimed, had done it this way for so long. Anyway, the jury made the award, making it "sacrosanct" for the trial lawyer, and, in his mind, it means he can deny all responsibility. In Alabama, "victimhood" had risen from the shameful status it had always held and had become the key to fortunes beyond one's wildest dreams—for the victim and for the lawyers. The trial lawyers reached deep to protect their playground. Between 1990 and 1994, Alabama trial lawyers contributed $5.1 million to state candidates. More than a million dollars came from five Birmingham lawyers, according to the American Tort Reform Association.

The 1994 judicial race involved a great deal of money. The plaintiff trial lawyers were very concerned about their ability to obtain contingent fees from huge damage judgments. The percentage they received from such awards ranged from 30 to 50 percent. They also alleged that any change in the system was an attack on the jury system and the rights of plaintiffs. Business interests were afraid that they were facing unfair judgments, which were increasing in quantity and dollar value in the court system. Over $1 million was spent on the chief justice race alone. The 1994 election was not lacking in contentious issues. It descended to personal, scurrilous attacks by one side. It ended only after an eleven-month litigation delay by the losing side.

This book is the story of the election that illustrates better than any other election in Alabama's history, perhaps in American history, the critical issues at stake in our judicial system. Perhaps the most interesting thing about this story is that many of the issues raised by the challenger during his campaign were not fully exposed until after the election was over. Issues like the misuse of the courts for personal gain (political or financial), the power of lawyers to change laws for their benefit, the arrogance and determination of one party in power to stay in power, and the incest of campaign contributions and political affiliations that bonds judges and lawyers were brought to light. It demonstrated the errors that result from one party's monopolistic control over a state's civil government, and the power that money, political affiliation, and loyalty to the "law-yer club" can have over judges, the court system, and judicial campaigns. It is the story of the Alabama chief justice election of 1994-1995.

Because I was so close to one of the players in this con-troversy, I have tried to quote others as much as possible. Perhaps that will help the reader to accept some of the facts I will be recounting. Otherwise, the reader may have difficulty believing my story. I have quoted extensively from newspaper articles, editorials, and television news statements. Watch as the facts develop in this book, and make your own decision as to whether my opinion about one particular party and the legal profession is correct. I think it will open your eyes.

The Players

I had known "the judge" for nearly all my life. My dad played cards with Perry Hooper, Sr. at the Montgomery Country Club. Hooper had also done business with my dad, who had been a stockbroker with Merrill Lynch. He had been active in Republican politics since the early fifties. By "active" I mean he made speeches and worked to build the party in a state that had practically no elected Republicans until 1964 and the Goldwater sweep. Some like to say that they were in the Republican party before it was popular. I like to say that in the late fifties and early sixties, Perry Hooper, Sr. *was* the Republican party, at least in the Montgomery area. He had a bulldog character. He told me many times that he never ran from a fight. When he was in his sixties, he saw some punk bumping into people and accosting them as they walked down the aisle at Food World. Judge Hooper let this punk know to stop. He even had to get physical with him. Judge Hooper didn't run from political fights, either.

In 1964, Hooper was the first Republican elected to public office in Montgomery County in 100 years. But that election was not a fluke because he continued to be reelected by a solid majority in a county that, since he retired, has yet to elect another Republican office holder. Everyone called Perry Hooper, Sr., "the judge." He was probate judge of Montgomery County for ten years and circuit judge of Montgomery County for eight years. He was elected probate judge in 1964. He ran for and won reelection in 1970. He ran for and was elected circuit judge in 1974. He ran for and won reelection in that office in 1976 and 1982. He retired as circuit judge in 1983. There was talk, at that time, of his running for U.S. Senate, but other circumstances which I will discuss later, intervened.

The judge was of a generous spirit, sometimes almost recklessly so, as you will understand when I explain the Jerry Hamilton situation. He earned criticism in 1970 for not giving any jail time to the State Treasurer, Melba Till Allen, who was prosecuted under the new Ethics Law. He thought the law was vague and found Mrs. Allen a sympathetic figure. When I left the Air Force in January 1994, I went to Judge Hooper to see if he knew anyone in Montgomery who might hire an attorney. As I sat with him in his office, he waved his hand for me to follow him and said, "Come on." He took me upstairs and showed me some unused office space. Judge Hooper offered me an office, rent-free, to help me get started in private practice. His generosity required little thought; it was second nature to him. He acted on his Christian convictions when people needed help.

Judge Hooper had white hair, and he truly acted in kindness to people in need. When I started working in his building, he had a black man who did some part time work maintaining and cleaning the building. He respected someone getting out and trying to make a living. If you tried, he would do whatever he could to help you. He often referred to the Bible: "We're supposed to visit those in prison," or "Jesus said to love our neighbor." He truly believed the Bible was the Word of God and tried to apply it to his life. He thought a great deal about evangelism, which was a major part of his motivation to share the gospel with others. Once, as Jack Campbell, Hooper's campaign manager, Scott Whitely, a worker in Hooper's campaign, and I walked with him after he had bought us lunch, he spontaneously began singing a gospel tune called "Down by the Riverside," a song about getting baptized and laying all one's burdens down. He took the time to explain to us that he liked that song, even though he was Presbyterian. He was a strong believer in conservative principles, by which he meant the ideas and philosophies of the founding fathers that made this country great. "Classic America" he called it. He was a free market advocate. He was sixty-eight years old and sometimes acted it. He had been a judge for eighteen years between 1965 and 1983 and a lawyer for over forty years. However, if you explained a situation to him that presented complex legal questions, he instinctively found the heart of the matter in a flash. He saw legal and political matters clearly when others merely saw a morass. Such acute insight banished any doubts about his mental abilities being affected by his age.

He did not hire me as an associate, but he said I could share some of the business that came through his door. He was a sixty-eight-year-old retired judge, and he did not need to have a booming practice. So I thought his offer quite generous. Not long after I began working in his office, Judge Hooper mentioned his intentions to run for chief justice of the Alabama Supreme Court. I can't remember how many times during the legal battle after the election that he said he hadn't run so that HE could be chief justice. He decided to run for the office because he wanted to make a difference. Otherwise, as he often said during the legal battle after the election, he would have retired and set off for the beach to walk in the sand with his lovely wife, Marilyn. He turned sixty-nine on 8 April 1994, the date of qualification for the Republican primary. In Alabama, no one can run for or be appointed to a judgeship after turning seventy. It was his last chance to run for judicial office.

Judge Hooper was conservative in his economic views, favored family values, and was very religious. I liked his philosophy. When he decided to run for the office of chief justice, he said, "Based on some recent actions and decisions by Alabama's judiciary, I'm very concerned about the direction in which the judiciary is headed." He strongly believed in judicial restraint. He said a thousand times: "The court cannot strike down a law passed by the legislature of the state of Alabama unless it is violative of the fundamental law beyond a reasonable doubt." That was his attitude toward law. Judges must interpret the law, not make the law. Making law is the job of the legislature. The Constitution of Alabama of 1901 strongly affirmed the principle of separation of powers, and Judge Hooper loved to quote it.[1]

Judge Hooper thought Montesquieu's exposition of this principle to be the most influential on the founders.[2] He was vehement in his arguments against the usurpation by the judiciary of the prerogatives of the legislature. As the Alabama

Constitution and Montesquieu put it, such usurpation resulted in tyranny and the destruction of the rule of law. He considered it vital that the legislative and judiciary branches remain separate, and, while he understood that the legislature could be tyrannical, he saw the threat to separation coming primarily from the judiciary. Specifically, he saw Alabama courts threatening the Constitution of Alabama, the laws of Alabama, race relations in Alabama, the business climate in Alabama, and job security in Alabama. It was not until after the general election of 8 November 1994 that the populace of the state received a much-needed education in just how badly the lawyers and the courts could wreak havoc in Alabama.

Seeing such serious problems develop, he decided to leave a comfortable judicial retirement and run for statewide office. He was told that he would no doubt lose and be savaged by the trial lawyers in the process. He quoted Sophocles, with a twinkle in his eye: "One must wait until the evening to see how splendid the day has been." Throughout the campaign and the ensuing legal battle, he often quoted that line. Judge Hooper's battle eventually proved the truth of that statement.

I offered to help with his campaign. I was something of a neophyte in Alabama politics, having served in the Air Force outside the state for five and a half years. Before that, my only experience with a political campaign involved two city council elections in which I had worked as a volunteer. I knew that, in 1993, a Democratic attorney general had indicted and prosecuted the first Republican governor of Alabama since Reconstruction. This fact reflected plenty about Alabama politics, but I had much to learn.

Judge Hooper kicked off his campaign with announcements in Montgomery, the capitol of the state, Birmingham, Huntsville, Tuscaloosa, Mobile, and Dothan. The newspapers quoted key statements from Hooper's press releases. The 8 April *Tuscaloosa News* reported:

> I am gravely concerned about the direction of the state's highest court. I am concerned that direction is away from the mainstream people of Alabama . . . Alabama is twelfth in the nation "when it comes to million-

dollar damage suits and we ranked as one of the top in
the country with $65 million awarded in damages last
year . . . Hooper said he is reentering politics at the
urging of friends and family and because "if a battle is
to be won, you have got to be willing to wage the
fight."

The *Huntsville Times* reported Hooper's observation that
"civil verdicts are more excessive and more unrealistic than
ever before in the history of this state." He went on to note,
"Such court decisions hurt business and, more importantly,
cost Alabamians jobs while the main benefactor is some trial
lawyer who literally becomes a multimillionaire overnight."

The *Birmingham News* reported: "Hooper said he would
not have been a part of 'a secret settlement' to end a lawsuit
aimed at putting more blacks on the state's appellate courts."
The *Montgomery Advertiser* reported "When the Legislature
passes laws, Perry Hooper would be very, very reluctant to
declare them unconstitutional."

High civil damage awards, jobs, and the state's economic
status, a secret affirmative-action type settlement of a lawsuit
involving the state's appellate courts, and the separation of
powers between the legislature and the judiciary were the issues around which the campaign ultimately revolved. They
laid the groundwork for a less-than-peaceful election fight for
the five seats up for election on the Alabama Supreme Court
in 1994. More issues, however, would be revealed as time went
by, than Hooper realized when the campaign began.

Hooper also referred to "battle." The races for seats on the
state's highest court had become battles, in recent history, in
Alabama. The key antagonists in those battles were the business community and the plaintiff trial lawyer community. The
business community considered the litigation climate in Alabama intolerable. In 1987, during the administration of the
first Republican governor of Alabama since reconstruction,
after so much tort reform legislation had been enacted into law
around the country, Alabama followed the lead of other states
and passed tort reform legislation. However, over the following seven years, those reforms were quickly undermined as the

Alabama Supreme Court struck them down as unconstitutional.

For over a hundred years, only Democrats had served on the Alabama Supreme Court. In 1992, the chairman of the Montgomery County Republican Executive Committee, Mark Anderson, ran for a seat on the supreme court. The campaign was bloody for Anderson who had little money and who was bludgeoned by his opponent's campaign commercials alleging he had been sued for malpractice and numerous improprieties as a lawyer. Anderson was sued during the election campaign, and after the general election was over, nothing came of that lawsuit. It only costs about $100 to file a lawsuit against someone, and if filed in the summer before an election, it will not come to trial before the date of the general election. The plaintiff can always let the lawsuit die a natural death without expending too much effort or time, and would rarely face inquiry as to whether the filing was frivolous. Nothing came of the lawsuit against Anderson, but it provided excellent campaign fodder for his opponent.

That was the type of battle that Hooper faced by entering this race. Friends and family told him that the trial lawyers would do anything to protect their asset, Sonny Hornsby, the Democratic incumbent heavily backed by plaintiff trial lawyers. They would trash Hooper and his family. Did he really want to put himself and his family through that grief? He faced an incumbent who was backed by the most powerful, ruthless, well-financed special interest group in the state. The odds of Hooper winning were low, to say the least. Yet Hooper could not simply sit back and let the state be controlled by such interests. As it turned out, no one could have imagined how far that group was prepared to go to assure Hooper's defeat.

Sonny Hornsby was a former president of the Alabama State Bar Association. More importantly, for this election, he was also a former president of the Alabama Trial Lawyers Association. In fact, he had lobbied the legislature against tort reform when it was being debated in the mid-1980s. Therefore, he was the darling of the trial lawyers, which meant his campaign got big money from the trial lawyers. It also meant he would do whatever it took to win.

Hornsby was an up-and-comer in the Alabama Democratic party in the sixties. In 1960, when he was a University of Alabama Law School student, he attended the Democratic National Convention. He went as a committed delegate of John F. Kennedy's. However, on the first ballot, he voted for Arkansas Governor Orval Faubus. Faubus was governor of Arkansas when the federal government had to send in the National Guard to allow blacks into a Little Rock High School. Even though Faubus' name had not been placed in nomination, Hornsby said he voted for Faubus as a "protest against advocates of forced integration." He planned to vote for Kennedy on the second round, but Kennedy was elected on the first round, so Hornsby never had a chance to vote for him. Hornsby said that Faubus' win in the Democratic primary for governor reaffirmed his "faith in a great Southern governor." After his graduation from law school, Governor John Patterson appointed Hornsby as an attorney in the state insurance department.

Apparently those of his own party found Hornsby somewhat abrasive, perhaps a little dictatorial. During the campaign for chief justice in 1994, Hornsby provided telling examples of his personality. In the mid sixties, when George Wallace was "king" in Alabama, Hornsby was something of a dissenter within the Democratic party. As a young state senator, he publicly opposed Wallace, calling his antics inflammatory. His opposition to Wallace was not necessarily a philosophical difference on race. It was more of a pragmatic disagreement. He said that Wallace's actions caused more attention to be directed toward the state's racial politics than if Wallace had not been such a lightning rod for controversy. It was a rare Democrat in those days who criticized George Wallace publicly. In 1965, he told the Alabama Senate: "What we need is a real stand, not a grandstand. The strategy employed by the governor has set our state back 100 years." He called Wallace's racial politics "bluff, blunder and backdown."

In spite of his criticism of Wallace, Hornsby was no shrinking violet when it came to racial politics. In response to a resolution that recommended local school boards await the outcome of a federal civil rights suit before signing civil rights "compliance agreements," he told the Alabama Senate: "We ain't gonna pass any nigger resolutions." He also sponsored a bill to allow churches to eject anyone they considered trespassers. The purpose of that bill was to make sure white churches could keep blacks off their premises. The Hornsby of the 1960's would never have supported a settlement of a lawsuit that would impose a quota of a particular race on the appellate courts of Alabama; in 1990 Hornsby did. Hornsby did not run for a second term as state senator. Many thought he saw his inevitable defeat because of his public opposition to Wallace.

Sonny Hornsby seemed to change his political views to fit the time period in which he found himself. Perry Hooper, on the other hand, remained unchanged. As probate judge of Alabama in the 1960, his conservative principles compelled him to believe that a poll tax was not unconstitutional, but he held no animus toward the black race, and he supported their right to vote. Unlike Hornsby, he would not have made a speech using the term "nigger." In 1994, Hooper still thought a poll tax was not unconstitutional but supported everyone's right to vote.

Until 1988, Hornsby disappeared from the political scene in order to, as he described it, perfect his skills as a trial attorney. In 1988, he ran for chief justice on a platform to reform the juvenile justice system. At that time, juvenile crime was beginning to get out of hand. Hornsby picked up on a truly hot button issue. During his term as chief justice, he confirmed his affection for large damage verdicts. He even argued in his written dissents that Alabama should allow *additur*. *Additur* is the ability of a trial judge or appellate judge to add to a damage award when that judge thinks that the jury awarded too few damages to a plaintiff. That doctrine was radical, even for the Alabama Supreme Court, which had historically rejected such a doctrine. Low damages verdicts were never a problem in Alabama.

Judge Hooper was a plaintiff trial lawyer in private practice. There is nothing wrong with being a plaintiff trial lawyer. It is a noble part of a noble profession. Therefore, when I use the term "trial lawyer" in this book, I use it to refer to a politicized group of attorneys which uses its political and financial muscle to protect unlimited lawsuit damages. This group advocates with zeal and without regard for either the merit of the argument or the detriment to the people and economy of Alabama that unlimited money damages may impose.

The Alabama Trial Lawyers Association (ATLA) is highly politicized, but that does not mean every member of ATLA is a member of the elite group I will be referring to in this book. It does, however, mean that their dues go to advance the particular political agenda I'll discuss. It also means that ATLA overwhelmingly supports Democratic candidates for office. The Democratic party is much more attentive to the demands and desires of the plaintiff trial lawyers than the republican party. In fact, the Republican party sponsored tort reform legislation in the U.S. Congress. The Democrats almost uniformly oppose such legislation. Even though Judge Hooper himself was a trial lawyer, ATLA was the leader of the attack upon him during the campaign.

I attended a Montgomery County Trial Lawyers Association meeting not long after leaving the Air Force. As an Air Force lawyer, I was accustomed to being around a very professional group of people in the legal community. A couple of minutes into the talk, the guest speaker, the president of ATLA, looked around the room as if he had forgotten to mention something and said, "Oh, by the way, I assume everyone in here is a Democrat." He was wrong, of course, but I was so shocked that I said nothing and decided the wise course was to listen and learn about this fellow and the other lawyers who associated with him. I was not impressed with someone who would so politicize the legal profession that he simply assumed that everyone listening to his voice was a member of a particular political party. To me, his assumption that everyone in a particular legal organization was of a particular political persuasion was unprofessional and the height of presumption.

When Hornsby was asked about Hooper's comments about Alabama's legal problems, he replied with the familiar ATLA line that Alabama has no problems. He said, "We are in the mainstream of American jurisprudence today." He said that *Forbes* magazine had listed Alabama in a different light from what Judge Hooper portrayed. Never mind that *Forbes* had described Alabama as "tort hell." Judge Hooper obtained his statistics from a national weekly legal newspaper called the *National Law Journal.* Hornsby also said that the Alabama Supreme Court had reduced some damage awards by as much as 66% and had nullified others. That meant that as far as Hornsby was concerned the Alabama Supreme Court, not the legislature, had the power to reduce exorbitant awards to the amount it considered appropriate. Every shrewd businessman who read that statement wondered whether he should get ready with campaign contributions for the incumbent judges on the supreme court in order to prevent his business from being gouged by such damage awards.

It would be shocking to think that an incumbent chief justice of a state's highest court would have such a crass view of the legal system. I would not make the claim that Sonny Hornsby had extortion of the business community in mind when he made that statement. However, the dynamics of the campaign contribution process among businesses, lawyers, and judges, and the appearances of impropriety that process creates were a couple of the major themes of this election campaign. A state supreme court can make or break a business when reviewing a big lawsuit. The supreme court can make a lawyer's career when deciding a case that lawyer has filed with the supreme court.

A business in an Alabama court faced wildly unpredictable judgments. While I was still in the Air Force, I spoke with a man whose son had a business and was being sued for inadequate workmanship on some homes in Macon County. He asked me if there was anything a person could do to a lawyer who admitted he had no case against his son's business, but who continued to pursue the case in court anyway. He said that his lawyer had told him that, because the lawsuit was in Macon County, their only option was to settle the case. Obviously, a father's opinion his son in a lawsuit should be taken with a grain of salt, but it is distressing when people have the viewpoint that no matter how meritorious a defendant's case, some counties will always find for the plaintiff.

The BMW case educated me, also. A doctor in Birmingham, Alabama had purchased a brand new BMW for approximately $40,000. During the first year he owned the car, he took it to an auto detailing shop and the shop foreman told him that the car had been repainted. The man sued BMW. BMW had repainted the car because it received acid rain damage during the boat trip from Germany. BMW had examined the laws across the country and had found that the strictest law in any state at that time allowed for a safe harbor for automobile dealers. According to those safe harbors, sellers of cars need not notify the customer of the repairs, if those repairs equaled 3% or less of the price of the car. In other words, if the repair performed by the manufacturer/dealer cost 3% or less of the price of the car, the dealer was not duty-bound to inform the purchaser of the repair before selling the car. Alabama had no comparable law, but there was nothing in Alabama's statutes or cases that indicated it would take a different position than other states. BMW spent $300 repainting the car, which placed the repair well within the safe harbor of 3 percent of the price of the car. The former owner of the BMW dealership testified that he thought the car's value had been reduced by approximately $4000. A jury awarded the doctor four million dollars in punitive damages. The Alabama Supreme Court reduced the verdict to two million dollars. However, the United States Supreme Court remanded the case to the Alabama Supreme Court in 1996, saying that the two million dollar punitive damage award was grossly excessive and violated due process granted to defendants under the Fourteenth Amendment to the United States Constitution. It was the first decision in the history of the United States Supreme Court to reverse the punitive damage award of a state court.

Sonny Hornsby did not vote on any case involving tort reform legislation that came before the Alabama Supreme Court during his tenure as chief justice. That does not mean he had no influence on the other justices. It means he felt his partisan lobbying work against the legislation would color any vote he cast in such a case and would make it look as if his decision were predetermined. He did not need to vote. The supreme court had no trouble garnering the required votes to strike down much of the legislation. During the 1988 race for chief justice, he was asked what his position toward the 1987 tort reform legislation would be if he won the seat. He replied, "It's a done deal. The legislature has spoken." In the next five years under his leadership as chief justice, the supreme court undid most of that "done deal." During the campaign of 1994, Hornsby came to symbolize the entire trial lawyer/judge/campaign contribution/large damage award connection that became a major issue in the election and one of the keys to Hornsby's downfall.

Notes

1. "In the government of this state, except in the instances in this Constitution hereinafter expressly directed or permitted, the legislative department shall never exercise the executive and judicial powers, or either of them; the executive shall never exercise the legislative and judicial powers, or either of them; the judicial shall never exercise the legislative and executive powers, or either of them; to the end that it may be a government of laws and not of men." 1901 Ala. Const., Section 43.

2. "Again, there is no liberty, if the judiciary power be not separated from the legislative and executive. Were it joined with the legislative, the life and liberty of the subject would be exposed to arbitrary control; for the judge would be then the legislator. Were it joined to the executive power, the judge might behave with violence and oppression. . . . There would be an end of everything, were the same man or the same body, whether of the nobles or of the people, to exercise those three powers, that of enacting laws, that of executing the public resolutions and of trying the causes of individuals."

Montesquieu, "The Spirit of Laws," as published by the Colonial Press, 1900, quoted in *The Christian History of the Constitution of the United States of America,* compiled by Verna M. Hall, edited by Joseph Allan Montgomery. (San Francisco: Foundation for American Christian Education, 1966) p. 135.

Chapter Two

The Campaign

The media has the idea that a judicial election should be very sedate, no rocking the boat. That's how it had always been in Alabama, except in 1988 and 1992. The media seemed to think that any sign of disagreement would indicate to the public some type of problem in the courts. It would undermine the trust the public had in the judicial system. This attitude persisted even after the thirty years of controversial rulings by the federal courts. People had been disagreeing with the courts on a massive scale, especially in the South. To say that disagreeing with the courts, publicly, would denigrate the courts in the eyes of the public was the epitome of blindness. It was the responsibility of the courts to maintain the appropriate dignity. If those courts did not apply the law properly, the people were right not to trust them. But, that position assumes that the people have some sense. Many in the media and the legal community think the people have no sense.

The Democratic party had a historic lock on the judicial elections in Alabama. Disagreement would be minimal in such an environment. However, with the rise of the tort reform battles of the '80s, the increased power of the Alabama Republican party, and with what appeared to be politicized decisions issuing from the Alabama Supreme Court, conflict and disagreement were inevitable. The public airing of differing opinions on the role of the courts would be a healthy example of democracy in action and the education of the public as to the importance of those courts. The public is not nearly as stupid as some assume, and the courts' reputation had already been tarnished. An airing of the issues and concerns was the only way to resolve the problems and, hopefully, restore the reputation of the courts. Some who sincerely, yet naively, opposed such democratic debate worried about the reputation of the courts; others feared the ramifications of the exposure of the courts to criticism and a voting public that was becoming better educated. Many simply did not want the public to become educated about what was happening in the judicial system. That way, things could continue smoothly, as before, without disruption. The lawyers' playground could remain undisturbed.

Judge Hooper knew what issues he wanted to address, and he did not shy away from those issues. Everyone knew that tort reform and the punitive damages that a few plaintiff trial lawyers were reaping in Alabama would be a big issue. But there was also the appellate court-packing scheme, which was negotiated by the attorney general and approved by Sonny Hornsby. There was another issue involving campaign contributions that we did not even know about until a newspaper in south Alabama broke the story later during the election.

Hornsby claimed to be truly concerned about the problem of punitive damages in Alabama, even though he denied that there was a problem. He quoted some statistics that made Alabama's situation look quite rosy. He also set up a commission to look into alternative dispute resolution, like mediation and arbitration. He said, "If we can get people to settle their cases rather than having war in the courtroom, then certainly we'll have a better business climate in Alabama."[1]

I thought the chief justice had told us that the business climate in Alabama was just fine, and that all this talk about excessive punitive damages and running business out of the state was just demagoguery. He alleged that the poor business climate in Alabama was caused by business. "Sixty-four percent of the lawsuits in Alabama are brought by businesses, and ninety-eight percent of those lawsuits are settled short of trial. But with mediation, 'we want to move it back and settle that case closer to the time it's filed,' Chief Justice Hornsby said."[2] He denied that this move was in response to Hooper's challenge and concern about the business climate in Alabama. The Alabama Bar Association president "backed him up saying that the project had been in the works for years." The timing of the announcement still seemed strange. So Hooper put out a news release asking: "Why has it taken six years for Chief

Justice Hornsby to form a commission on the issue of alternative dispute resolution when alternative dispute resolution has existed for many years longer than that? This is an obvious ploy to avoid the issue of exorbitant damages and to mislead the people of our state in an election year."

Here is the history behind the appellate court-packing scheme. The problem appeared before the 1994 elections, the year that five supreme court justices' seats were up for election. In the latter part of 1993, the U.S. Justice Department told the State of Alabama that it had not obtained pre-clearance of changes to its voting laws. Under the 1965 Voting Rights Act, any time Alabama changes any law affecting its method of electing officials, it must obtain pre-clearance from the U.S. Justice Department before the new law can go into effect. In 1969, 1971, and 1975, Alabama added judicial seats to the Court of Civil Appeals, the Court of Criminal Appeals, and the Supreme Court. These changes were part of two fairly massive statutory enactments by the legislature affecting the voting laws of Alabama, and every other aspect of those changes had been sent to Washington for pre-clearance. In 1975, Alabama passed an entirely new judicial article to amend the Alabama Constitution and thoroughly change its judicial system. This change was well known and influential in the country's legal community. No one knows how the matter of the number of judgeships was left out of the pre-clearance process. No one could find the necessary paperwork. Justice Gorman Houston was so sure that the state had already obtained pre-clearance that he offered to go to Washington at his own expense and try to prove it. He did go, but the U.S. Justice Department had no paperwork either. Many were suspicious why and how something like this could happen, especially considering the timing—right before a major election of justices to the Alabama Supreme Court.

Also interesting was the fact that the two seats that would be affected by this so-called lack of pre-clearance were the seats of the two non-plaintiff trial lawyer supported justices, Houston and Maddox. These were the two most conservative justices on the court. So Hornsby informed them that if a lawsuit prevented the election in November, it would be

Maddox's seat that was affected. Houston was not up for election again until 1998.

The U.S. Justice Department decided that Alabama had not obtained pre-clearance of these changes. What were the changes? Adding judges to the appeals courts and the supreme court. It did not matter that such changes had nothing to do with the actual method of electing these judges to office. That method of selecting judges remained totally unchanged. Apparently, at that time, the Clinton Justice Department was doing everything it could to meddle in the voting laws of the states. They later did the same thing in Arizona, in counties where the popular vote did not result in the election of Native Americans to judgeships. These counties had fewer than a dozen Native American lawyers in each county at any one time. These Native Americans had always elected whites, and apparently, no Native American had ever run for judicial office.

The problem of pre-clearance set up the perfect stage in Alabama for a particular special interest group to take advantage of the problem. They filed suit on 27 January 1994 on behalf of all black people alleging that Alabama's method of at-large election of justices was inherently discriminatory and should be changed. They brought suit in federal district court for the Middle District of Alabama and added that certain parts of Alabama voting laws had not been pre-cleared by the U.S. Justice Department. It is hard to believe that some Justice Department official went through reams of pre-clearance paperwork from Alabama, from the '70s, to try to find one minor aspect that had not been pre-cleared. Nevertheless, someone found such a problem. The case was called *Hoover White v. The State of Alabama*.[3]

With a major judicial election less than a year away, the U.S. government might delay the election or even invalidate prior elections. At least, that was what the Alabama attorney general gave as the reason for settling the lawsuit so quickly. Politically, he probably wanted to avoid a district-type of election system, which would put Republicans as well as blacks on the appeals courts. District-type elections had been the solution in such cases in the past. At that time, the Democrats had a near monopoly on the courts and did not want to see any Republican elected to those offices. Hooper did not want district elections, but he also did not think the lawsuit was appropriate.

Here is how the settlement came about. On 8 December 1993, Jimmy Evans, the Alabama attorney general, sent a letter to Steven Rosenbaum of the U.S. Justice Department. Actually, Donald Watkins, a noted black civil rights attorney, wrote it. The first line read, "Alabama Attorney General James H. Evans, at the request of Alabama Supreme Court Chief Justice Sonny Hornsby, has appointed me to represent the State of Alabama in its efforts to obtain pre-clearance of Acts 987 (1969), 75 (1971) and 93-346 (1993)." Hornsby received a letter from the Alabama Lawyers Association, a black lawyers group affiliated with the Democratic party, stating their position on the at-large election system. The Alabama Lawyers Association disagreed with Watkins.

The letter from Evans to the U.S. Attorney General of the United States told of the great political strides that had been made by blacks in Alabama. Evans stated: "It is the state's position that the current at-large election system does not unnecessarily limit the opportunity of black voters to elect candidates of their choice for the reasons discussed below." He said that the political power of blacks in the state was such that there was no reason to change the present system of at-large election in the state of Alabama. The plaintiffs filed their lawsuit on 27 January 1994. Evans moved quickly to offer a settlement to the plaintiffs. On 1 February 1994, he wrote a letter to the chief justice telling him about the settlement idea. Four days is mighty quick to work up a proposed settlement of a complicated case. In that letter he noted, "I am preceding [sic] with the offer of judgment unless I hear from you to the contrary by 2:00 P.M. tomorrow." Yet, in a 24 February 1994 *Montgomery Advertiser* article on the matter, Evans denied that there had been any settlement offer. As of 1 February 1994, no one knew about the proposed settlement except Jimmy Evans and Sonny Hornsby.

It was bad enough for elected officials to try to institute an affirmative action program in the appeals courts. However, their method of accomplishing this goal was equally bad. Chief Justice Hornsby received the letter from Attorney General Jimmy Evans on 1 February 1994. On that day, he met with all the members of the appeals courts to apprise them of the settlement agreement. He told the assembled justices and judges of the plan, and Mark Montiel, a judge appointed to sit on the Court of Criminal Appeals and the only Republican on any of the appeals courts, raised an objection. Montiel was appointed by Governor Guy Hunt. The chief justice told Montiel that he considered silence best. Hornsby said that because the attorney general was acting as their attorney in a settlement matter they should keep all communications with their attorney quiet.

Hornsby said: "Well, Judge Montiel, this is simply a communication from the attorney general to his client, and those communications are normally kept secret."

Montiel said, "I believe the people of Alabama are the true client in this case. They're the ones who have been given the right to elect their own justices by the Constitution of Alabama."

At that point, Associate Justice Mark Kennedy piped up: "Mr. Chief Justice, I think it would be appropriate if you ordered Judge Montiel not to speak of this matter outside this group."

Hornsby: "Mark, that's right. I'm gonna have to tell you not to talk about this settlement proposal to anyone."

Montiel: "Mr. Chief Justice, I would just remind you that judges also have the right to freedom of speech."

After that meeting, Hornsby took Montiel aside and, in a fatherly manner, told him that he was a bright, ambitious young man, and he didn't want to ruin his future in any way. Nevertheless, Montiel held a press conference to blow the whistle on the whole scheme. Evans then delayed his planned settlement offer. Hornsby sent a letter back to Evans saying he had no objection to the settlement.

Once the controversy had died down somewhat, Evans went ahead with the settlement proposal. Interestingly, on a day not long before he had decided to run for chief justice, Judge Hooper met Lanny Vines walking down the street. Lanny Vines was one of the richest plaintiff trial lawyers in Alabama and one of the four most generous contributors to judges running for election to the state's highest court. Lanny candidly told Judge Hooper that he had helped Jimmy Evans write the settlement agreement in this case. Why would a wealthy plaintiff trial lawyer be involved in writing the settlement of a civil rights suit involving the state appellate courts?

Judge Myron Thompson, U.S. Federal District Judge for the Middle District, presided over the case. Other parties intervened in the case. The federal court set up a method by which the public could object to the settlement. Judge Hooper participated in the objection process. Before that however, Hooper held a press conference. It wasn't an ordinary press conference. Present were the three other Republican candidates for the supreme court, the most there had ever been in one judicial election since Reconstruction. Harold See, a law professor at the University of Alabama; Mark Montiel, a judge on the Court of Criminal Appeals; and B.J. Russell, a local attorney who had served as a judge on the Court of Civil Appeals, joined Judge Hooper in front of the supreme court building. All four had similar judicial philosophies, so it was an ideal opportunity to express a united front to the public, particularly on this issue.

At the 10 September 1994 news conference, Judge Hooper criticized the settlement for its violation of the Alabama Constitution and Alabama law. He also pointed out that the at-large system of voting did not discriminate against blacks. Blacks rarely attempted to run for such offices, and those who had run had always been reelected (after being appointed at an earlier date). Montiel spoke about his experience in the meeting with Hornsby, and Hornsby's admonishment to not let word of the settlement leak out. He never used the words "back room deal," but that is what it sounded like. After the other two Republican candidates explained their opposition to the plan, Judge Hooper returned to the microphone to answer questions and recap.

We noticed that Sonny Hornsby himself attended the news conference, and Judge Hooper, with an unplanned remark that surprised all of us, invited Hornsby to the microphone to comment on the settlement. Unbelievably, he accepted and, in his best trial lawyer voice, began to harangue those assembled as if he were giving closing argument before a jury. He said the Republicans were using the race card and not wanting to move into the future. He called their comments demagoguery, even though they simply told what had happened and why they thought the attorney general's and the chief justice's actions were improper. At one point, he turned and looked at Judge Hooper and said that anyone who said he was in any back room of the supreme court building cutting secret deals was a "bald-faced liar."

Hornsby was able to steal the headlines and get some pretty good quotes into the big newspapers like the *Birmingham News*. He said, "I am very saddened at the demagoguery that is being foisted on the people of Alabama by men who are asking to be on the highest court of this state . . . I'm ashamed of you. You ought to be ashamed of yourself to raise the ugly race issue again in 1994, and that's all it is. You are playing the race card." This coverage did not help him however. The settlement plan was clearly a racial quota scheme, which gave the governor power to appoint up to six appellate judges. The Alabama Democratic Conference (ADC), the black wing of the Democratic party, would get two seats on the nominating commission, and the predominantly black Alabama Lawyers Association would get one seat. The Alabama State Bar would get one seat, and those four members would select a fifth member. If the governor did not select an appointment, the chief justice had the right to make the appointment. The entire lawsuit and settlement plan was about race. How could Judge Hooper and the other Republican candidates inject race into an issue that was already based on nothing but race?

Judge Hooper kept the same expression on his face the entire ten minutes that Hornsby spoke—a great big grin. He looked like the Cheshire cat. I wondered how he kept that look on his face while Hornsby acted the part of a demagogue. Later, I remembered the advice he had received from a friend at the beginning of the campaign. Someone who knew Hornsby told him that if he could smoke Hornsby out, he could beat him. That press conference was the beginning of the "smoke-out."

We started to see the real Sonny Hornsby after that event, and it wasn't pretty. Hornsby got the headline in the newspaper the next day, but it didn't look seemly for the chief justice to engage in such contentious off-the-cuff debate. He knew that in Alabama, he could lose his position based on the appellate court-packing issue alone. Racists would not like it. Non-racist people of Alabama would not like something that smelled like a secret deal and subverted the constitution. They had proved that in the 1986 election, when they elected the first Republican governor of the state in over 100 years. In that year, the Democrats had allegedly handpicked their nominee, instead of going with the winner of the Democratic primary. In addition, in 1994, affirmative action was on the wane across the country as people began to see its detrimental effects.

The candidates expressed their positions well. Hooper truly cared about the constitution and the back-door insult the settlement posed for blacks. Montiel wanted district elections (Hooper did not), which would have helped both Republicans and blacks. Harold See was a law professor who could not stand to see such a mockery made of the constitution and laws of Alabama. Russell, perhaps more than any other candidate, expressed concern for blacks and thought this settlement did more harm than good. He said, "How could a good conservative black man become a member of the appeals courts with this settlement? It would be impossible."

There were some less flattering portrayals of Hornsby's performance. The *Montgomery Advertiser* reported, "After a ten-minute speech, his voice raised, his face reddened, the chief justice returned inside the Supreme Court building, vowing not to discuss the matter again." In contrast, here was the report of Hooper's response to Hornsby's speech: " 'At least we got a dialogue going,' Mr. Hooper said later." Even though it was Hornsby who stooped to name-calling and crashing the other side's press conference, later editorials tarred both candidates with the label "uncivil." The media seemed opposed to any airing of controversy between judicial candidates, even if the controversy was focused on issues of importance to the state. Because Hooper and the Republicans had raised the issue in such a public and provocative way, the media blamed them for being uncivil also.

Notes

1. *Montgomery Advertiser,* July 7, 1994.

2. Ibid.

3. The case history: White v. The State of Alabama, 851 F.Supp. 427 (M.D. Ala. 1994); 867 F.Supp. 1571 (M.D. Ala. 1994); 867 F.Supp 1519 (M.D. Ala. 1994); 74 F.3d 1058 (11th Cir. 1996); 922 F.Supp. 552 (M.D. Ala. 1996).

Chapter Three

Campaign Contributions

Hooper faced an entrenched judicial power, controlled for over 100 years by one party, and bankrolled by the special interest able to generate the most money from the most numerous sources in the least amount of time—the trial lawyers. Hooper knew he would have to give the voters a reason to not vote for Hornsby. He had to go on the attack. He obtained some commitments from business interests with plenty of campaign money. Without that funding, Hooper would never have been able to run the television commercials he needed to counter the trial lawyers' ads, especially their attack ads. Other campaign methods he used were bumper stickers, large four-foot by eight-foot "HOOPER" signs, and visits to editors of the rural weekly newspapers. Hornsby restricted his campaigning almost exclusively to television. It is possible that Hooper's small tactics made a big difference at the end. But what really made the difference for Hooper was Hornsby himself.

The media clearly did not like the idea of issue-driven campaigns, with candidates battling it out in public. That attitude on the media's part played right into the hands of the incumbents. Also distasteful to them was the money aspect: business money versus trial lawyer money. To the media, this meant that candidates were bought and paid for by whoever provided the campaign funding, or, at least, it meant it appeared as if they were bought and paid for.

The media constantly lamented the amounts of money used for judicial campaigns and how it appeared as if the judiciary had lost its respectability because of that money. They linked the amount of money used in the judicial campaigns to the legitimacy of those campaigns. In their minds, the more money there was in a judicial campaign, the less legitimacy. What the media, and many others, had not yet realized was that the judiciary had become the supreme power in the United States. Any agency or institution that takes upon itself the power of judging the legitimacy of every other entity, including the executive and legislative branches of the civil government, is setting itself up for a power grab. It does not matter who is doing the grabbing for power. The effort may be from noble or from ignoble motives. Nevertheless, a power grab requires money. Money buys influence. But there is a limit to what an interest can do with money. Money could not buy what Sonny Hornsby already had—the chief justice seat.

Business interests claimed they were simply trying to restore balance to the courts, and there was certainly some history that indicated balance was needed. Trial lawyers claimed they were simply trying to maintain the delicate constitutional balance they had worked so hard to obtain in the courts, protecting the right to trial by jury. Of course, their success in that department didn't do any harm to their pocketbooks either. That is what made their motives suspect—the money they stood to gain or lose.

Neither Hornsby nor Hooper faced any opposition in the Democratic and Republican primaries. However, there were a couple of primary races relevant to this discussion. One incumbent justice, Henry Steagall, planned to retire at the end of his term because of age and, therefore, his seat was open in 1994. One candidate for the Democratic nomination for his seat was Terry Butts, a circuit court judge from Coffee County. Judge Eugene Reese of Montgomery County, the author of the most intrusive school equity funding decision in the nation, was the other Democratic candidate. He claimed to be targeted by the trial lawyers. This claim was questionable because Reese received a little less than half his campaign contributions from trial lawyers. He said the Alabama Trial Lawyers Association (ATLA) had tried to get him to run against Justice Maddox, but he refused. He also said there was an organized telephone effort against him by the ATLA. The ATLA president, Lee Pittman, denied the accusation, saying that the ATLA doesn't endorse candidates. The media endorsed Reese almost unanimously because they were in love with his equity funding decision. Much of the rest of the state thought it was an example of supreme judicial arrogance at the trial court level.

Butts' campaign commercials blasted Reese with allegations by a murder victim's relative that he was hard on the victim's family during the trial. Butts made Reese look like a coddler of criminals and abuser of victims. It was a questionable but ingenious tactic. We do not know whether it was an accurate portrayal of Reese as a trial judge. But it was effective. Reese lost the primary. It was a sign of what to expect from the trial lawyers in the general election—attacks on the decisions and actions of former judges, like Judge Hooper.

Hugh Maddox's seat was also up for election. He had been a sitting associate justice for over twenty-four years and a frequent dissenter to some of the more activist actions by the court. He dissented consistently with the court's decisions to overturn the damage caps imposed by the legislature. The trial lawyers opposed him. In spite of his opponent having all the money he needed to win and the endorsement of all the correct Democratic groups, Maddox decided to voluntarily cap the contributions to his campaign at $500. In the Democratic primary in Alabama, if a candidate lacked the money and the endorsement of the right groups, he was a goner. Maddox had neither money nor endorsements. Maddox won. Surely his experience as an incumbent justice was in his favor, but it was still an amazing victory. As far as conservatives were concerned, there was one blemish on Justice Maddox's record— he had not voted in the Guy Hunt appeal. Instead, he released his dissenting opinion after the primary election was over. Some said that decision to delay releasing his dissent was a political move. Others said he did the pragmatic thing and prevented a loss in the primary. The results of the Reese race and the Maddox race were encouraging. Hooper ran, not on a pro-business plank, but on an anti-judicial arrogance plank. Like Maddox, he disagreed with the ease with which the supreme court struck down the laws of the legislature. Unlike Reese, he did not believe a circuit court judge could act as a super "board of education" for the entire state.

But the first big break in the chief justice campaign came about without any initiation from us, and it lead to our best television coverage. On 17 July 1994, the *Mobile Press-Register* (now the *Mobile Register*) reported that several lawyers in the Mobile area reported being contacted by Hornsby for campaign contributions, and they felt very uncomfortable. The chief justice of the Alabama Supreme Court was calling lawyers for campaign contributions. The threat that his position posed to these lawyers, as the highest judge of the state had its effect—shakedown. Judge Hooper figured Hornsby was simply trying to get some defense lawyer contributions so that his campaign contribution reports wouldn't contain only contributions from plaintiff trial lawyers.

The method Hornsby used was shoddy, however. He would follow up his phone calls with a fax message about the money. Here are some quotes from the article: "Lawyers Dislike Hornsby's Pleas," was the headline.

> Alabama Supreme Court Chief Justice Sonny Hornsby has stirred up grumbling among some Alabama lawyers who claim he twisted arms by personally calling them to ask for money for his reelection campaign. Hornsby, like some other politicians, also suggested the amount he wants each lawyer [in the firm] to give, attorneys said. And he has followed up his calls with notes sent by facsimile, sometimes the same day . . . Some lawyers said they felt leaned on heavily by a judge who would hear their cases on appeal. 'This is beyond dignity—it's flat arm-twisting is what it is,' said one Mobile attorney, who spoke only on condition of anonymity, saying he feared retribution in court.

Judge Hooper read the story while he was in Gulf Shores at a Baldwin County Republican Committee meeting. Gulf Shores is close to Mobile, so he read the Mobile newspaper that morning. The story said that the writer had tried to get Judge Hooper's opinion on such solicitations of campaign contributions, but that he could not be reached for comment. Judge Hooper couldn't leave the story like that. He had to respond to let people know he didn't agree with that sort of thing. A month earlier, a good friend of his had told me that we should send a letter to every lawyer in the state asking for support. When I told Judge Hooper about that advice, he immediately reacted negatively and said, "No, I'm not going to do that. I don't like that. That's not my style." Without a second thought, he turned down the opportunity to reach over 10,000 potential voters and financial supporters who could easily fill his campaign coffer.

Later, a couple of lawyers showed up at a fundraiser or two. Judge Hooper did not think it wrong for a lawyer to give to a judicial campaign. They had a right to contribute like anyone else. But he thought the personal solicitation of campaign funds was wrong. He thought Hornsby's "arm-twisting" was more stupid than anything else. He said, "The chief justice doesn't need to ask for money. He'd 'uv gotten all he needed. What he was trying to do was get defense lawyer contributions to make his giving look balanced."

Judge Hooper's attitude was that a lawyer must represent a client zealously. If he thinks a campaign contribution would help his client, then he is likely to give it. What if he does not give, but his opponent in a case does? Would there be a subtle bias in that judge's mind, even if unintentional, against his client? When the chief justice himself (or a candidate for that position) personally contacts a lawyer for money, the pressure is intense for that lawyer to give something to him. The pressure would be on that lawyer to give, even if he did not want to support that judge or candidate. Even if that were not a danger, what about the appearance of impropriety, the appearance of buying the judge? Judge Hooper had to clarify his position immediately.

We called a news conference for him to explain his position on the issue of personal solicitation of campaign funds. Hooper said, "I'm not going to personally solicit money from lawyers because after I'm elected in November, I do not want to find myself in the position of hearing cases of law firms which I have asked for money." He said, "the court system must retain the highest level of integrity if the public is to maintain its confidence in the institution."[1] He added: "When Sonny Hornsby personally calls law firms and tells the partners of that firm they should each give him $500, he has placed the full weight of the chief justice's office on that firm. I don't believe that's right."

Hooper also said that he had never personally solicited campaign funds from any lawyer when running for circuit court judge. We tried to make sure that his memory was accurate on that statement, and he said he was "pretty" sure. It fit his character of being averse to fundraising. After being a circuit court judge for as long as he had been in 1982, he didn't need to raise funds. People contributed. The only campaigning he did in 1982 was to put up a few billboards.

Hornsby said that he had no improper motive in making calls and saw nothing wrong with it. He said he would not stop asking attorneys for campaign contributions. He called Hooper's claim that direct solicitation by the chief justice was different from a campaign committee soliciting donations "cosmetic." Hornsby's press conference, which he held later the same day as Hooper's, did more harm than good. The *Montgomery Advertiser* ran this headline: "Hooper: Foe Abusing Power." The *Birmingham News:* "Hooper Blasts, Hornsby Defends Solicitation of Funds from Lawyers." The *Mobile Press-Register:* "Hornsby Rival Blasts Jurist's Fund-raising." Elbert Peters, the chairman of the Alabama Republican party, demanded that Hornsby release his phone records to make sure that he had not made these calls using state phones. Hornsby released the records which showed $77 worth of long distance calls from his state office in May and June, but all the names were blacked out to protect people's privacy.

There were other editorials about this, and there would be more. The *Montgomery Advertiser* ran an editorial called "Twisted Arms." In it, they quote Hornsby: "I think the overwhelming majority of lawyers appreciate a phone call from the chief justice . . . There are hundreds of lawyers with cases pending before the Supreme Court. On a daily basis, we make a distinct effort to avoid any apparent conflict of interest between the business of the Court and campaign business."

The editors at the *Advertiser* declared:

> Actually there's a world of difference between a cordial call to say hello and a call to solicit funds, and we suspect Hornsby knows it . . . If Hornsby were a trial judge and a witness replied to a question so vaguely, he would have declared the reply non-responsive and in

no uncertain terms ordered the witness to answer the question . . . For them [judicial candidates] to get the majority of their funds from attorneys and special interests likely to have cases before them—as the majority of judges routinely do—should shake the faith of the public in the court system to its core. But Hornsby has pushed the reliance on fund-raising to new depths. We know of no other sitting judges who have set out to systematically call attorneys personally to request funds . . . We call on Chief Justice Hornsby not only to abandon this practice, but also to push for Alabama to adopt the ABA's Model Code of Judicial Conduct which so clearly prohibits it.[2]

Of course, the media used the news to call for an entire revamping of the judicial campaign system. Judge Hooper just thought it was bad for a judge to personally solicit funds. During the campaign, Harold See exposed that Justice Mark Kennedy had received a campaign contribution of $12,000 from a law firm that had argued a case before him the very day they delivered the contribution. A couple of years later, Kennedy became the subject of an article in *Reader's Digest* about the worst judges in America.

This press coverage of Hornsby's fund-raising turned into perhaps the single most important campaign issue for Hooper, with the exception of an issue Hornsby tried to use against Hooper. It was a traumatic event from Hooper's past, which Hornsby saw fit to dredge up in the sleaziest way. It was a classic trial lawyer stunt, like the one used against Mark Arderson in 1992.

Judge Hooper knew of this potential for abuse of the legal process to slander a challenger. He emphasized this to his potential financial backers. Sam Duvall, a member of Hooper's campaign team and a veteran in Alabama politics, went further in his assessment. He said that the other side would literally stop at nothing to defeat Judge Hooper. In addition, they could raise hundreds of thousands of dollars, in one weekend if necessary, to obtain a quick new TV commercial or accomplish anything else they desired to accomplish. We had our work cut out for us.

The stealth campaign started just like the campaign against
Anderson. One day in the summer of 1994, we received a
letter from a Montgomery trial lawyer, Knox Argo, demand-
ing that Judge Hooper provide compensation to Mississippi
Valley Title Insurance Company. The letter alleged that Hooper
had made mistakes and committed fraud in his work for Don
Martin, a real estate developer who had been convicted and
imprisoned for criminal fraud in his real estate dealings. Hooper
had acted as closing attorney for many of Martin's real estate
deals in the '80s. Hooper had quit because Martin had asked
him to move into the same office with him, and Hooper didn't
think that was right.

Martin moved massive amounts of property in his business, buying up cheap and foreclosed properties. He put tre-
mendous pressure on Hooper to get massive numbers of clos-
ings done quickly. He appeared to Hooper and many others to
be in good financial condition. However, he came to Hooper
one day and told him he had gotten in too deep. Hooper took
him to the head of the bank department to explain the situation. Hooper thought he could possibly find a way out of the
predicament. Martin had apparently sold properties he didn't
yet own. After going to the bank, he went to see another
attorney in town, who recommended bankruptcy. That's when
the house of cards came crashing down. Creditors now felt
defrauded, and the state brought a case against him.

Hooper had done some of the work of examining the
titles. The problems came because of the various names Martin used for his businesses—C & C Land Company, C Co.,
Martin, etc. If, for example, a secretary mistyped the owner as
C & C Land Co. instead of Martin, then the simple solution
was to prepare a deed of correction. However, once Martin
entered into bankruptcy, everything was frozen, and all kinds
of problems arose. Mainly, it looked as if he was trying to get
out of covering his obligations by going into bankruptcy. There's
a name for that: bankruptcy fraud. The title insurance had to
come into play in order to cover for Martin's over-extension of
his business.

Hooper had been involved in all the negotiations among
the players involved, including Mississippi Valley. They had

every opportunity to claim that Hooper was at fault and should somehow be a party to a settlement. But they didn't take that opportunity in 1990. They settled the matter among themselves. At that time, there was no mention of fault or liability on Hooper's part. Then, all of a sudden and out of the blue, Mississippi Valley decided to sue Judge Hooper. It didn't add up, unless you took into account the political angle—in the summer of 1994, Hooper was running for the Alabama Supreme Court. In that light, the lawsuit made sense.

Argo filed the lawsuit on 16 August 1994, claiming that Mississippi Valley had incurred losses of more than $850,000. The headlines on 17 August 1994 blared: "Court hopeful accused of misconduct, fraud." Even though it was low key, that was pretty good free advertising for Hornsby. Both Knox Argo and Mississippi Valley's chief executive office declined to comment. How easy would it be for Argo to get Mississippi Valley to sue? All he had to do was offer to file the action in court at no cost to the company. If they won, Argo would receive a percentage of the winnings, and if they lost, Mississippi Valley would lose nothing.

Title insurance covers losses to a lender because the mortgaged property was insufficient to cover default by the borrower. Martin and all his companies were in the same boat. He and his companies were sinking. Whether his name, or C & C Properties, was on the title was irrelevant to whether he had made a fraudulent business transaction. It might have affected what the insurance company paid for a particular loss. The losses were not due to mix-ups concerning names of titles. The losses were due to Martin's business practices. He obtained mortgages on properties he did not yet own, and when the scam did not work out, he filed bankruptcy, leaving his creditors holding the unpaid debts. That is bankruptcy fraud. Hornsby's campaign ads alleged Hooper goofed up on the simplest work a lawyer can do. This was hypocritical of Hornsby. The mistakes of names Hooper was alleged to have made are easily corrected by a deed of correction, unless the owner goes into bankruptcy, which is what Martin did. One day near the end of the campaign, we received a phone call from a Wetumpka man who had hired Hornsby to help him with the purchase of his house. The title was not clear, however, and he asked Hornsby to fix it. He could not get satisfaction from Hornsby for several months, so he called the state bar. He found another lawyer who would do the work for him that Hornsby left unfinished. Simple work for an attorney.

Hooper responded by saying, "In my forty-one years in the legal profession, I have never been sued either personally or professionally until now. It is more than suspicious that a suit would be filed against me eighty days before the November 8 election involving work I did as much as nine years ago." He added: "The suit tells me that Sonny Hornsby knows he's in trouble in the polls." The Don Martin story reappeared in a Hornsby campaign commercial, but Martin was small potatoes compared to what Hornsby would use later in his TV commercials. I assume that Hornsby thought the Jerry Hamilton story would be his silver bullet.

Notes

1. *Birmingham News,* July 20, 1994.

2. *Montgomery Advertiser,* p. 2F, July 24, 1994.

"Good Mornin' to You, Sir"

If we had not run our commercial, perhaps Hornsby would not have run his. Judge Hooper drew him out. He had to. Judge Hooper was the underdog challenger. He had to show why he was the better candidate than Hornsby. The television stations running the ads gave each candidate the chance to see the other's ad. The day we began to run "Good Mornin' to You, Sir," Hornsby began to run the Jerry Hamilton ad.

Karl Rove & Co., a well-known Texas company specializing in campaign help for Republican candidates, helped us with our campaign. They hired John Deardourff, a well-known Republican media consultant, to prepare Hooper's commercials. Hooper's main commercial had one actor, who played a lawyer getting a call from the chief justice. The hypothetical in the ad was Deardourff's creation; the exact scenario never took place. However, it is important that I point out that the facts supporting the hypothetical situation presented by Hooper's ad were entirely true. In fact, upon first being challenged by the media coverage about his practice of calling attorneys approximately three months before the election, Hornsby said he had done nothing wrong and would continue to make the calls. He changed his practice about one week before the election.

In the commercial, a lawyer's secretary tells him that the chief justice is on the phone. The only voice you hear is that of the lawyer receiving the call. He answers the phone in a flatteringly sweet southern accent that sounded uncannily like Hornsby himself: "Judge Hornsby? Good mornin to you, sir." Then, in a dumbfounded and somewhat shocked voice, he said, "You want what?" It then showed him writing on a pad that the chief justice wanted $500.00 from each lawyer in his firm. The man then says, "Now you know judge, we do have a case pending in your court." He then responds with, "It doesn't matter?" The lawyer says, "Yes, sir. I'll get the money to you right away, sir." Then there was a paste up on a black background and a voice-over: "Isn't it time to replace judges like Chief Justice Sonny Hornsby?"

It was devastating. It was also funny. It was consistent with the facts as we knew them. It demonstrated the pressure a lawyer is placed under in such a situation, and was the exact criticism that Hooper had for Hornsby's practices.

Hornsby held what he thought was an ace in the hole. On the day Hooper ran the "Good morning to you, sir" commercial, Hornsby ran the Jerry Hamilton spot. Before I describe the commercial, I need to describe the actual events involving Jerry Hamilton that occurred in the early 1980s. I studied the case quite thoroughly because Hooper knew it would become an issue during the election. Hooper had told us what he remembered, and I have filled in the gaps with studies of the newspapers and court records of the time. It was a disturbing memory for Hooper because the incident had upset him and his entire family.

Jerry Hamilton was arrested for a burglary of *Roper's Jewelry*, a Montgomery retail store, on 17 August 1981. Hooper's recollection of the facts from the sentencing hearing are as follows: Hamilton was drunk at the time of the crime. He broke a window at the jewelry store and sat down and waited for the police to show up. He was charged with burglarizing a jewelry store and stealing a $30.00 watch and a $10.00 watch. Hamilton pled guilty and appeared before Hooper for sentencing. Just that year, the legislature had passed a new habitual offender law, that required that the defendant receive a higher penalty if he had prior felonies on his record. However, no one was familiar with all the details of that law because it was so new. According to the assistant district attorney present at the sentencing hearing, he tried to get Judge Hooper to sentence Hamilton using the habitual offender law and Hamilton's two prior felonies. However, in Hamilton's record in the Montgomery County Courthouse, there is mentioned a 1972 felony and some bad check misdemeanors. Misdemeanors do not affect anyone's sentence under the habitual offender law. There was another Jerry Hamilton, however, who had several prior felonies. I first thought that the district attorney had confused the two, and he may have. The possibility of such confusion demonstrates why the habitual offender law requires that the prosecution prove the prior felony by means of a certified record. Hamilton had another prior felony, but that felony was committed in Lee County. That record was in Opelika. Also, there was absolutely no mention in Jerry Hamilton's case action summary and no record in the entire file showing that the district attorney presented to Judge Hooper any documents showing any prior felony. Without a certified record of the prior felony, the law prohibited the judge from sentencing a defendant under the habitual offender law. It was the district attorney's responsibility to make sure they provided the proper information to the judge for sentencing purposes.

Hooper saw the offense as extremely minor and felt that Hamilton was simply a drunk who needed some help to get his life together. Judge Hooper had always followed his Christian beliefs in his actions and judgments as a judge. One of those beliefs was to have mercy when possible. If someone committed a minor offense that didn't involve physical harm to another, then they deserved a lighter sentence. It was also more practical because the jail was packed full, and this was the period when the federal courts were telling states to build more and bigger correctional facilities because crowded conditions were cruel to the prisoners. The county jail contained prisoners who should have been in the penitentiary (sentenced to more than a year in prison), but the penitentiaries were also full. Judge Hooper was instrumental in obtaining a new courthouse for Montgomery County, but that came later. For the time being, there was simply no room for a drunk who broke a window. However, Judge Hooper said he believed in throwing the book at anyone who committed rape, robbery, or murder.

Until the new county jail was built, Hooper had to sentence the minor offenders to probation. Also, Judge Hooper brought several prisoners to his church to see if they could change their lives by learning the scriptures and receiving the influence of Christian teaching. He had some success stories with prisoners who had turned their lives around, and he thought Hamilton was a good candidate. Hamilton had gone through a difficult divorce, and he had a cute son.

Judge Hooper sentenced Hamilton to sixty days in jail or until a place could be found for him in an alcohol rehabilitation program, $300.00 restitution, and a year and a day of probation. The exact wording in the case action summary was: "A year and a day, sentence suspended, split sentence, sixty days in county jail and restitution of $300.00 and to be under Mr. Lynn Thompson's alcohol program." It was signed Perry O. Hooper, Sr. Significantly, the sentencing hearing occurred on 30 October 1981.

Hamilton spent about a week in jail before he entered a alcohol rehabilitation program. After he completed rehab, he obtained a job in the courthouse moving books from the old courthouse building to a building across the street where excess law books were stored. Judge Hooper thought he would be good at that type work, and it would give him something productive to do to keep him off the bottle. He also needed work to pay his restitution. There was nothing unusual about the job. Even today, inmates, not just people on probation, work for the courts. Hamilton later helped with other jobs. He even did legal research for the district attorney's office. Judge Hooper did not supervise him in this work. The courthouse employed him. The only contact Judge Hooper had with him was inviting him to church.

There was also a court reporter who worked in the courthouse. Her name was Missy DeVaughn. She worked for different judges on an as-needed basis. She was not Judge Hooper's personal court reporter. Judge Hooper barely knew her. She seemed like a nice country girl to him. He had no knowledge of any relationship between her and Hamilton.

On 30 November 1982, the assistant district attorney, Frank Hawthorne, Jr., filed to revoke Hamilton's probation because he had not paid his court-ordered restitution. I have a copy of the motion from the circuit court. Remember that Hamilton's probation was ordered to be a year and a day, beginning on 30 October 1981. That would place his probation's final day on

31 October 1982. Even if it were argued that he didn't begin his probation until after getting out of jail in 1981 (an improper argument because it was clear from Judge Hooper's order that the probation began immediately), then the end of his probation, at the latest, was 7 November 1982. In either case, District Attorney Jimmy Evans was almost a month late filing for revocation of Hamilton's probation, perhaps a whole month. It is never the job of the judge to keep up with probationers. How could a judge do something like that? That is why there is a probation officer who keeps track of probationers to determine if he should recommend to the district attorney that someone's probation be revoked. It is, however, the district attorney's responsibility to notify the judge when someone has violated probation. There is no other way for a judge to know. The judge is not an investigator checking up on probationers. That would be a full-time job. Judge Hooper, following well-established case precedent, had no choice but to deny the district attorney's request for revocation of probation because Hamilton's probation had ended. For Judge Hooper to grant the district attorney's motion would have been the same as a judge ordering a man back to prison after he had served his entire prison sentence, because the man didn't clean his cell before he left. It was simply out of the question, legally and practically.

As time went by, Hamilton continued to work in the courthouse and apparently was able to befriend many of the people there. Hooper says that Hamilton was something of a con man, very slick. He convinced Hooper that he needed a car to go back and forth from work in order to pay his restitution. So Hooper co-signed some type of car note for him. Judge Hooper was not sure when this occurred, but it apparently occurred after Hamilton's probation ended. Judge Hooper said he didn't normally do that type of thing, and that it was a mistake. Later the police picked up Hamilton for driving under the influence. While in jail, Hamilton lit a newspaper to get the jailer's attention. Hooper, not knowing what Hamilton had done, went to see the district attorney for Autauga County, where Hamilton was arrested. Hamilton was an employee of the courthouse, so Judge Hooper wanted to know what was happening with him. Glen Curlee was the district attorney, and he told Judge Hooper that he didn't think there was much to the arson charge against Hamilton. The arson charge was for lighting the newspaper. Judge Hooper asked Curlee what he planned to do with Hamilton. He emphasized that he did not try to influence Curlee and did not think a circuit judge for one county could influence the district attorney for another county. Curlee said he didn't plan to present the charges to the grand jury. Later, because Curlee was away for the day, the charges were presented to the grand jury, and Curlee had to have them dropped.

On 11 April 1983, Missy DeVaughn did not return home to Clanton after work. Her husband became worried and contacted the police. On 13 April the story hit the newspapers. Hamilton's sister said Hamilton had come to her house with blood on his clothes, and he did not have his own car. The police arrested him and charged him with kidnapping. Missy was last seen leaving the courthouse with Hamilton on Monday night. Hamilton was thirty-seven years old, and Missy was twenty-three. The family of Missy DeVaughn, which lived in Clanton, Alabama, was understandably very scared and distraught. The Montgomery police found Missy's car in the Jackson Hospital parking lot in Montgomery on Monday night. The investigators from Chilton and Lee counties were looking into leads in Troup County, Georgia. Lee County is just across the border from Troup County. The newspaper said Hamilton had probably kidnapped Missy. Judge Hooper knew employees of the courthouse and a lawyer who said they saw Missy leaving with Hamilton voluntarily. Another witness said he saw Hamilton force her into her car. The newspaper said that the district attorney's office had been trying to revoke Hamilton's probation since 30 November 1982. The district attorney also said that Hamilton had not served his full sixty-day sentence in jail and had not paid his restitution.

I do not know how the subject of Hamilton's probation not being revoked came up. Either the district attorney's office volunteered the information, which could have led a smart investigative reporter to discover that the district attorney had fallen down on the job, or the newspaper itself asked that question after checking into Hamilton's record. That check would have been incomplete if they were relying on the district attorney for information. In any event, the search for a devil other than Hamilton began. There appeared a need to blame someone in the legal system. Instead of focusing on the district attorney's office, they focused on the judge, Perry O. Hooper, Sr.

After his arrest, Hamilton confessed to the murder, but he would not tell investigators where the body was. He eventually took them to where he had said the body was, but they could not find it. His two lawyers had to ask to be taken off the case because they claimed a conflict of interest. Ira DeMent, the soon-to-be federal judge, was appointed to replace them. The news stories on the case dragged on and on because the authorities could not find her body. Finally, Hamilton took the authorities into Georgia, just across the Alabama State line near Auburn. They found her body somewhere in Georgia or Alabama in November 1983, almost seven months after Missy's disappearance.

Strange stories continued to crop up. For instance, not only was it discovered that Hamilton did legal research for the district attorney, but the courthouse's law library also contained a cot and several personal items. There was speculation that Hamilton had lived in the courthouse. All this information was reported as if Judge Hooper had gotten Hamilton the job at the courthouse, gotten him a car, let him live in the courthouse, and then demanded he work on his campaign for circuit judge. It was also alleged that Hamilton worked in Perry Hooper, Jr.'s campaign for the legislature. Judge Hooper helped this drunk get a job, like he would help any drunk who came before his bench, and, from then on, except for inviting him to church, he barely saw the guy, didn't keep up with him on a regular basis, and certainly didn't expect any favors from him in return. If he had anything to do with the guy, it was simply out of Christian charity for a drunk who had fallen on hard times with alcohol, his family, and the law. As for campaign activity, Judge Hooper doesn't remember anything like that. He didn't even run a campaign in 1982, except to put up a few billboards. His attitude, though, was that if Hamilton wanted to help with Perry Jr.'s campaign, that was Hamilton's right.

In almost every mention of this story by the *Montgomery Advertiser,* Judge Hooper's name appeared. He was no longer in the courthouse, where the district attorney's office was and where he might have been able to better control what was being said about him. He became tired of hearing misquotes about himself. So he went to the *Advertiser* and asked them to do an accurate story. They asked if he would be willing to do a Question and Answer format and he agreed. Early in the case, there had been an ethics complaint filed against Hooper. That probe eventually cleared Judge Hooper of any kind of wrongdoing in the matter. But the stories continued anyway. Hooper pointed out in the article that it had always been his policy as a judge not to comment on a case because cases should not be tried in the newspaper. However, because this case had been in the newspaper already, he wanted to let his side be heard for a change. He explained that he first met Hamilton when Hamilton came before him for sentencing. He looked over his probation report and saw that he deserved the sentence he gave him. He explained that he did not see Hamilton's actions as true burglary. He broke a plate glass window while he was drunk. No one in the courtroom, including the district attorney present, objected to the sentence. On 1 November 1982, Hamilton completed his sentence of probation. No one brought to Judge Hooper's attention anything about his nonpayment of restitution. One month after the completion of Hamilton's probation, the district attorney filed a motion to revoke his probation. Hooper stated: "That's like saying, 'Let's close the gate after all the chickens are out.' I like to say it's like saying a twelve-inch ruler will be decreed a thirteen-inch ruler. You can't do it. The sentence was complete." He then explained that he was reviewing 1900 probation revocation requests at that time.

Hooper also told the *Advertiser* that he did not think that Judge Price's decision to revoke Hamilton's probation six months after his sentence had expired was correct. He said that, in certain cases, judges receive public pressure to do the politically correct thing. This case had more than its share of public pressure, to say the least. Hooper then explained that the judge cannot be the district attorney. The district attorney has the responsibility of not only petitioning the court for the application of the Habitual Offender Act, but also of proving the previous conviction with a certified copy of that conviction and sentencing. If a defendant has not been sentenced in accordance with the prior conviction, the district attorney can appeal that decision like any other. No one appealed or made any objections to Hooper's sentence of Hamilton.

From the first day that Missy DeVaughn was missing, newspapers reported that Hamilton might be involved and the media mentioned Hooper and the sentence he gave Hamilton in 1981. Ellen Brooks, the chief deputy district attorney at that time, mentioned this information to reporters from the *Montgomery Advertiser*. Why? Were they setting up the story for the spin later? Later, it was discovered that Hamilton had done work for the district attorney's office. The *Advertiser* reported: "The man accused of kidnapping and possible murder of Missy DeVaughn researched and left notes on jurisdiction questions involving crimes which cross county or state lines." Of course, the concern in this crime was that Hamilton had crossed into Georgia and then killed Missy. District attorney Jimmy Evans got the notes. But there was alleged to be a diary also. We don't know what happened to the diary, but the story that circulated in Montgomery was that the diary held very embarrassing information on a particular judge, not Judge Hooper, some lawyers, and perhaps even Jimmy Evans. According to this rumor, the particular judge was a former assistant district attorney for Jimmy Evans.

Judge Hooper mentioned the Ethics Commission: "The commission has found just what I thought they would find, that I have done absolutely nothing wrong. They found some things about other people that the public should probably know about. This whole episode came about through underhanded political motivation."[1] Before the results were issued he hinted that whoever was responsible for Hooper having the spotlight turned on him may end up at the receiving end of an investigation—"poetic justice." Unfortunately, that never happened. In addition, someone had called Hooper to ask him about running for the U.S. Senate. A rumor to that effect had circulated Montgomery for some time. The *Advertiser* even ran an article and cartoon about it. Then, the situation with Missy DeVaughn occurred. Judge Hooper felt that politics was involved in the attention being turned toward him. He had resigned his judgeship because he and his wife had prayed about it, and felt it was the best thing to do. He had told the other judges about it in January, long before the Hamilton story, so they could elect a new presiding judge.

At the top of the newspaper article, there was an inset with some very interesting information. Several lawyers talked about the case. For example, "Bill Skinner, who represented Hamilton in the burglary and theft case, said the judge was made aware of Hamilton's 1966 conviction in Lee County but was not provided with the proper documents to sentence him as a habitual offender." He also said the district attorney's office did not file a petition to enhance the punishment under the act. Judge Hooper said there was no objection from the district attorney, so I have to believe that the district attorney did not even ask for a delay in order to try and obtain the correct paperwork. He also said that, at that time, judges and district attorneys used their own discretion in invoking the act. A few months later, the supreme court ruled the enhanced punishment was mandatory. Skinner also confirmed Judge Hooper's version of the story by saying that the jail sentence was supposed to last only until Hamilton could get into an alcohol rehabilitation program. He also backed up Hooper's contention that Hamilton could not be punished after his probation ended for not paying restitution. Maurice "Red" Bell said he was the one who got the arson charge dismissed against Hamilton. He had it all arranged with district attorney Glen Curlee that no indictment would be returned. An indictment was issued because Curlee was not with the grand jury one day, but Curlee then "promised to drop the charge at arraignment." Curlee said there was no arson. In the center of this section was a picture of Hooper and a quote next to the picture: "I have had many others come to our Sunday School class and they have not turned out in the tragic way that this has. They've turned out successfully."

The story about Hamilton and Hooper began because someone told the media Hamilton should have had his probation revoked in 1982. The media would not have had sufficient legal sophistication or time to go back to old files in the court clerk's office and study the story. They surely did not study the records later. How did the media get the information? Someone had to tell them. Only the district attorney's office and the probation office had that information since they are responsible for supervising probationers. It was later revealed that Missy DeVaughn's father was looking for answers to why Hamilton's probation was not revoked. How would he have known to ask? He didn't know Hamilton. He didn't go to Hooper to ask questions; he went straight to the Ethics Commission. Who had the information? Who had a great deal to lose if the public discovered where the responsibility for pursuing Hamilton as to his probation violations? Who was in control of the information in the courthouse? The district attorney's office. Who was considering a run for the U.S. Senate? Who was no longer in the courthouse? Who was the judge in Hamilton's case? Judge Hooper. It was a perfect set-up. The district attorney's office could use Hooper to deflect attention from itself. The only thing that could have upset it would have been a nosey reporter who didn't trust the district attorney's story and who could understand the legal rules and responsibilities of everyone involved with probation. In other words, there was no one to check up on the district attorney's version of the story. To this day, Missy DeVaughn's father blames Judge Hooper for his daughter's death. Politics has a way of imposing casualties upon bystanders.

So there's every reason to believe that the office of Jimmy Evans placed the blame for Hamilton upon Judge Hooper. The district attorney's office had made two mistakes: not doing their full job in seeking habitual offender status for Hamilton, and being late seeking to revoke his probation when he had not paid his restitution. If his office had the political motivation to place the media on Hooper's scent, it would have solved two problems: how to keep the district attorney's office from being blamed for Hamilton being on the street and how to keep Hooper from running for the U.S. Senate. Those were two big incentives for a politically motivated public official. In 1994, Jimmy Evans was attorney general for the state of Alabama.

The press, however, is the real culprit for the spotlight being placed on Hooper. If they had done just a meager amount of study of Hamilton's files at the courthouse and tried to understand a little about probation and the Habitual Offender Act, the stories could have been written in an entirely different light. If they had wanted to be objective, the stories would have focused on the tragedy of the murder first. Ultimately, no one was to blame for this murder except Jerry Hamilton. He had no serious record, and everyone who knew him in the courthouse was shocked that he could do such a thing. However, if there was blame to be cast for not putting him in jail for a longer period of time, it rested with the district attorney's office for Montgomery County.

Most of the information I have related is available publicly. I obtained it from copies of the *Montgomery Advertiser* and the documents in the Montgomery County Courthouse. Where I obtained information from Judge Hooper that was not available publicly, I have so noted. Another event occurred after the DeVaughn kidnapping that made Judge Hooper's action in the Hamilton case appear bad. A week after the kidnapping, Judge Price found Hamilton delinquent in his restitution payments, and a week after that, he revoked his probation. There was no need for this. Hamilton was already in jail facing kidnapping and murder charges. Judge Price ignored established precedent as to the issue of probation revocation. His decision came almost six months after Hamilton's probation had expired. Did that decision mean that anyone who had not paid their restitution was subject for the rest of their lives to being thrown in jail? What if the district attorney had waited six decades instead of six months to revoke his probation? The requirement to pay restitution had always only applied during the term of the person's sentence. Perhaps it is arguable that restitution has no term; otherwise a deadbeat criminal could simply string the court along until his sentence ends and get away without paying. However, that is why there is a probation office to inform the district attorney's office, before the probation term ends, that someone has ceased to pay restitution. Then the district attorney can inform the court before the expiration of his sentence and throw him in jail if necessary. That clearly did not happen in this case.

Price's decision was completely without precedent. Nevertheless, for the unlearned public, it made Hooper's decision look bad. Judge Price was a new judge; in fact, he was Hooper's appointed replacement. The media had made the Hamilton case the litmus test for how a judge should be assessed. Leniency toward criminals was not in public favor. Therefore, one possibility was that Judge Price, in the face of a case with such public notoriety, was simply terrified to do anything else. Second, Judge Price was a Democrat. Even though Judge Hooper called Judge Price his friend, it is possible that Judge Price fell in line with the political agenda against Judge Hooper. At that time, it seemed as if the Democratic party walked lockstep with each other whenever necessary to accomplish a political objective. The entire fiasco prevented the most successful Republican officeholder in Montgomery County from running for the U.S. Senate.

But Judge Price's decision was not the only shock. Skinner, Hamilton's lawyer, appealed Price's decision to revoke probation, thinking that the Alabama Court of Criminal Appeals would surely reverse Judge Price. The district attorney's office contended that Hamilton extended his probation by not paying restitution. My research showed that there had never been a case on appeal that required anything of a person who had served the entire term to which he or she was sentenced. Yet, the Alabama Court of Criminal Appeals decided to make a new rule with this case. Without mentioning a single case as precedent, the Court of Criminal Appeals said there had been no formal discharge of Hamilton from probation, Hamilton had not paid his restitution, and Hamilton had not served his full sixty days in jail. In addition, he had been arrested for driving under the influence, arson, and kidnapping, all of which happened after his sentence had ended. The court used the word "satisfactory" from the code section on probation to say that his probation could be revoked if he did not make satisfactory fulfillment of his probation. But that word from Alabama Code § 15-22-54(a) and (b)[2] applies to a person still serving an unfinished sentence of imprisonment which has been converted into probation. When a probationer is not serving his term in a satisfactory manner, the district attorney comes before the judge with the probation report and tells the judge he has not made satisfactory fulfillment of his conditions of probation. The judge can then revoke the probation. But how can a judge revoke something that has already been completed? What would the punishment be? Normally, a person whose probation is revoked must then serve his sentence of imprisonment that is still incomplete. What unfinished term of imprisonment would Hamilton serve? His one year and one day sentence was long over. Of course, the Alabama Court of Criminal Appeals didn't have to worry about such practical questions. Hamilton would be in federal prison for a long time for the murder of Missy DeVaughn. His confinement for burglary in 1981 was irrelevant by this time.

Judge Price's decision in the Hamilton case began a whole new rule for probation cases. Perhaps from a pro-victim standpoint, Judge Price's decision was a good one. But then why have the courts been so reluctant to use it? In order to make sense of the *Hamilton v. State* decision by the Court of Criminal Appeals,[3] later courts had to impose additional conditions upon the application of the principle that is called "formal discharge"[4] from probation. Otherwise, the principle would have expanded beyond all sense or constitutional boundary. However, the courts did not always achieve that goal of restricting the *Hamilton* case.[5] Some would argue that Judge Price's decision was a good one even though precedent did not support it. My point is that Judge Hooper followed the law as it existed in 1981. Once Hamilton's probation period was over, Alabama law clearly said that his probation could not be revoked. After *Hamilton*, the law on the issue became very confusing. That is because the law changed in *Hamilton v. State.*

Hamilton was an anomaly. No case in the casebooks before or since was just like it. Perhaps lawyers did not appeal cases like *Hamilton*. But when there exists a questionable appellate court opinion, lawyers are anxious to appeal so that they can attempt to change the precedent. Questionable cases are easier to attack and obtain reversal. I suspect that the trial judges have simply not followed *Hamilton*. They probably have not been willing to revoke probation after the probation period has ended. They are probably also careful of what they say about probationers finishing payment of their restitution. No judge is perfect, however, and some judge has surely had a case that followed the facts of the Hamilton probation situation. I suspect that not only have judges refused to use the *Hamilton* decision, but so have district attorneys.

The Court of Civil Appeals could have reversed Judge Price, and Hamilton still would have remained in prison for the rest of his life. The decision's purpose was not to protect the public. Judge Hooper, who followed the law in existence at the time he decided that Hamilton had finished his term of probation, suffered the effects of this new court precedent. He was the one who was publicly tarred and feathered for that decision in the press. Any first year law student could have studied the records, as I did, and come to the same conclusion. Lawyers and judges know better, or at least they should know better. When it came to Sonny Hornsby, who was up for reelection as chief justice, the highest judicial official in the state, not only did he miss the law, but he could not even get his facts straight.

Notes

1. *Montgomery Advertiser,* August 14, 1983.

2. Section 15-22-54(a) & (b), Alabama Code of 1975: "(a) The period of probation or suspension of execution of sentence shall be determined by the court, and such period may be continued, extended or terminated; provided, that in no case shall the maximum probation period of a defendant guilty of a misdemeanor exceed two years, nor shall the maximum probation period of a defendant guilty of a felony exceed five years. Upon the satisfactory fulfillment of the conditions of probation or suspension of sentence, the court shall by order duly entered on its minutes, discharge the defendant. (b) The court granting probation may,

upon the recommendation of the officer supervising the probationer, terminate all authority and supervision over said probationer prior to the declared date of completion of probation upon a showing of continued satisfactory compliance with the conditions of probation over a period of said probation."

3. *Hamilton v. State*, 441 So. 2d 1035 (Ala. Cr. App. 1983).

4. A formal discharge in previous cases had a fairly clear definition. Now, it could be conditioned upon a moral injunction to the probationer, e.g., Hooper's advice to Hamilton that he should go ahead and pay his restitution even though he had completed his probation. § 15-22-54, Ala. Code 1975, mentions discharge: "Upon the satisfactory fulfillment of the conditions of probation or suspension of sentence, the court shall, by order duly entered on its minutes, discharge the defendant."

There is something strange in the case history. *Chapman v. State*, 199 So. 2d 865, 43 Ala. App. 693 (App. Ct. 1967) discusses "discharge," but its discussion in the casebook differs from its discussion in a computerized legal publication. What's interesting about the difference is that the computerized version sounds like the *Hamilton* case. That's significant because a 1967 case similar to *Hamilton* would supply the needed precedent to legitimate *Hamilton*. The Michie computer disk quotes the statute: "Upon satisfactory fulfillment of the conditions of probation or suspension of sentence, the court shall by order duly entered on its minutes, discharge the defendant." That quote does not even appear in the casebook, which was in existence long before the computer version. The only reference to "discharge" in the casebook version deals with habeas corpus: ". . . entitled to his discharge on habeas corpus."

This *Chapman* case involved a man who was sentenced to seven years in the penitentiary for assault with intent to commit murder. He was granted probation (amazingly) for a period of ten years. Eight and a half years later he was convicted of manslaughter in the first degree and received five years in the penitentiary for this crime. The court also revoked his probation and ordered him to serve the original seven years for the first conviction for assault. This case is totally different from the Hamilton case because Chapman still had a year and a half to finish his probation. In the *Chapman* case, the man was still on probation when he committed the crime. There is no question that Chapman's probation should have been revoked. Yet, the Michie computer version is a summary that sounds very different from the casebook version and reads similar to the *Hamilton* case. The portion of the computer version I found unusual was: "The period of probation or suspension of execution of sentence shall be determined by the court and may exceed the length of the sentence and such period may be extended by the court but shall not exceed a period of three years from date of sentencing. Upon satisfactory fulfillment of the conditions of probation or suspension of sentence, the court shall by order duly entered on its minutes, discharge the defendant."

Why would the computer version be different from the casebook version?

5. Consider *Smitherman v. State*, 639 So. 2d 569 (Ala. Cr. App. 1993). *Smitherman* involved the revocation of Smitherman's probation more than five years past the date of his sentence. Even the opinion in *Hamilton* stated that the Alabama statute did not allow the extension of probation past the maximum five-year limit. The author of the opinion, Mark Montiel of all people, allowed the extension because Smitherman had been detained for not paying his restitution three and a half years after the sentencing date. However, at that time, the trial judge did not revoke his probation. Yet, Montiel used that event as a justification for extending the time period for revoking his probation beyond the maximum five-year period. The opinion read: " 'Probation revocation proceedings may properly be initiated after the actual probation period has expired where there had been no formal discharge from probation.' " *Young v. State*, 552 So. 2d at 880; see also *McCasky v. State*, 589 So. 2d 790, 792 (Ala.Cr.App. 1991). The appellant's failure to pay restitution from December 19, 1991, to July 30, 1992, when his probationary term would have ended, was a violation of a condition of his probation. The appellant never received a formal discharge from probation, and the maximum number of years in which to bring a revocation action had thus not expired." *Smitherman*, at 571. He also added that the court had given Smitherman no formal discharge from probation, an idea first used in Hamilton.

Aiding and Abetting Murder?

On 10 October 1994, before the Jerry Hamilton commercial aired, the *Birmingham Post-Herald* ran a story about the case. It contained the same mistakes made by the Montgomery Advertiser in 1983. Time does not always bring about a correction of errors in history. In this case, the truth had become fuzzier with time. The passage of time resulted in a loss of interest in what really happened. Players had changed and moved away. All that was left was the perception perpetrated by the newspaper stories. Considering how much time had passed, it would have been even more difficult than in 1983 to get the story straight.

The article did not repeat the erroneous statement that Hooper improperly refused to revoke Hamilton's probation in 1982. The article told of James P. Ammons, a chiropractor in Clanton at the time of the murder, who had moved to Crestview, Florida. He said that he had made some commercials about Judge Hooper because Hooper's "the one that kept Jerry Hamilton out of jail when he should have been in jail, and my daughter wouldn't have been killed." He did not say how he came to know that Hooper was running for chief justice. He spoke by phone with the reporter. At the end of the conversation, he said he had not yet seen the finished commercials. " 'They're supposed to send me a copy for me to OK before they're used,' he said." He didn't say who "they" were, nor did he say where he got the money to pay for the commercials. Hornsby's campaign would not respond to calls from the newspaper. Judge Hooper didn't want to say anything until he had seen the commercials. The article did make some explanation as to the true source of the commercials: "A source close to the Hornsby campaign, who spoke on condition of anonymity, said Ammons was taped by the chief justice's campaign organization."

As I said before, Hooper went to view Hornsby's commercial at a television station. Hooper chose the day for his own commercial to run. On that very day, Hornsby ran his Jerry Hamilton commercial. I did not see Hornsby's commercial when it first came out because I was too busy. My wife saw it and told me it was bad. Jack Campbell, Hooper's campaign manager, had seen it and told me it looked like some sleazy production with eerie music in the background and pictures of Missy DeVaughn flashed up for dramatic effect. On a Sunday, I watched the public television news program "For the Record." A panel of journalists were discussing the chief justice election. Specifically, they focused on TV advertising. They showed our commercial about the lawyer getting the fundraising call from the chief justice. After it was over, the moderator of the panel had a grin on her face. The other journalists seemed to enjoy it also.

After talking about its effectiveness, they showed the Hornsby commercial about Jerry Hamilton. It was worse than sleazy. It was the worst thing I had ever seen. I became so angry that I got up and called Jack on the phone and told him that commercial meant "war." I no longer just wanted Hooper elected. My goal was to make sure that Hornsby did not get reelected. In my opinion, a man who could run a commercial that distorted the facts and misrepresented the law was not fit to practice law, much less be chief justice. The *Tuscaloosa News* reporter on "For the Record" said Hornsby's commercial was the worst example he had ever seen of how low a judicial election could go. But he had to admit that it was pretty effective. It was sixty seconds long. Hornsby could afford to pay for that length of commercial.

The commercial began with a 1983 newspaper picture of Perry Hooper, Sr. It was centered in the frame and surrounded by a black background. It was tinted orange, I assume, for some sort of horror picture effect. Eerie music played as the narrator spoke. In the middle of the first sentence by the narrator, a newspaper picture of Jerry Hamilton faded in. It also was tinted orange, and it was next to the picture of Judge Hooper. It was the worst picture they could find of Hamilton, and it looked bad. Narrator: "Circuit Judge Perry Hooper, Sr. put convicted felon Jerry Hamilton back on the streets and stopped a district attorney's effort to revoke Hamilton's probation." Then, an action scene appeared in the background. It was a scene of prison bars closing or opening.

Other than Judge Hooper and his family, I was more incensed by this commercial than anyone because I had carefully researched the facts and the law. The first claim was totally misleading. The statement portrayed Judge Hooper's decision to not revoke Hamilton's probation as a decision to release him from confinement—"put convicted felon Jerry Hamilton back on the streets." Of course, that was not what happened. Hamilton was already on the streets. The average viewer, who was not as knowledgeable as I, would think Hamilton was probably a convicted killer at the time of his hearing before Hooper. That was the impression one was left with. Hornsby's commercial followed the newspaper conclusions about Hooper's actions instead of the actual facts and the law at that time. A lawyer is ethically obliged to be careful to not take a third party, like a newspaper's analysis of a case, at face value. Hornsby didn't follow that basic rule of ensuring that he was restating the law and facts accurately. Hornsby was the chief justice.

Before the narrator's next statement, the background scene switched to show a gavel coming down and striking a judge's bench in slow motion. Then, after that, in the middle of the narrator's statement, there appeared a hand signing a document, signifying Hooper signing a bank note. Narrator: "He personally intervened with another judge to free Hamilton, and he signed a bank note so Hamilton could buy a car." At this point, a very strange scene appeared in the background. Hooper's and Hamilton's pictures disappeared. There was very eerie music playing in the background, a violin with menacing drumbeats. The hazy scene showed a young woman being thrown down in slow motion and then a knife coming to her throat. She had a distinct resemblance to Missy DeVaughn.

Then a picture of Missy DeVaughn appeared. The narrator continued: ". . . perhaps the same car he used in the kidnapping and murder of young court reporter Missy DeVaughn."

Here is where Hornsby was not even as accurate with regard to the facts as the newspapers. Hooper never talked to another judge about the case. He talked to a district attorney, not a judge. In their reports of the abduction, the newspaper reports were also clear and consistent concerning the car he used. He used Missy's car. The allegation that Hooper "intervened" to "free Hamilton" was shaky at best. The district attorney, Glen Curlee, and Hamilton's lawyer, stated that Hamilton would have been released no matter what; there was no case against him. It's bad enough that Hornsby got the law and court records wrong, but he could have at least used the facts as reported by the newspapers.

The photo of Missy DeVaughn disappeared, and the commercial moved to an interview with Dr. J.P. Ammons. He sat in what looks like a home, with a green plant behind him. He was an older man, almost decrepit in his manner of speaking. In the commercial he said, "Nine days before Jerry Hamilton murdered . . . kidnapped and murdered my daughter, Perry Hooper went to Autauga County and got him out of jail." Then the black background reappeared with bold white letters saying, "Judge Perry Hooper . . ." Then these words appeared beneath the others: "got Jerry Hamilton out of jail." Then Ammons continued talking: "I mean, he didn't pull the trigger or use the knife, but he certainly aided and abetted." At this point, the picture returned to the Ammons interview: "I honestly think that Hooper is as guilty of murdering my daughter as Jerry Hamilton, simply because he was derelict in his duty."

There is no way that these words represent anything other than the mistaken and grief-filled thoughts of the very sad father of a murdered and beloved daughter. Dr. Ammons had learned nothing of what really happened, of the negligence of the district attorney's office. He still blamed Hooper. The words "aided and abetted" are words full of legal meaning. Chief Justice Hornsby should have known that. However, the law concerning slander is very weak with respect to public figures. Hornsby knew this. But those words go too far, even in a political campaign. Ammons also had his facts wrong about the Autauga district attorney meeting. Hooper went to Autauga County approximately four months before the murder, not nine days.

Then the eerie music began again, and a new and different newspaper photo of Hooper appeared. This time he was looking straight at the camera. It was actually a good picture of him. A black background surrounded the picture. The camera zoomed in for a close-up of the photo and as the narrator spoke, his words appeared at the bottom of the photo until it grew large enough to fill the screen. The narrator's final words appeared on the screen: "Why did Perry Hooper protect Hamilton?" Then after those words appeared: "What hold did Hamilton have on Hooper?" The next words did not appear on the screen. Narrator: "Do you want Perry Hooper to be chief justice of our supreme court?" The commercial ended with the ominous drumbeats of the eerie music.

It was the worst piece of political advertising trash I had ever seen. For anyone to trash a good man's reputation like that was awful, but this commercial was produced by the chief justice of the state's highest court. One fellow who called in a couple of weeks later to a local news show, "People's Poll," on the chief justice election expressed my feelings best. He said, "Sonny Hornsby ought to be arrested for putting out that commercial." It went way beyond the bounds of normal political attack ads.

Strangely enough, however, this commercial was exactly what Hooper wanted. A balanced ad that put together all the questionable things in Hooper's career, things that accumulate in any person's life, would have been much more effective. Hooper had again drawn Hornsby out, and he hoped this ad would produce a backlash against Hornsby. We wondered why he had done it. We decided that he had read the polls and become desperate. But there may have been more. Hornsby may have taken the attacks about the appellate court settlement personally. He certainly seemed to take it that way at the news conference he crashed on the judicial building steps. Anyway, he began to run the ad early in the campaign.

Hooper's ranking in the polls dropped precipitously after that commercial began to run all over the state. At times, the campaign seemed to become desperate, even helpless, as the ad did its dirty work. Hooper ran his ad, but Hornsby had much more money available to run his ads. He had already been running his "feel-good" ad about the administrative improvements he claimed to have made in the court system and its computer system. Then this Jerry Hamilton ad appeared. There was also the Don Martin ad about Judge Hooper's relationship with the local real estate mogul who went too far out on a limb financially, filed bankruptcy, and was convicted of fraud. Of course, Hornsby's commercial brought up the lawsuit and all the loaded words used in the complaint. We believed the lawsuit was entirely political, a home-cooked subject for a commercial. There was no time for a trial before the election, so the commercial presented no proof, merely innuendo and accusation.

This takes a toll on a candidate's family. The Jerry Hamilton commercial particularly took a toll on the Hooper family. They had lived through that trauma once, in 1983. It was bad enough that this courthouse worker had killed Missy DeVaughn, but all the allegations and publicity that seemed to place so much blame on Judge Hooper were too much. Guilt by newspaper story.

Judge Hooper conferred with some good legal minds. It was clearly a slanderous ad, but the standard of proof for slander of a public official is high—"actual malice." In a political campaign, people tend to expect some exaggeration. But this ad was bad even for politics. Hooper made the decision to follow the Alabama Code and write to Hornsby to demand that he publicly, to the same extent that he advertised, retract and apologize for publicizing the slander. This was the first legal step required before Hooper could file a lawsuit. We knew Hornsby would never apologize in the middle of a major campaign. A lawsuit would have been a long shot, but Hooper was seriously considering it. He had endured enough. He sometimes joked that even if he didn't win the chief justice election, he could get rich off a successful lawsuit against

Hornsby. The use in the ad of the words "aiding and abetting" a kidnapping and murder was, on its face, libelous. Hooper sent the following letter to Hornsby:

> "Dear Chief Justice Hornsby:
>
> A political advertisement on behalf of your candidacy, broadcast widely on television, falsely accuses me of 'aiding and abetting' a kidnapping and homicide. These statements are false and defamatory; have been published maliciously; and this libelous and defamatory publication of yours has been made with knowledge that this charge is false or with reckless disregard of whether it is false or not. See, *Camp v. Yeager*, 601 So. 2d 924 (Ala. 1992).
>
> "Pursuant to § 6-5-186, Alabama Code, I hereby demand that you make a full and fair public retraction of this charge in as prominent and public a place or manner as the publication of this advertisement occupied.
>
>
>
> Yours truly,
> Perry O. Hooper, Sr."
>
>

This letter complied with Alabama law regarding libel. Judge Hooper received help in drafting it from Montgomery attorney Maury Smith and others. It referenced the clearest and most vicious part of the ad. Accusing someone of a vicious crime is *prima facie* damaging to one's reputation. In other words, if Hooper went to court, he wouldn't have to prove those words damaged his reputation. He would still have to prove knowledge of their falsity, and malice on Hornsby's part. Hornsby could always argue that he was not being malicious and that all he did was try to win an election. The letter was hand delivered to Hornsby, and it was also released to the press with an explanatory press release. It is interesting that Hornsby responded by saying that he stood by the ad. Nevertheless, a few days later, the ad stopped appearing. It did not appear again until about two weeks before the election, but it had been changed. It no longer included the words "aiding and abetting." Gone was the reference to the possibility that Hamilton used his own car to commit the crime and the

reference to influencing a judge. These were small changes in
an ad so full of egregious accusations, but significant in that
the changes were made quietly and after Hornsby had publicly
stood by the original.

Before the letter was written, Judge Hooper held a press
conference about the TV ad, in which he revealed:

> When I was considering the race for Chief Justice, I
> sought advice from family and friends. Most of the
> advice encouraged me to run. But some warned me it
> would get rough and personal, that the trial lawyers'
> coffers were huge, and that they would say and do
> whatever it took to win—particularly if they thought I
> was leading in the polls. Last Thursday, Sonny Hornsby
> and the trial lawyers unleashed their most vicious as-
> sault against me with a TV ad that contained misrep-
> resentations of the truth. If Sonny Hornsby runs a
> good campaign and defeats me on the issues, that's
> fine, and I'll accept the judgment of the voters of Ala-
> bama. But to dredge up this eleven-year old case and
> try to defeat me with vicious personal attacks is simply
> unconscionable.

> I have been in public service long enough to stomach
> rough politics, but it is not fair to subject my wife,
> children and grandchildren to such distortions, innu-
> endoes, and malicious tactics as Sonny Hornsby and
> the trial lawyers have used. I am referring to the case
> of Missy DeVaughn who was murdered by Jerry
> Hamilton some eleven years ago. The ad suggests that
> I got Hamilton out of jail—a total falsehood—that I
> somehow aided and abetted in her murder, which is
> ridiculous. If there had been any wrongdoing on my
> part, you better believe that Jimmy Evans would have
> prosecuted me in his usual headline-grabbing manner.
> I grieve for the DeVaughn family. I know that if some-
> thing happened to one of my family members, I would
> be devastated. But the idea of using a non-factual ver-
> sion of this case is wrong. I ask Mr. Hornsby to with-
> draw this ad immediately. His use of this issue cheap-
> ens the office of chief justice and demeans judicial

candidates all over Alabama. He should be ashamed to resort to such gutter tactics.

My duty in this campaign is to point out the fundamental differences between Sonny Hornsby and myself. When the people of Alabama are able to compare us, I will be elected on November eighth. I am a Republican. He is a Democrat. I have not and will not personally solicit money from lawyers. Hornsby also ignores the truth in an ad in which he claims he supports the election of judges by all the people. I oppose the court-packing scheme where minority judges are hand picked by a committee controlled by Joe Reed. But Hornsby agreed to the secret settlement without allowing this to first go to federal court where we would have had a better chance to preserve our system of electing judges. Let it be said for the record that I favor at-large elections for judges and do not support election by districts. Does Hornsby believe that he can tell any lie that he wants to and the public will simply believe him? I believe the tort reform laws passed in 1987 are constitutional. His court has ignored the will of the legislature and has rewritten rather than interpreted the law. If Alabama is ever to expand our industrial and small business base we must bring fairness—not excess—to our verdicts. My campaign has focused and will continue to focus on these issues. I urge Mr. Hornsby to withdraw his misleading TV ad and to get to the real issues.

The ad had an initial beneficial effect on Hornsby's standing in the polls. Our ad and the media coverage of Hornsby's solicitation of lawyers had done its work, and Hornsby had needed something to pick up his ratings. After running his commercial for several weeks, Hooper's ratings in the polls started to pick up. We hoped the backlash against Hornsby's sleaze commercial was working in Hooper's favor.

Hornsby could afford several different commercials. We thought one was a fraudulent attempt to steal one of our key issues. It began with a picture of Hornsby working at the supreme court. The words on the screen and the narrator said,

"Chief Justice Sonny Hornsby is fighting to keep our courts free and independent." It then changed to a zoom-in of Sonny talking to the camera and saying, "Since 1868, all the people of Alabama have elected all the judges of Alabama. Today, there are forces at work to allow the federal courts to take over our state court system and take away the right of the people to elect their judges. I support the continued election of all the judges by all the people of Alabama." It ended with the narrator saying, "Chief Justice Hornsby, working for Justice."

If he had not used such absolute language, I would have assumed that the commercial was referring to the desire of some Republicans, like Montiel, to have district elections for the appellate courts. However, his use of the words "all the judges" means he was referring to the appellate court settlement, which he personally approved. He could have said, "I support the continued statewide election of judges." That would have left out some facts, but it would have been less egregious. This misuse of words is a perfect example of what plaintiff trial lawyers like Hornsby allege to sue insurance and car companies all the time. Did Hornsby learn the wrong type of morality from his years as a practicing trial lawyer? Or does the finger pointing at a business or insurance company guilty of fraud contain four pointing back at the accuser? Hornsby was not above this slick use of words to mislead the public and retain his seat on the highest court of the state.

During the week before the election on Novermber 8, 1994, NBC News ran a story about Hornsby's fundraising practices. Tom Brokaw on the 6:00 evening news was shaking his head in disapproval. We couldn't believe it. It was perhaps the worst thing that could have happened to Hornsby so close to November 8. NBC aired a short spot of Hooper calling the practice evil. They also gave time to Hornsby. When the interviewer asked Lanny Vihes why he gave so much money to judicial candidates, Lanny said, "Good guv'ment." It was not convincing. That news show plus Hooper's "Good mornin' to you, sir" commercial narrowed the margin between Hooper and Hornsby appreciably.

Chapter Six ────────────────────────────────

How to Steal
An Election—Almost

The night of the election, I went home at about 5:00 P.M. to get ready for the election night festivities at Judge Hooper's house. My wife and I arrived at what we hoped would be a victory party and grabbed something to eat. The election results had already begun to come in. Hooper and the other Republican candidates for the supreme court were behind. But it was still early. At some point in the evening, Hooper began to gain on Hornsby. At about 10:30 or 11:00 P.M., he was ahead of Hornsby by 6,027 votes with 53 percent of the 3303 precincts reporting. That lead increased to 7,000 by midnight. His lead continued to increase through the early morning hours. At one point, Hooper turned to a campaign aid and asked, "Well, are you ready to go to work at the supreme court?" At about 3:30 or 4:00 A.M., with 87% of the precincts reporting, Hooper was leading by about 13,000 votes. My wife turned to Sam Duvall and asked if it was safe to say we had won. He said, "With a lead like that this late in the returns, I don't think they can steal it from us now." The other supreme court races were close but the Democratic candidates were still ahead.

Television station WAKA had a panel of newscasters discussing the races. One veteran political watcher named Frank Brewer prophetically said that a factor not yet considered was absentee ballots. He said, "There's notorious counties as far as absentee ballots. . . . They're paper ballots. . . . At one time, if they got tired, they just went home." He was referring to the poll workers going home. That meant they had all night to create new absentee ballots. He added, "We still have five counties with more registered voters on the rolls than adult residents of the county. . . . We'd have to have more than a

75

five to six thousand vote lead to be comfortable."[1] The news-
caster even mentioned a problem with a voting machine in
Wilcox County. A report was made that if a voter pulled the
Democratic lever on that machine, he could not split his ticket
to vote for an individual Republican candidate. That was a
warning of things to come.[2]

Bob Howell of WSFA News revealed a particularly disturbing event. Late in the coverage, at about 3:30 A.M., he said
that some of the poll workers in certain counties were going
home to bed. That would prevent the reporting of the counties' results until morning. I remembered an incident Jack had
told me about from his days of poll watching. The polls where
he was working closed, and all the votes had been collected.
A poll worker said that he was taking the results to the county
courthouse as he was required by law to do. However, there
was a delay in his arrival, so Jack called the sheriff who found
the poll worker at home busily filling out ballots with which
to stuff the ballot box. I couldn't get that story out of my mind
when Bob Howell said that. I hoped that the Republican
party's poll watchers were being careful to do their job.

The next day the *Montgomery Advertiser* reported the mood
at the Hornsby "victory party." "Sonny Hornsby was locked in
a fierce battle late Tuesday night in his race for a second term
as chief justice. At 12:30 A.M. today, Republican Perry Hooper
Sr. led by about 7,000 votes at the end of an unusually bitter
judicial campaign. With seventy-five percent of the state's 3,303
precincts reporting, unofficial returns showed the chief justice
had 427,868 votes; Mr. Hooper, 434,930—effectively a 50-50
split. . . . By 11:00 P.M. the once-buoyant crowd surrounding
Chief Justice Hornsby at a downtown restaurant became sub-
dued. The chief justice himself stood in front of a television,
surrounded by staff scratching down figures on a notepad. . . . 'I
don't know where it's coming from. It's about 5,500 votes
now,' he said." The Thursday edition also reported on that
party: "An increase in drink orders coincided with the abrupt
shift, waiters there said."

At about 10:00 A.M. the next day, Hooper was ahead by
fourteen thousand votes. At that time, the only boxes left to
count were Republican boxes. We thought it was over. With

97 percent of the precincts reporting, we were still ahead by 10,000 votes. Then I received a call from my wife. She said that with 98 percent of the polls reporting Hooper was ahead by only twenty-five votes. How could that be, we asked? Within a half-hour, Hornsby was ahead by 1200 votes. During the day, Hornsby's lead changed until it rested, temporarily, at 698 votes.

We could not understand how the lead had changed so drastically. In one hour, the votes in the chief justice race changed by about 10,000, and the votes in the race between Kennedy and See changed by about 7,000. It was rumored later that 4,000 write-in ballots were counted late. Those voters casting write-in ballots had placed Johnny Ford, the well-known black mayor of Tuskegee, on their ballots for state auditor. That was not enough to change the result that drastically. In addition, such ballots would also have negatively affected the Republican candidate for governor, the top of the ticket. However, no such effect registered. It would also have helped the incumbent Democrats running for the courts of appeals. Those races were below the supreme court races on the ballot. No such assistance registered. At some point on the morning of Wednesday, 9 November 1994, it appeared that some votes were added to the supreme court races but not to any others.

We also began to hear about problems at various polls. In Wilcox County, over 100 absentee ballot applications were not even submitted by registered voters. The absentee ballot manager would not let John Grods, the Republican poll watcher, and an attorney, challenge ballots that were improperly filled out. If a poll watcher is unable to challenge a ballot, there is no way to later identify who cast the ballot during a contest. There is little that one can do in a contest if you don't know how the fraudulent voter voted. On election day, the absentee ballot manager, which is often the circuit clerk, separates the identifying envelope from the ballot and throws it away. That process keeps the ballot confidential. However, Alabama law provides that the absentee ballot manager who opens the ballot must keep challenged ballots attached to the envelope. That way, in an election contest, the legislature can determine that the identified voter was truly the one casting the ballot, that the voter was registered, and that there was no fraud involved in the casting of the ballot.

In Greene County, massive numbers of absentee ballots which could be traced to no voter were delivered to one post office box. Absentee ballots accounted for approximately 25% of the total vote for Greene County—approximately 1,450 absentee ballots out of a total of approximately 4,833 votes cast for the county. The normal percentage is about 7% to 8% of the total votes for a county. In 1994, there were 7,642 registered voters in Greene County, while Jefferson County (including Bessemer) had 383,089 registered voters. Yet, Jefferson County had a total of 3,564 absentee ballots cast in the 1994 general election.[3]

Also, a woman named Pam Montgomery found absentee ballots sent to fourteen people at a post office box used by the local Democratic party in Eutaw in Greene County, 24 absentee ballots sent to the acting chairman of the local Democratic party, and 8 sent to the address of the Greene County Sewer and Water Authority. We also heard about strange activities taking place at the polls in Montgomery County. Jacqueline Gandy of Montgomery, while visiting her mother at a nursing home, found a woman by the bedside of a comatose woman. The woman had filled out an absentee ballot for the woman in the bed. However, Mrs. Gandy was sure that the bedridden woman was unable to understand and give instructions as to how she wanted to vote.

Perry County was another hot spot. The *Marion-Times Standard* on 9 November reported the results of the election: "As the general election approached, Perry County's notorious absentee-voting machine geared up for its final effort of the election year." The circuit clerk's office mailed 2,122 absentee ballots. Sixty were returned as "insufficient address." Those numbers showed that 16% of the population of Perry County was prepared to vote absentee. Two thousand sixty-two ballots equaled 24.76% of the registered voters of the county. The legitimate reasons for voting absentee are absence from the county on election day and illness that prevents someone from voting at their normal polling place. Were 24.76% of the voting population of that county too ill to vote or out of the county on 8 November? It's a rural county, so it is not full of professional people travelling to business meetings. The results of the supreme court race from that county as of 9 November were: Hornsby—3275; Hooper—1227; Kennedy—3276; See—1103; Cook—3246; Montiel—1186; Butts—3333; Russell—1050. That type of spread between Republican and Democrat in a rural Alabama county is typical. Think about what effect over 2,000 absentee ballots could have on the elections in that county. From the results, it looked as if only a little over 4,500 people voted. That means the absentee ballots made up about 40% of the vote.

We learned of more problems around the state. A man named Harold Raley, who was running for the Alabama House of Representatives, was told by a group that for $5,000, he could get about 1,500 votes by absentee and at the polls. In Dale County, one voting machine had failed to record the votes for a Republican state senate candidate. We did not learn until later whether that affected the supreme court races. It did. We heard that there were problems in other counties, like Madison, the county in which Huntsville is located. We couldn't learn all the details until the certification process had been completed. Madison County planned to hold certification the Monday following the election. We did our best to keep track by calling the counties and local Republicans.

We would later learn some interesting facts from Justice Houston. On the day following the election, Houston went to see Bill Bowen, a judge on the court of criminal appeals, to see how he had done. Bowen said that he was behind by about 10,000 votes, and he had probably lost. He later found Justice Kennedy and his staff mourning the results of the election. They told Houston he was behind by about 7,500 votes, and the only remaining boxes were strong Republican ones. Justice Houston then wrote a letter of congratulations to Harold See. After delivering the letter, he was told that Hornsby and Kennedy were now ahead. Justice Houston heard from a court building employee that Joe Reed had told members of the Alabama Democratic Conference to write in Johnny Ford's name for state auditor, and the voting machine caused those ballots to be kicked out. When those votes were counted the next day, they allegedly helped the Democrats because they were straight Democratic ballots. Justice Houston then went to see Bill Bowen, expecting to see that his votes had changed. But Bowen's vote totals had not changed at all, and he was still behind by the same margin. Justice Houston also called Fob James' office, whose vote total had not changed at all. Why would the vote totals change for the supreme court candidates but not the governor or the lower appellate court races? Also, according to the Alabama secretary of state's numbers, the total number of write-in votes for Ford came to only 4,176. That was not enough votes to change the results in the Hooper and See races. Joe Reed is the unchallenged leader of the Alabama Democratic Committee (ADC), the black portion of the Alabama Democratic party.

I spoke by phone with Collin Luke, an attorney in Birmingham with expertise in election law. I told him the vote gap (698 votes), and he said that we should do everything we could to investigate what happened at the polls. Math errors uncovered at some polling places might be enough to change a lead of only a few hundred votes in a race involving more than 1.12 million total votes. By correcting such errors, we could realistically change the result of the election even without raising the specter of vote fraud and a major project of dubious success like an election contest in the legislature. It is important to understand how votes are tallied at the county level to see the potential effect math errors have.

In Alabama, different counties use different methods of voting. Some use the old machines with levers. Some use the newer machines that receive a paper ballot filled out like a multiple choice computer page with boxes filled out by pencil. The machine reads the ballot and counts the votes in each race. I heard that there were three counties in Alabama that still used paper ballots that the voters stuffed in a box. Those were the most dangerous targets for fraud. All absentee ballots are paper ballots. They are not counted electronically.

The results from each machine or box are recorded by the poll workers and then delivered to the county courthouse. The results are also usually posted outside the polling place. At the courthouse, the probate judge often listens as someone calls out the results, and he records them. He then gives both parties and any independent parties a chance to review the results the following Friday to see if there are any discrepancies. After that, the probate judge certifies the results from the county. A math error can occur anywhere along that path before the results are reported to the office of the secretary of state. After giving the parties a chance to review the results, the probate judge sends them to the secretary of state, who has until fifteen days under state law after the date of the election to compile the results, count the votes, and certify the winners.[4] In 1994, that meant the secretary of state had until 23 November 1994 to count and certify the statewide elections, an important date with respect to later events.

There were too few Hooper campaign workers to go to all sixty-seven Alabama counties to check on the results at each polling place. So they started calling the local county Republicans and told them just how close the race was. Someone needed to check the results at every step of the process—the polling place results, the probate judge's numbers, etc. They needed to act immediately because some probate judges sent their results in before the Friday following the election. Sometimes the polling place results did not remain posted on the outside of the polling place. This job of going to every polling place also required a good bit of travel throughout a county. We made sure they understood that the law of Alabama specifically allowed them to analyze the certification results of the probate judge. If there were poll watchers at the polling places, then they could compare the probate judge's figures with the figures kept by those Republicans poll watchers. On election day, we had trouble with local officials in Wilcox County denying poll watchers access to the absentee ballots, even though the Birmingham attorney who was present showed the officials a xerox copy of the Alabama law on the matter. Fortunately, we had no trouble getting access to review the certification process. It helped that this election had no lack of media attention. There seemed to be a story about the election on the TV news every evening and an article in the paper every morning.

The most difficult task was that some counties had very few Republicans residing there, willing to be involved. Some counties would threaten to call the sheriff if someone attempted to exercise their rights. In Wilcox County, the poll watchers were threatened with jail for wanting to challenge absentee ballots.

The Hooper campaign was abuzz. They were calling probate offices all over the state, trying to get the most accurate and up-to-date figures as quickly as possible. The people we spoke with were amazingly patient with us, especially considering the fact that Hornsby's people and the media were making the same calls. Sometimes we heard a local official say that we were the fourth and fifth people to call about the chief justice election that particular day. Hooper's attorneys advised him to get a restraining order to protect the security of the ballots. By law, the local officials were required to secure all the ballots until the local certification was complete. Then the probate judge was to turn them over to the sheriff for safe-keeping for at least six months. After that they could destroy them.

We were afraid, however, that certain counties that were notorious for strange election results might still try to add ballots. There was plenty of time before Friday for a county to add to the results in some fashion. For example, an unscrupulous person could simply add some absentee ballots to the absentee ballot box. Once the identifying envelope of an absentee ballot is separated from the ballot, there's no way to determine whose ballot was cast properly or improperly or when it was cast. If investigators discover 200 absentee ballots in the box, there may be a record of only 150 absentee ballots being cast. But there is no way to distinguish the true from the false. The courts don't look kindly on throwing out potentially lawful votes.

The plan formed fluidly as the campaign encountered events. Hooper planned to contest the election, if possible. To do that he had to find fraud, and in order to find fraud he had to preserve the ballot materials. At the same time, we would try to correct as many errors in the vote records and tallies as possible to see if that might change the result. Hooper went to court in Shelby County where he knew he could get a reliable judge to hear his request for an injunction to keep the ballot materials secure in case a contest was necessary. Judge Al Crowson was a Republican circuit court judge, and Hooper filed his request for a restraining order to preserve the ballot materials inviolate before Crowson's court. Hooper also filed in federal court, just in case a state circuit court judge's order didn't carry enough weight with the bolder vote-stealers in the state. Judge Howard, a federal district judge in Mobile, issued an order similar to Judge Crowson's, but it was not issued until the afternoon of Thursday, 17 November. The written order was issued Friday, 18 November.

According to the newspapers, on the Wednesday afternoon following the election, Hornsby lead Hooper by 698 votes (560,856 to 560,158). According to our tally, Hornsby was ahead by only 304 votes. Jim Martin, the Republican candidate for state treasurer, was behind by only about 1,200 votes. The secretary of state had recently initiated a system by which counties could fax their results into his office to give him a preliminary total. But some counties didn't have fax machines or hadn't sent their figures in as quickly as expected. By the Thursday after the election, the secretary of state had his preliminary figures, showing Hornsby ahead by 698 votes. Bennett publicly declared what he called unofficial preliminary returns. On Thursday evening, with only 304 more votes than Hooper, Sonny Hornsby declared himself the winner. He made the announcement even though there were significant questions as to the numbers that had come out of the counties. Later events proved that his people were checking up on the results from each county just as we were. Hornsby knew that the difference in the results had changed in only two days from 698 to 304. However, the county results were not official until after their certifications were complete. They were supposed to be completed on the Friday following the election. However, some waited until Monday or Tuesday of the next week. There appeared to be no illicit motive for this delay. Perhaps some larger counties found it more expedient to wait.

Hooper was not yet ready to concede the election based on two things: the race was too close, and there were too many questions as to the legitimacy of the results. Jack Campbell told the media: "There's enough stuff out there. I just feel like you're going to see Allied Van Lines backed up to the supreme court building in January." The chairman of the Alabama Democratic party, Bill Blount, said that today's voting mechanism made stealing votes impossible. Sonny Hornsby said, "Recognizing that these [unofficial preliminary results] are unofficial, we nonetheless have no reason to expect them to change. This has been a hard-fought and well-won campaign." He spoke too soon.

There had never been a contest of a statewide election in Alabama history. Such a prospect involved gathering enough facts and witnesses to show that the election had been altered by fraud or mistake. It was a formidable task. Neither Hooper nor Hornsby wanted to go through such an ordeal. Such a procedure involved the House of Representatives choosing five members and the Senate choosing three members for an eight-member committee to investigate and make a report to the entire legislature. The legislature would then choose the winner. Hooper didn't want to contest because Democrats made up the majority of the legislators from whom the committee would be chosen to decide the issue. And the Senate was full of trial lawyers. Hornsby didn't want to contest because the House and its Speaker were solidly pro-business and anti-trial lawyer. In addition, the overwhelming majority of the fraud that occurred helped Democrats obtain office, not Republicans. Republicans did not have enough experience or control of the local offices in these rural counties to accomplish election fraud, even if they had wanted to. Absentee ballot fraud seemed historically to be a monopoly of the Democrats.

In only eight rural counties, out of 67 total counties in the state, 21% of all the absentee votes were cast. Those counties were Henry, Winston, Lowndes, Wilcox, Bullock, Hale, Perry, and Greene counties. Statewide absentee ballots represented little more than 3% of the total votes cast in the governor's race. Absentee ballots represented about 25% of the total votes cast in the State in November 1994 in the four most populous counties of Alabama. These counties make up 36% of Alabama's total population. In those four counties—Jefferson, Mobile, Montgomery, and Madison—9,600 absentee ballots were cast. In the eight rural counties mentioned above, 8,500 absentee ballots were cast. In each county, absentee ballots made up the following percentages of the total votes cast:

> Hale—30%
> Greene—30%
> Lowndes—16%
> Bullock—19%
> Henry—20%
> Perry—28%

In July 1995, before the U.S. House of Representatives Oversight Committee on Voter Registration and Elections, residents of Greene County appeared and told about election practices there. Pam Montgomery said that prior to the 8 November 1994 election, 400 absentee ballots were received at the circuit clerk's office. She said that on election day five men walked into the Eutaw Post Office and put three suitcases on the counter, opened them and began pulling out absentee ballots. She claimed that those absentee ballots represented 25% of all the votes cast in Greene County. Mrs. Montgomery told the committee: "We tend to think of America as the shining example of democracy where the majority rules. I am sad to report to this committee that this no longer is the reality in Alabama."

The 1996 election also demonstrated the incredible scope of absentee ballot abuse. Here are some statistics from the 1994 and 1996 elections comparing the percentage of total votes that absentee ballots made up in certain counties:

	1994	1996
Bullock	19%	5%
Greene	30%	5%
Hale	20%	4%
Henry	13%	7%
Lowndes	16%	7%

| Wilcox | 18% | 5% |
| Winston | 15% | 6% |

Notice the drastic reduction in the rate of absentee voting in each county. Every Republican running for statewide office won in the 1996 election. The only explanations that seemed to make any sense of these figures were: (1) there were fewer local elections (where Democrats have been strongest) involved in the 1996 election; (2) the Republican attorney general elected in 1994 promised to pursue voter fraud, and he proved that he would do so by bringing indictments in Wilcox County[5] and pursuing investigations in other counties. The Alabama Republican party also made sure it had poll watchers at sensitive polling locations all around the state in 1996. The percentages for the two elections show the powerful effect that absentee ballots can have on an election.

I had first hand knowledge of Hornsby's inability to find fraud or any errors that favored him, based on my experience in Wilcox County. On the Monday after election week, Bill Moulton, an investigator hired by Hooper's attorneys and I, were investigating what happened in some south Alabama counties. Our task was to make sure that the probate offices, clerks, and sheriffs were following orders to keep the ballot materials secure. We were also hoping to meet people who might be witnesses of fraud. We traveled to Macon, Houston, Henry, Dale, Bullock, Covington, and Wilcox Counties. While we were interviewing the probate judge of Covington County, she received a call from someone who thanked her for finding an error in the county vote total that, when corrected, gave Sonny Hornsby one more vote. That was about the best Hornsby could do in his search for errors.

Even more interesting is what happened in Wilcox County. While waiting for the probate judge to give us copies of some information, I waited in the part of the office holding the records of title. A man was telling another man about the election in which a Democratic nominee for the Wilcox County Commission had lost to an independent candidate. This independent candidate, Reginald Southall, had run and lost the Democratic primary. As an independent in the general election, Southall won by eleven votes. Southall received thirty-four votes at the polls, while David Wright, the Democrat, received 565 votes at the polls. So how did Southall win? He received 597 absentee votes, while Wright received only fifty-five absentee votes. The man in the records office was talking about helping Wright contest the election. In the middle of the discussion, he pointed at me and said, "He knows about it." I wondered how this fellow could know me. Apparently, the word was out about us.

This same fellow pulled me aside later and said that he was a trial lawyer and that he had supported Hornsby. He claimed to have second thoughts about that support. He said that, after the election, he had received a phone call from Hornsby's camp asking him if he could get those absentee ballots thrown out. He told them: "Look fellows, you get those ballots thrown out and you lose. Every single one of those ballots cast for Southall was a straight Democratic ballot except for the race for county commissioner." He said the only audible sound on the other end of the line was "Oh." Almost all the errors and fraud, when corrected, were in Hooper's favor. How could Hornsby hope to successfully contest the election if the secretary of state certified Hooper the winner? If Hornsby lost over 500 votes (Southall's absentees), his 304 vote margin was gone.

Hornsby tried an interesting tactic in Dallas County. We had learned that the probate judge had admitted that he mistakenly excluded 100 votes that were cast for Hooper on election night. Either a poll worker mistakenly wrote down eighty instead of 180, or someone called out the number eighty at the courthouse, or the person recording the number heard eighty. Nevertheless, 100 votes were left out. The probate judge said that he could not correct the error because he had already sent in his certified results to the secretary of state's office. Hooper had to go to court to try to get the probate judge to change his figures and add 100 votes that legitimately belonged to Hooper. Hornsby hired J.L. Chestnut to represent him. Chestnut was the attorney who had successfully appealed cases that the U.S. attorney had brought against accused vote stealers back in the 1980s.[6] At a hearing on 14 November, Chestnut asked for a delay of the hearing until Friday, 18 November 1994, so that

Hornsby could attend. Judge Jack Meigs granted the delay. Chestnut added a gem of a comment to the media. He said that "he was concerned about possible disenfranchisement of black voters." The case in Dallas County involved a 100-vote math error. We were dumbfounded to hear that correcting that error might disenfranchise black voters.

The majority of the errors after being corrected fell in Hooper's favor. On 11 November 1994, Shelby County Judge Al Crowson ordered all election materials seized. He justified his order by citing a 100-vote error in Hornsby's favor in Dallas County, 800 absentee ballots in Wilcox County that were challenged because they were not sealed or lacked an affidavit, and a failed voting machine in Butler County that failed to record votes for Republican Mark Montiel. There was an allegation that forty-seven felons, who may not legally vote under Alabama law, had voted in Hale County. We heard of improper "assistance" being given to voters in Montgomery County and money being passed in Elmore County. Then there were always the vote brokers. These were people who would go to a candidate and offer to get them a certain number of votes, say a thousand, at a dollar a vote. The vote broker would then send for a thousand absentee ballots. Before 1 January 1995, when a new state law went into effect, there was no limit as to how many absentee ballots a person could request from the circuit clerk's office. The vote broker would then go to the elderly at nursing homes for example. Some of these people knew what they were voting for and some didn't. It would also be possible for someone to fill out completely fraudulent absentee ballots by using the names of persons still on the registered voters list who were dead or unable to vote for some reason.

Even after Hooper had Crowson's order in hand, there were still major problems in several counties, including Wilcox, Covington, Henry, Lowndes, Perry, Clarke, Sumter, Cleburne, Hale, and Marion. The counties should have had the sheriff place the ballot materials in a jail cell for safekeeping. However, we found that some counties had the materials, which included the voting machines' electronic data packs, in cardboard boxes in unsecured rooms or open, public areas. Those problems provided added motivation for Hooper to go to federal court.

A brazenly illegal method of obtaining fraudulent votes would be to go to the courthouse and write down the names and addresses of all those who had requested an absentee ballot. The law requires that that list be posted at the courthouse, so that poll watchers can make sure that those voting absentee are registered. The vote thief could go to the voter's mailbox and actually steal the ballot out of the mailbox, fill it out, and send it back to the courthouse. If the legitimate voter seeks to again obtain an absentee ballot or tries to vote at the polling place on election day, that voter will not be able to legally vote because, according to the list of absentee voters, the voter is shown to have already voted. We heard several reports of people going to their polling places and being turned away because they were told that they had already voted. One woman in Macon County told us that her husband continued to receive an absentee ballot every year. The problem was that he had been dead for five years, and she had reported this fact to the Board of Registrars, the entity with the duty of updating the registered voters list. But they had apparently not updated those records.

On Friday evening of 11 November, Hooper held a press conference. He stated his intention not to concede Hornsby's claim of victory: "We have endured lies in this campaign, but I'll be damned if I will accept outright thievery. While Alabamians slept Tuesday night, forces were at work to overturn the will of the people." Hornsby responded by saying that it was sad for us to blame our defeat on poll workers who were "honest people who provide a public service." We never said that poll workers were the source of any fraud. There are many people who can gain access to absentee ballots and fraudulently create votes. Hornsby couldn't resist adding one more dig at Hooper: "This has been a long process, and I empathize with Mr. Hooper and his family. They have to have been through a lot in the last couple of days, and I wish them well." By the following Monday, he was singing a different tune.

On Monday, 14 November, it was confirmed that a machine in Dale County, a "vote accumulator," had not received all returns. The Circuit Clerk found the malfunction after an unofficial preliminary total was sent to the Secretary of State. Not only did the math error catapult the Republican candidate for state senate into office but it also gave Hooper a net gain of 295 votes. That cut Hornsby's lead to nine votes. If we could get the Dallas County 100 added, Hooper would lead by ninety-one votes. Madison County later found a large error in Hooper's favor. We had done it. We had found enough errors to change the results of the election. Now, Hornsby would have to contest the election. The question I kept asking myself was "What will they pull next?" We soon found out.

Notes

1. There's an old joke about two officials going through a grave yard collecting names for the absentee voters list off the tombstones. One complained to the other about not being able to read some of the names and said he wasn't going to list those names. The other became indignant and said, "Now Joe, you know that fella has just as much right to vote as the rest of these folks in here."

2. The bias of the legal community in the election was evident in the news coverage. WAKA's coverage was excellent in every respect except one. One of the members of their expert panel was local Montgomery attorney, Jay Lewis, a former newsman who was brand new to the legal profession and to whom they turned to get the lawyer's perspective on the judicial elections. He always had nothing but praise for the incumbent judges and nothing positive to say about the republican challengers. He spouted incorrect facts. For example, he said that Harold See had never practiced law. Not only was that incorrect, but it also came straight from Justice Kennedy's attack ads. See had practiced law for several years before becoming a law professor and teaching future lawyers at the University of Alabama. It is also interesting to note that at the time Justice Kennedy was appointed to a district court judgeship by his father-in-law, George Wallace, he had been out of law school for about one year. Mr. Lewis didn't mention that fact.

Mr. Lewis went on to explain that the reason See was making such a good showing was "not See's good reputation," but the alliance of big business, insurance companies and their PAC's pouring big money into the coffers of the GOP challengers. Never mind that Kennedy had over twice as much campaign money as See. I suppose trial lawyer money for Lewis is untainted. It was quite galling to see this intentional display of partisanship in a forum that was supposed to be neutral and objective.

3. I obtained these figures from the Alabama Secretary of State's office and the circuit clerk and voter registrar offices for Greene and Jefferson Counties. The percentage of votes cast in Greene County that were cast by absentee ballots was over 30%. The percentage of absentee ballots compared to the total number of registered voters in Greene County was over 19%. That last percentage in Jefferson County (registered voter population, 1994 = 383,089) was 0.93%.

4. "All returns of elections required by law to be sent to the Secretary of State must, within 15 days after an election, be opened and counted in the presence of the Governor, Secretary of State, and Attorney General, or two of them." Ala. Code 1975, § 17-14-20.

5. On August 25, 1997, a mother and daughter plead guilty to rigging absentee ballots during the 1994 Wilcox County Commission race between Reginald Southall and David Wright. Southall was the fellow who received 34 votes at the polls but 597 votes by absentee ballots. Wright, on the other hand, received 565 votes at the polls and 55 votes by absentee ballots. During the trial in which Wright contested the election, handwriting experts testified that as few as six people were responsible for the 597 absentee ballots cast for Southall. Wright and Southall settled that contest by agreeing that Southall would serve the first half of the County Commission term and Wright would serve the second half. By the time the trial would have finished, the term would have been almost halfway completed anyway. So it made sense for Wright to settle with Southall to save on attorney's fees. Southall apparently knew he would lose in a trial.

6. Interestingly, that U.S. Attorney was the same man who defeated Jimmy Evans for the Office of Attorney General of Alabama in 1994.

Hornsby's Desperation Bid

We had heard a rumor that Hornsby's son was so discouraged about the results of the race that he was on the floor weeping. It sounded preposterous. We didn't know if it was true or simply a clever trial lawyer ruse to get us to lower our guard and slow our efforts. By Monday, 14 November, however, we realized the report that the Hornsby camp was disconsolate was true. They had known the correct numbers before we had. They had a ready-made network of agents throughout the state, the trial lawyers, ready to do whatever was necessary, at no cost, to help Sonny. This was the grassroots aspect of the ATLA, and it added to their effectiveness in gathering information and taking legal action virtually anywhere in the entire state.

The official election results were due to the secretary of state's office by 18 November, and, by law, the secretary of state had the responsibility for certifying the statewide totals by 23 November, fifteen days after the election. Hornsby had time to plot a new strategy to keep Hooper from being certified the winner. A few in the media now knew just how far ahead Hooper was. WAKA TV, for example, reported that Hooper was ahead by 268 votes. Others knew that if the Dallas County 100 votes were added to Hooper's total, it would put him ahead by at least ninety-one votes. On Monday, 14 November 1994, Hornsby knew he had lost.

Publicly, the only thing the Hornsby people reported, after they figured out that Hooper was ahead and they knew that the numbers weren't going to change, was that they were concerned about approximately 2,000 unwitnessed and unnotarized absentee ballots around the state that had not been counted. This was a new message. Before this, the Hornsby campaign had dismissed any discussion of fraud or irregularities in the voting process.

Most people know that absentee ballots in Alabama have historically been subject to horrendous abuse. The only constraints on that abuse are the individual consciences of the voters, workers, and officials; the fear of prosecution by the state; the vigilance of poll watchers; and the witness/notarization requirement for absentee ballots. If this was a public relations ploy by Hornsby, it wasn't very smart. Public opinion was on the side of tightening up the absentee ballot process to combat the abuses, not loosening it. It didn't make much sense.

I should have gotten the hint of what was to come, however, from a statement by Secretary of State Bennett. On Tuesday, 15 November, the *Montgomery Advertiser* reported that he said that unwitnessed absentee ballots would only be a factor in the election if someone contested and the courts got involved. The Alabama Code specifically prohibits courts from deciding contests of statewide races. In fact, section 17-15-6[1] specifically prohibits the secretary of state from obeying any judge's order that would interfere with his counting and certifying of the election.

The word "chancery" basically means an equity court, which in Alabama is the circuit or trial court. Circuit courts have the broadest jurisdiction and the broadest power to consider all the facts of a case and construct appropriate remedies in those cases. Yet, the law specified that even that court could not interfere with the certification process by an election official, and Bennett, as secretary of state, was the highest ranking election official in the state of Alabama. To say a court lacks jurisdiction is the strongest way of saying that a court has no authority to hear and decide a case. In essence, this statute specified that Bennett, or any other election officer, can thumb his nose at any judge's order that "[seeks] to ascertain the legality, conduct, or results of any election." If any judge finds him in contempt, he can appeal directly to the Alabama Supreme Court. He need not file a bond, so it would cost him virtually nothing to appeal the contempt order. He has a duty as secretary of state to protect the election process from being interrupted by someone who doesn't like the result and tries to use the courts to stop the democratic process. If there's a problem with the conduct of the election, the loser can follow the statutory process and contest the election with the legislature. If Bennett was immune from the orders of anyone, even a judge, who attempted to prevent him from performing his duty, why did he say something about the courts getting involved and stopping the certification process? Bennett was a Democrat like every other major state office holder in Alabama at that time. He was not ignorant of section 17-15-6.

Bennett set Thursday, 17 November, as the date he would begin tallying the results of the election. Our biggest concern at the time was an honest vote. In order to avoid any allegation of tampering with the results, Bennett hired a well-known accounting firm, Jackson Thornton, to handle the actual compilation of the numbers. It also lengthened the time required for the process. What we did not know was that on Wednesday, 16 November 1994, the day before the results were to be counted, a Montgomery attorney and active Democrat named Joe Espy went into Montgomery County Circuit Court on behalf of an absentee voter. He filed for a temporary restraining order (TRO) to stop the counting of the votes. Ostensibly, an absentee voter whose vote was not counted brought the action against the secretary of state and the Montgomery County election officials. However, Hornsby's own campaign spokesman had mentioned these ballots a couple of days earlier, so we knew who was really behind it. This was Hornsby's way of challenging the election before he lost, in a courtroom instead of in front of the legislature.

At 5:30 P.M. (the Montgomery County Clerk's Office closes at 5:00 P.M.), Judge Joe Phelps held an emergency hearing in his private office and decided to issue the TRO. The basis was that unwitnessed, unnotarized absentee ballots had not been counted at the local level and approximately 2,000 voters had been disenfranchised thereby. That number of ballots could make the difference in a race that was separated by less than 300 votes, especially when the overwhelming majority of absentee ballots in Alabama are cast for Democrats.

Judge Phelps, who had contributed $500 to Sonny Hornsby's campaign, issued the TRO after a one-hour hearing. The transcript states that during that hearing he thoroughly studied the law on the matter. He ordered the TRO in spite of the clear and absolute language of section 17-15-6 of the Alabama Code. Consider the problems this type of precedent could set. Could any loser of an election now allege a problem with an election and then go into court to have the counting of the votes stopped? All a loser need do is find a surrogate plaintiff to claim an inability to vote for some reason. Then, that private citizen could file a lawsuit as a voter. That way it would not look like a contest. Such actions by candidates have the potential to shut down the entire elective process. Nowhere in the Alabama Code is a circuit court given specific and special powers that would allow that court to ignore section 17-15-6.

On Thursday morning, 17 November 1994, Secretary of State Jim Bennett stopped the counting of the votes, which Jackson Thornton had already begun to do. That was the first we heard of any TRO. The deadline under state law for the secretary of state to complete his count and certify the results was 23 November. Our understanding was that there would be a hearing on these absentee ballots the following Tuesday, 22 November. We were confident that if an honest vote count was held that day, Hooper would be certified the winner, and Hornsby would have to go through the onerous process of contesting the election with the legislature if he wanted to. It was apparent to us that he did not want to.

That Thursday morning, the questions from reporters for Jim Bennett came fast and furious. I was in the hallway near the offices of the secretary of state in the capitol. I took the opportunity during this question time to ask Bennett: "What about Alabama Code Section 17-15-6?" He turned and looked me in the eye with a somewhat startled look, then dropped his head and turned away and mumbled, "Uhh, we don't know if that applies before or after certification." The whole point of that code section was to prevent a delay in certification.

Bennett had probably spoken with someone in the attorney general's office. The attorney general acts as legal counsel for any state office needing legal advice. So he was probably getting legal advice from Jimmy Evans's office, which would not be very objective. He had already come up with a story as to why he was not following the statute.

Late in the afternoon, at approximately 4:30 P.M., I was waiting at the secretary of state's office. The Hooper campaign did not receive notice of everything that was happening regarding the counting of the votes, so the campaign staff took turns waiting outside Bennett's office. The campaign thought a vote count could take place any moment, and Hooper needed someone present if it did. As Bennett was speaking with some people in the hallway, I overheard him say something about a hearing at 5:30 P.M. at the courthouse. That was news to me.

I called Jack. He said he knew nothing about a hearing. Then I called Al Agricola, who said he would call the courthouse to confirm the time and date of the hearing. Al discovered that there was a 5:30 P.M. hearing, set before Judge Eugene Reese. Judge Reese had not been available the night before; that was why Judge Phelps heard Espy's original petition. Al said he would contact the state Republican party to see if they wanted him to represent the party before the circuit court. I went to my car where I had some copies of cases dealing with absentee ballots. I studied them in the short time before the hearing and then went over to the courthouse. Jack had gotten on the phone. The media were there in force. The courtroom was crowded.

I asked Al if he would allow me to sit at the counsel table. I had copies of a couple of cases that I thought might be important that I gave to Al, but I had not had sufficient time to carefully study them. They turned out to be the key precedent used by the plaintiff. Al Agricola had to ask to intervene in the case on behalf of the Alabama Republican party because the only named parties to the case were the two plaintiff voters, Jim Bennett, and the Montgomery election authorities, all Democrats.[2]

The hearing lasted for about an hour. Joe Espy[3] requested permission to make an opening statement. I assume that was for the benefit of the media people present. His statement was dramatic and eloquent in its concern for those voters whose absentee ballots were not counted because they were unwitnessed. He spoke of the fundamental right to vote, the purpose of the voting rules, and the innocent mistake some people had made by not having their absentee ballots witnessed or notarized. His legal argument rested on a couple of Alabama cases that held that Alabama follows the "substantial compliance" doctrine.[4] Therefore, according to Espy, voters need not comply with the statute governing absentee ballots.[5] He also made an eloquent statement of the importance of preserving the integrity of the election by preserving the integrity of absentee ballots. He made it seem as if he were representing the great and noble cause of democracy. His oratory was moving, but I was disgusted.

Al also asked for permission to make an opening statement, which Judge Reese granted. He laid out the facts as clearly as he could. The plaintiffs were trying to avoid the election contest provisions of Chapter 14 of Title 17 of the Alabama Code. Section 17-15-6 withdrew jurisdiction from the circuit court to hear such matters. If the matter involved the ministerial duties of an election official (like our case of the 100 Hooper votes that went uncounted in Dallas County) as opposed to duties that require the official's discretion, then the circuit court could order the votes counted. But this case involved the legal interpretation of at least two Alabama Supreme Court cases, not a ministerial duty of a local election official. Espy said it was hard for him to believe that we would come into court to say that "legal" votes should not be counted. He said that he did not set forth rhetoric but law dealing with the court's jurisdiction in this case.

Judge Reese said he had spent the entire day reviewing the case, the statutes, and the supreme court cases, and he concluded that his court did have jurisdiction. He said several times that this was not a contest of an election. He even said that his court was not there to decide who the winner of the chief justice election was "or assuming we are talking about any other statewide election where the parties have made their arguments and comments that have been made through the media." He also told Espy: "Whatever the results hold, if they hold Mr. Espy's clients or whoever he may be interested in or Mr. Agricola's, any of your clients, whoever they may be, if they win, they win, so be it."[6] Al asked to take an interlocutory appeal to the Alabama Supreme Court to determine if Reese's court had jurisdiction. Judge Reese said that wasn't necessary; Al could appeal later if he received an adverse judgment.

Espy called his first witness, Debbie Hackett, the Circuit Clerk and the authority responsible for the handling of absentee ballots in Montgomery County. She testified about the application procedure for receiving an absentee ballot. The affidavit is printed right on the envelope, so it is called an affidavit envelope. In answer to Espy's question regarding the source for the instructions to not count these particular ballots, she said she did not know if the instructions were obtained from the secretary of state's office. She said the instructions had been used as long as she had been in office. She knew that about ninety-eight absentee ballots in Montgomery County had not been counted because they were not notarized or witnessed.

Marc Givhan, the assistant attorney general representing the Alabama secretary of state, was present and asked her if she had received personal instructions from Mr. Bennett. He also asked if the materials she held on the procedure had been printed before Bennett became secretary of state. She answered that she had received no personal instruction from Bennett and that the materials had been printed before he was appointed to that office. He never asked about the importance of the witnessing requirement for preserving the integrity of absentee ballots, and he seemed totally unconcerned with the effect this case might have on Alabama law regarding the issue.

Al asked her why she did not count these ballots if the secretary of state had not personally instructed her. She said the statute says that the ballots should be witnessed and that was the way she had done it since 1983. She stated that the uncounted ballots are set aside and are available in the event of a contest of an election. The polling officials who have been counting longer than she has been circuit clerk determine which ballots do or do not get counted. Then Espy called Liddie Hall, a poll worker in Bullock County, to testify that she saw absentee ballots uncounted, set aside, and a list made as to why they were not counted. Espy offered the list into evidence.

Espy then called Bert Estes, the chief clerk in the Montgomery Probate Office. He substituted for Probate Judge Hobbie on the election commission because Hobbie was running for reelection himself that year. He confirmed Debbie Hackett's testimony. Of course, Marc Givhan had to again ask questions to protect Secretary of State Bennett. Al asked about the election school that is held each year before elections to train poll workers. Estes said poll workers are instructed not to count unwitnessed absentee ballots when counting ballots at the courthouse. Again, he said that they had done it that way for a number of years and that no one had ever complained before.

Espy then began his closing statement. He said that he had included an affidavit from the circuit judge who sat on the *Williams v. Lide* case.[7] He also included copies of the actual absentee ballots in that case. I did not get to see those affidavits at the time of the hearing. Espy argued that the statute and the law on the matter were so clear that it was clear error for the local election officials not to count unwitnessed absentee ballots. Espy said: "I have the utmost respect for Mr. Givhan and the utmost respect for Jim Bennett in his attempts to fulfill his duties. I don't want in any way to question that." I assume Bennett did not like what was being planned and had asked for assurances from all the players—Jimmy Evans, Joe Espy, Hornsby—ahead of time so that he would not be hurt legally or politically by this scheme to change the voting rules. Espy also made it clear that he had fully complied with Alabama Rule of Civil Procedure 65, regarding notifying the parties of his motion for a temporary restraining order. There was good reason for him to clarify that. Bennett had said that he would not stop the count of the votes on Wednesday evening until he had received a hard copy of Judge Phelps' TRO. Once he received that on Thursday morning, he stopped the count. Attorney Mendolsohn, who represented Estes and Hobbie, said that his clients did not take a position on whether the ballots should be counted or not.

Al then called Ms. Vickie Balough, election analyst for the secretary of state's office. The secretary of state himself did not attend. She testified that the procedure for not counting absentee ballots had been handled the same way for six years at least, the time she had worked in the office. Espy cross-examined her, trying to intimidate her. He asked her: "Am I to understand that you advised election officials in this election to reject and not count votes of absentee voters where the signature was not notarized or there were not two witnesses?" It appeared that Espy might be trying to not only protect Bennett but scapegoat Ms. Balough for any alleged wrongdoing that could be conjured up in this charade of a hearing. She answered that it was her practice to so advise local election officials.

Givhan said that his office had not been notified of the hearing the day before and neither had Bennett's. Espy claimed to have telephoned both offices before he obtained the TRO. Otherwise, it is possible that Espy would not have qualified to obtain the order based on lack of notice. Reese expressed little concern.

Bennett's later public statements and testimony in federal court supporting Hooper indicated that he wanted honest elections. Bennett's nonappearance at the hearing could be explained by his knowledge of the action beforehand but his refusal to come to the hearing to either help or hinder this plan to gut Alabama law on absentee ballots. He may have been disgusted by what was happening, but, unable to do anything to stop it, he acquiesced and chose not to actively participate. Bennett may have been pushed into not protesting by Jimmy Evans' office. Not long after this hearing, Bennett hired his own attorney to advise the secretary of state. Perhaps it was his experience with Jimmy Evans that caused him to add a lawyer to his staff. Givhan was trying to protect Bennett from any charges of ignoring the hearing, so he came up with the excuse that Bennett didn't receive sufficient notice. Yet I heard Bennett tell someone about the hearing an hour before it was scheduled to begin. Still, he chose not to attend. Espy explained again that he had provided notice to all the parties involved.

Al made his closing statement arguing that the proper forum for determining whether these ballots should be counted was the legislature. He argued that even under the substantial compliance doctrine of *Williams v. Lide*, unwitnessed absentee ballots did not comply with the absentee voting statutes. It was strange that Marc Givhan went to great lengths to defend Mr. Bennett but never rose to the defense of Alabama's statute for preserving the integrity of absentee ballots. Defending state law was a much higher priority than defending Jim Bennett. If he had stood up for that law, there would have been no need to make a defense of Bennett. In that case, it would have been clear that Bennett was simply obeying state law concerning the witnessing of absentee ballots. There would be no need to defend someone for obeying state law. But Espy had to make it look as if something was wrong with enforcing the law.

Judge Reese emphasized that he had spent the day reviewing all the case law and the authority on the matter. For the fifth or sixth time, he reiterated that the hearing was not an election contest and that he did not want to count votes. He stated that he would not take part in a partisan debate between Republicans and Democrats. Even though there was really only one statute at issue in the case, he said there was obviously conflict in the statutes. He said he had to follow the supreme court in their interpretation of the law, which means substantial compliance. For Judge Reese, that meant counting unwitnessed absentee ballots. He reiterated that he had no clue how the votes would come out. He ordered Espy to prepare the written injunction and get it to him by nine the next morning.

Alabama had had its share of problems with absentee ballots, but never had it seen a court order the voting officials to count questionable, unwitnessed absentee ballots. This was not nighttime stuffing of the ballot box. This was a daylight raid on the existing law itself.

When Judge Reese pronounced his order granting the TRO, I was shaken. I found it difficult to stand when the bailiff told the courtroom: "All rise." All that we had worked for to correct the errors of the election disappeared as this judge ordered the unwitnessed, unnotarized absentee ballots counted immediately. He wanted an order prepared and in his office by 9:00 the next morning. He signed the written order on 18 November 1994, but it was dated 16 November 1994. We did not know why. On 18 November, the absentee ballots came flooding into Bennett's office.

The nine days since 8 November had been an up and down experience; sometimes we were ahead and sometimes we were behind. We had finally gotten to a secure position as far as the numbers of votes were concerned. Then Judge Reese issued this TRO. Even though it was a defeat, it was also a vindication. Hooper had argued during the campaign that the courts were too intent on making the law instead of interpreting it. I was convinced that was what Reese had done. Now Hooper was experiencing it firsthand.

Notes

1. "No jurisdiction exists in or shall be exercised by any judge, court or officer exercising chancery powers to entertain any proceeding for ascertaining the legality, conduct or results of any election, except so far as authority to do so shall be specially and specifically enumerated and set down by statute; and any injunction, process or order from any judge, court or officer in the exercise of chancery powers, whereby the results of any election are sought to be inquired into or questioned, save as may be specially and specifically enumerated and set down by statute, shall be null and void and shall not be enforced by any officer or obeyed by any person; and should any judge or other officer hereafter undertake to fine or in any wise deal with any person for disobeying any such prohibited injunction, process or order, such attempt shall be null and void, and an appeal shall lie forthwith therefrom to the supreme court then sitting, or next to sit, without bond, and such proceedings shall be suspended by force of such appeal, and the notice to be given of such appeal shall be fourteen days." (Emphasis added.) Ala. Code 1975, § 17-5-6.

2. *Odom v. Bennett*, No. 94-2434-R (Montgomery County Cir. Ct. 1994).

3. Joe Espy was no stranger to election contests. In 1986, Bill Baxley ran for the democratic nomination for governor against Charlie Graddick. Baxley accused Graddick, the attorney general at the time, of soliciting republicans to vote in the democratic primary and contested the election. Graddick won the primary based on the number of votes. A Democratic Executive Committee on Contests was formed to look into the contest. Baxley was the establishment favorite of the Democratic Party. Graddick was perceived as the more conservative of the two. The Contest Committee declared Baxley the winner of the primary, and the backlash against such "handpicking" by the democratic party was enough to propel a little know republican into the governor's office that year. It was the first time in over 100 years that a republican had won a governor's election in Alabama. Joe Espy was the attorney for that Democratic Executive Committee on Contests.

4. *Wells v. Ellis,* 551 So. 2d 382 (Ala. 1989); *Williams v. Lide,* 628 So. 2d 531 (Ala. 1993).

5. Alabama Code § 17-10-7 explained the requirements for the proper way for an affidavit to be filled out when sending in an absentee ballot:

> "Each absentee ballot shall be accompanied by an envelope upon which shall be printed an affidavit. This affidavit which shall be used in general, special or municipal elections shall be substantially as follows:

'State of Alabama

County of

I, the undersigned, do swear (or affirm) that:

  (1) I am a resident of County in the State of Alabama.
  (2) My place of residence in Alabama is:
  _____(street)
  _____, Alabama
  (city or town)   (zip code)
  (3) My voting precinct (or place where I vote) is:
  (4) My date of birth is:
                              month   day   year
  (5) I am entitled to vote an absentee ballot because:

Check only one:

I have moved from Alabama less than thirty days prior to the election.

I will be out of the county or the state on election day.

I am physically incapacitated and will not be able to vote in person on election day.

I work a required workplace shift that conflicts with polling hours.

I further swear (or affirm) that I have not voted nor will I vote in person in the election to which this ballot pertains.

I have marked the enclosed absentee ballot voluntarily and that I have read or had read to me and understand the instructions accompanying this ballot and that I have carefully complied with such instructions.

Moreover, I further swear (or affirm) that all of the information given above is true and correct to the best of my knowledge and that I understand that by knowingly giving false information so as to vote illegally by absentee ballot that I shall be guilty of a misdemeanor which is punishable by a fine not to exceed $1,000.00 and/or confinement in the county jail for not more than six months.

(Signature or mark of voter.)

(Printed name of voter.)

"Note: Your signature must [emphasis added] be witnessed by either: A notary public or other officer authorized to acknowledge oaths or two witnesses 18 years of age or older."

6. He ignored what was apparent to everyone else—that the plaintiffs were simply fronts for Hornsby's plan to avoid a contest in the legislature. That accusation is supported by the fact that Hornsby's campaign spokesman had spoken of these ballots two days prior to this hearing and that it is well known to most Alabamians that absentee ballots generally favor democrats.

7. *Williams v. Lide*, 628 So. 26 531 (Ala. 1993), involved an election for the Dallas County Commission. Curtis Williams

received 2,269 votes to John Lide's 2,265 votes. Lide contested the election in circuit court, and the trial court granted Lide a judgment which said that the legal vote was: 2,272 votes for Lide, 2,262 for Williams. Williams appealed raising these issues: the voting rights of convicted felons, the legality of certain challenged votes, the legality of certain absentee votes, and the exclusion of a particular witness's testimony. Williams claimed that 13 absentee ballots should not have been excluded because of deficiencies in the accompanying affidavits. the trial court used the three-element test of *Wells v. Ellis*, 551 So. 2d 382 (Ala. 1989), to admit seven of those ballots into evidence. The three elements of *Wells* (the *Boardman* factors) were: that the voter was not guilty of fraud, gross negligence, or intentional wrongdoing, the voter substantially complied with the essential requirements of absentee voting law, and any irregularities in the vote may not adversely affect the sanctity of the absentee voting law. *Wells* was based on a 1975 Florida case called *Boardman v. Esteva*, 323 So. 2d 259 (Fla. 1975). Williams presented testimony as to the ballots of four other voters whose affidavits lacked an element, and the trial court allowed those votes into evidence. The trial court then excluded two of those eleven ballots that were in evidence. Williams challenged the judgment by the trial court excluding those two ballots. Lide, in his cross appeal, challenged the trial court's decision that nine of those absentee ballots should count. However, the Alabama Supreme Court never had to make a decision as to Lide's cross appeal challenging those nine because it affirmed the trial court's judgment which gave Lide more votes than Williams. It only reviewed the question posed by Williams as to the two absentee ballots that the trial court did not count. If the supreme court had changed any of the trial court's judgment and changed the result so that Lide lost, it would have thoroughly reviewed the trial judge's decision to count those nine. In affirming the trial court, the supreme court did not need to address that challenge by Lide; he won anyway. The court said, "By allowing Williams to present testimony from absentee voters whose affidavits lacked the three elements deemed necessary, the trial court went a step further than it had to. Had the trial court been any more lenient, it would have effectively abolished § 17-10-7 [the statute requiring a witnessed affidavit for absentee voting] and necessarily, would have compromised the integrity of the election process." *Lide*, at p. 537.

Williams v. Lide did not stand for the proposition urged by Hornsby. The trial judge, John Bush, "admitted into evidence only those absentee ballots that were accompanied by an affidavit containing the voter's (1) place of residence, (2) reason for voting absentee, and (3) signature. However, if an absentee voter's affidavit lacked any of those three elements, the trial court permitted the voter to testify at trial to supply the missing elements (emphasis added)." *Lide*, at p. 536. Those three elements determine (1) whether a voter can vote in a certain county, (2) whether a voter can vote absentee because of illness or being out of the county on election day, and (3) the signature or mark that is essential to all affidavits. An affidavit without two witnesses or notarization is not an affidavit. Hornsby's people said that voters need only state the three elements and sign the piece of paper. Of course, such a piece of paper would not be an affidavit. Hooper's argument would not be that "substantial compliance" was wrong, but that doing away with the witness requirement was not compliance at all. The absentee ballots allowed to be counted by Judge Bush actually lacked witnessing and notarization, but that was not at issue in the supreme court's review as stated in its opinion. One example of a ballot not counted in that case was an absentee ballot which the voter did not seal.

Perhaps the most devastating part of the supreme court's opinion in *Williams v. Lide* was this statement: "the condition on which Lide's arguments are predicated has not occurred; therefore, the cross-appeal is to be dismissed as moot." *Williams*, at p. 538. As will be explained later, anything in the opinion dealing with unwitnessed absentee ballots was part of Lide's argument, and was therefore moot.

In the *Wells* case, the Alabama Supreme Court stated: "Alabama courts have not yet addressed the construction of the statute that authorizes absentee voting and sets out the manner in which that voting must be done (Ala. Code 1975, ° 17-10-1 et seq.). Our research, however, has revealed two primary methods of construction developed and adopted by other jurisdictions that have addressed similar statutes." *Wells*, at p. 383. *Wells* adopted the "substantial compliance" doctrine. Because the trial had not yet been completed when the Alabama Supreme Court reviewed it (an interlocutory appeal), there was no other detail to that case other than the adoption of the "substantial compliance" doctrine. Hornsby voted with the majority in both those cases. In no way, did it say to count unwitnessed absentee ballots.

The court in *Boardman v. Esteva*, upon which *Wells* was based, disallowed the counting of 88 absentee ballots. Why? Because "the official title of the subscribing witness was not indicated." Such were the facts of the case upon which the Alabama cases were based, but no one referred to those facts in *Odom v. Bennett*.

Interesting information developed about Florida's voting law in the 1997 Miami Mayoral election. Criminal investigation into absentee voting revealed "pervasive vote fraud 'across the board.'" A volunteer for one candidate, Suarez, was charged with trying to buy faked absentee ballots using the names of dead people. The fraud often manipulated the elderly. Agents arrested a peddler who voted in the name of a dead person and a secretary working in the law firm of the City Commission Chairman who falsified her address on a ballot. David Leahy, Miami-Dade County election supervisor, said, "We think it's probably a problem everywhere in the state. . . . The laws are intended to provide great accessibility to the process . . . but they didn't ensure the integrity of the process would be maintained." As a result of the abuses in that election, "[s]tate legislation was introduced to require identification and *a witness for a voter to obtain and cast an absentee ballot.* (Emphasis added.)" (Article by Will Lester, "The Associated Press," obtained through AOL News, Feb. 7, 1998.) On March 4, 1998, the judge threw out the results of that election and ordered that a new mayoral election be held. Notice that at the time of this particular mayoral election, Florida did not have a witness requirement for obtaining or voting an absentee ballot. So, even if one could stretch the *Boardman* case to allow for unwitnessed absentee ballots, it would not necessarily apply to Alabama, which did have a statutory witness requirement at the time of the 1994 chief justice election.

Chapter Eight

Hooper Gets A Reprieve

The policy of not counting unwitnessed absentee ballots was well-established. There was the statute § 17-10-7. There was also the Secretary of State's *Election Officials Handbook,* which had since 1980 contained similar language about unwitnessed absentee ballots: don't count them. There was also the 12 September 1980 attorney general's memorandum, which said don't count them. That policy was well-established state law, whereas the 1993 *Williams v. Lide* opinion was, at best, vague support for the position taken by Hornsby's supporters. The opinion had been published in the *Southern Reporter,* not a place that circuit clerks, most of whom are not lawyers, go searching for guidance on how to count votes. Even if one were to accept the argument that the Alabama Supreme Court had done away with the witnessing requirement in that case (a position I would not adopt), no one took any action to make sure it was adopted for future elections. No one had approached the legislature to change § 17-10-7. No one had approached the secretary of state to change his handbook. No one had asked for the attorney general's opinion about the case. No one had filed any type of action in state court to make sure that this new policy was publicized and adopted statewide. Not until the hearing before Judge Reese on 17 November 1994, nine days after the 8 November election, did anyone attempt to have its questionable holding applied.

After the hearing, TV reporters went to Al Agricola to ask his opinion of the decision. He stated that he had was bound by certain rules of ethics with respect to what he could say about a judge. Jack, who was not a lawyer and could speak his mind freely, was quick to say that Reese's decision was illegal and that we would not give up the fight.

We tried to arm ourselves sufficiently for the public relations war. Hornsby's campaign contribution report showed that both Judge Phelps and Joe Espy had contributed to his campaign. The *Montgomery Advertiser* called the hearing before Reese "an extraordinary Thursday night hearing."[1] It was the fourth time one of the parties in the chief justice election had gone to court. Hooper had gone into both federal and state court to have the election materials around the state impounded, and he had to go to court in Dallas County to challenge the probate judge's decision to not count the 100 votes that were mistakenly left out of the count there.

Hooper's campaign also began calling the Republicans in every county to inform them to get to the courthouse and be present as poll watchers when those absentee ballots were being opened. If they were opened without being challenged, the identifying envelope would be separated from the absentee ballot itself. Once the ballot was separated from the envelope, there would be no way to determine who truly cast a ballot and whether they "substantially complied" with state law or not. Hooper would have little chance in court if that happened. An election contest before the legislature would be extremely difficult, if not impossible.

At some point Espy inserted an undated memorandum into the case file in the Montgomery County Circuit Court. It contradicted what Hornsby's lawyers argued in federal court later. There were several errors in it. For example, he cited a case dealing with municipal court elections, *Sears v. Carson*, 551 So. 2d 1054 (Ala. 1989). Statewide elections are covered by an entirely different set of rules. Also, he confused discretionary duty with ministerial duty. These are terms of art used in the law to describe two types of duties of government officials. A ministerial duty is one that is clearly described in the law and that allows no room for discretion. Even if you accept Judge Reese's interpretation of *Williams v. Lide*, there's a problem with his ruling because of that distinction. Local election officials, even if they knew the case existed, would not have found *Williams v. Lide* to be clear direction as to how to do their ministerial duty. Even the attorney general and secretary of state had not recognized such a meaning in that case. If they had, they would have sent out appropriate guidance to the local officials. If it was true that the local officials could not have known that these votes should be counted, then how could a court charge the local officials with impropriety in not counting these unwitnessed absentee ballots. In his memo, Espy stated that the legal guidance in that case was so clear that the local officials were in clear error to not count those ballots? Yet, in the hearing before Reese, Espy said that these officials were "doing the best that they could." The strategy of Hornsby's lawyers, who later tried to defend that ruling, changed the rationale for their argument even further.

Bert Jordan had gone to Mobile on the Thursday that Reese ruled. He was trying to get a federal order preserving and safekeeping the election materials. The complaint in Mobile federal court asked for an "order requiring said defendants to preserve all materials relating to said election until such time as the plaintiffs [Hooper and Larry Roe, a Mobile voter] file an election contest." After leaving Judge Howard's court to return to Birmingham, he received a call that the other side was in Reese's court trying to get the absentee ballots counted.[2] At a reception that evening in Birmingham, he learned that Reese had ordered them counted. He worked with Al Agricola and Glenn Murdock until 2:00 Friday morning preparing the motion for a temporary restraining order based on Section 5 of the *Voting Rights Act*—preclearance. Al and Glenn spent the entire night preparing for Friday. Ralph Bradford was a co-plaintiff with Hooper on that action. The next morning, Hooper's attorneys went into the chambers of Judge Propst to get the order signed. Jordan asked for a three-judge panel to look at the matter. He and Al Agricola were preparing an order for Propst to sign, while a whole crew of plaintiff trial lawyers were in the courtroom to see what was happening. When those lawyers left the courthouse, another attorney overheard them saying that "some Nazis" were in Propst's court trying to get a TRO.

Judge Reese, with his order, had wiped out an entire sentence of state law regarding elections. It was now time for the federal courts to get involved. Because of its problems with voting and civil rights in the sixties, Alabama is on a list of states that must get any change in its election laws precleared by the U.S. Justice Department. Judge Robert Propst, a Democratic appointee, issued a TRO halting any tallying of the unwitnessed absentee ballots. By the time the state of Alabama and the counties received notice of this order, some of the counties had already counted their unwitnessed absentee ballots.

We learned from the news that the Alabama attorney general's office sent a letter to the Justice Department to ask that this change be precleared and that the action be expedited. We wondered how a change after an election could be precleared. The request to expedite the request was ostensibly because every election in the state was being held hostage by this legal controversy. Normally, such a request for preclearance takes weeks, even months to accomplish. At no time did the Alabama attorney general's office question whether this change should be precleared. It was a rush to judgment, and the Alabama attorney general had clearly aligned himself with Hornsby. As with all such haste to ratify a dubious judgment, this one was full of problems. For example, if the Justice Department precleared this change, and Hooper was later able to get Reese's decision reversed, then the Alabama attorney general would have to return to the Justice Department to get the reversal precleared. We later learned that the person in charge of preclearance at the Justice Department was from Alabama. His name was John Tanner, and he said that his staff would work through the weekend because "[t]he understanding that I have of this is that it is a very important issue and something that needs to be resolved real quick." Judge Propst, the federal judge in Birmingham, said that the law plainly says that signatures are required on the ballots: "I don't see how anything could be more vivid than that is."

On 21 November 1994, the *Wall Street Journal* reported that Alabama's chief justice election was a "virtual referendum on legal reform." It pointed out how close the race was—a difference of nine votes plus the potential boost for Hooper from the 100 Dallas County votes. It ended with the typical wailing by a political scientist that "the Hornsby-Hooper campaign has served to politicize the judiciary in a way that [it] hadn't been politicized before. This is unseemly." To these college professor-types, the exposure of corruption and political games in the courts is unseemly. Such commentators seem to think that the actual injustice of the system is less "unseemly" than the revealing of it. The voters of Alabama seemed to think the issues important. That was what was offensive to these elitist "experts"; the people did the choosing. Neither the elite nor the lawyers wanted the people to find out what was happening in their courts.

There were repeated calls for reform of the voting system. Some proposed stricter controls over politicians and their operatives going into nursing homes to get absentee ballots signed. Secretary of State Jim Bennett had already proposed a bill that the legislature had passed, that would allow only one absentee ballot to be sent to any voter. That would slow down the wholesale brokerage of absentee ballots; it would not stop it. It was to go into effect 1 January 1995. Bennett also proposed early voting on several news shows. Early voting allows the polls to open on a day before the election. Such a scheme might cut down on the number of legitimate absentee ballots, but it would do nothing to stem the tide of fraudulent ballots.

All we could do over the weekend was wait. Hooper's attorneys were hard at work preparing for the hearing on a preliminary injunction before the federal court in Birmingham. They had witnesses prepared to talk about fraud in Greene County, Wilcox County, and Cullman County. I delivered some documents to Hooper's attorneys on Tuesday morning and stayed to watch the proceedings. Judge Hooper was unable to attend. Al Agricola, Bert Jordan, and Glenn Murdock were the lawyers at this hearing. Rusty Johnston remained in Mobile, where Judge Alex Howard had issued an injunction against any tampering with the election materials around the state.

The attorneys felt that we were in good shape. Without preclearance, Reese's order was not going anywhere. We were sure they could not obtain preclearance over the weekend; we were wrong. Hornsby's lawyers had a preclearance letter from the Justice Department. I couldn't believe it. The U.S. Justice Department had done a legal review on a totally novel aboli-

tion of the notarization/witness requirement of state law by a
local trial judge in Alabama over a weekend. Something was
clearly wrong.

Hornsby's lead attorney was Joe Whatley, a noted civil
rights lawyer. He stood up to argue his case and simply said
that our argument was moot; they now had preclearance of
Reese's order. The three-judge panel, headed by Judge Propst,
read a copy of the letter before the hearing. They agreed with
Whatley that if the letter provided preclearance, then Hooper
had no case for keeping the preliminary injunction in place.
We clearly had no argument to the contrary. However, what
happened next took everyone by surprise, especially Hornsby's
lawyers. Judge Propst told Whatley: "This letter only preclears
the *Williams v. Lide* and *Wells v. Ellis* decisions of the Alabama Supreme Court. I and the other two judges on this panel
think that it does not preclear the *Reese* decision which we
view as stating a different result from those two cases." Propst
said that the supreme court decisions did not do away with the
notarization requirement. Hornsby's lawyers were shocked. The
lawyers and the judges discussed the situation back and forth.
Whatley argued that the Justice Department had precleared
the Reese decision. But it did not even mention the Reese
decision, and if that decision was different from the supreme
court decisions on which Reese relied, then there was no
preclearance of Reese's decision. During this discussion, a flab-
bergasted Judge Hancock asked Whatley: "Do you mean to
tell me that the United States Justice Department has precleared
the removal of any need for the verification of absentee ballots
in the state of Alabama?" Whatley simply replied, "Yes." I
knew at that moment that those judges knew what was going
on. I found hope in the fact that we were not the only ones
who saw Reese's decision as a departure from precedent.

During the lunch break, Whatley and associates went back
to the Justice Department to try to get another letter. The
court reconvened at 2:00 P.M. Whatley had a new letter. It said
that the previous letter was intended to include Reese's order
from *Odom v. Bennett*. In order to make things perfectly clear,
the letter said that "absentee ballots cannot be rejected on the
basis of the absence of two witnesses or notarization." It then

went on to say "The 16 November order in Odom specifically applied to absentee ballots cast in the 8 November 1994 election, and the change we precleared on that basis. The previous use of this standard in some counties and the reliance of voters in the state upon it are noted in our letter." How did they know that counties in the past had relied on such a standard? Whatley had spoken of Winston County, but his information was unverified and vague. He had absolutely no evidence of a pattern of reliance by any county in the past. How did the Justice Department obtain such information, especially since there was none? They had simply accepted whatever Hornsby's lawyers told them.

This perception by the federal judges made Espy's placement of that undated memorandum in the case file in Montgomery County somewhat moot. That memorandum contained different legal reasoning than he had given at the hearing itself on 17 November. It wasn't that the local officials didn't know any better and had innocently denied people the right to vote. Espy asserted that it was their ministerial duty to count these ballots and clear error not to do so. Local election officials were supposed to reach the conclusion that these ballots should be counted even though three federal judges had not come to that conclusion. Hornsby's lawyers now knew that the federal courts saw through Reese's legal reasoning and concluded that the precedent from the Alabama Supreme Court did not necessitate Reese's decision. That would be fatal to their case. So they began to focus solely on their only other basis for success: so many counties in the past had counted these ballots that it had become an accepted custom that they would be counted. The only problem with that theory was that there was no evidence that was the case. Yet the Justice Department had simply taken their word for it and had precleared a change in the election law and applied it retroactively to the 8 November election.

Judge Hancock was compelled to ask another question when he heard this. He asked if there had been a representative of the Alabama attorney general's office present at Reese's hearing. Marc Givhan stood and admitted to being present at that hearing. Judge Hancock then asked, with acid disbelief in his voice: "Why didn't you defend the law of Alabama in that hearing?" Givhan gave some nonsensical answer about other lawyers being there and agreeing with the interpretation. But he was clearly rattled by the question and made little sense in his answer. Judge Hancock had mercy on him and did not press the issue. It did not matter anyway. The deed was done. But Judge Hancock clearly wanted everyone to know of his indignation. Nevertheless, the panel had to lift the injunction. Hooper was knocked to the mat again. Speaking of being knocked to the mat, Justice Houston, who would reveal so much publicly about the Williams v. Lide case, had commented on the supreme court elections: "This election has sunk to the level of mud wrestling."

Al tried to proceed with the other aspect of our case and bring on witnesses. But Propst made the point that we would need to file a new or at least an amended complaint and give the other side time to respond. However, as he said that, he gave us a hint as to how to proceed. He said that Reese's order could be understood as a violation of due process. Propst said that a change after the election to allow unwitnessed absentee ballots to be counted would deny due process to some voters because of the voter's prior expectation that an unwitnessed ballot would not be counted.

There is also the "vote dilution" argument. The invalid votes would dilute the valid votes of those who followed the Code of Alabama when they voted. There is also the issue of the integrity of these absentee ballots. How does one prove who the voter was and whether he or she was properly registered? What about future elections? Wouldn't this make absentee ballot fraud much easier? That is what the ordinary Alabama voter saw in this case. No matter what anyone said, whether it was Judge Reese or the Alabama Supreme Court, it looked as if they were changing the rules set out by the legislature to keep elections honest.

Judge Propst later made his position even clearer with a written opinion. After that three-judge panel's decision to lift the TRO against Reese's ruling, Hornsby's attorneys and campaign staff were crowing about how those judges had approved the practice of counting unwitnessed absentee ballots. Lawyers have an ethical obligation to not misrepresent legal matters, even when they are not in court. Here is what Propst wrote in an unprecedented special written opinion that he released on the Friday following their decision: "[Section 5 of the Voting Rights Act, preclearance] was the only federal law addressed by this court. The attorneys, of course, were well aware of the foregoing. Their clients should have had no misunderstanding." In other words, the judges' decision addressed one narrow issue, and all the noise about their approving of unwitnessed absentee ballots was untrue.

He stated: "There may be some misunderstanding as to the role of this court." He explained the limited question that was before them: had Reese's change in the election law been precleared by the U.S. Justice Department as required by Section 5? That was all that three-judge panel was called upon to decide. Referring to the incompetence of the Alabama attorney general's office, he said in footnote two: "It is not clear who represented the voters of Alabama in said case. Of course, the same question might be asked concerning this case. This court respectfully disagrees with a conclusion that an 'affidavit' which does not include either of the prescribed attestations 'substantially' complies with the statute. Further, this judge does not agree that *Williams v. Lide*, 628 So. 2d 531 (Ala. 1993) so holds. Further, there was no evidence that *Williams v. Lide* itself had been precleared prior to 8 November 1994. This judge, having determined that the Montgomery County Circuit Court order constituted, in midstream, a change in voting procedures, had only one other issue to address on 18 November 1994." Again, that was whether the Justice Department approved of the change. This man was clearly trying to distance himself from the public representations made by Hornsby's campaign and his lawyers. Maybe he was concerned about his reputation or the reputation of the federal court. I don't know his motivation. It was clear he did not agree with what was happening.

He went on to explain the problem with the first letter received from the Justice Department early in the morning of 22 November 1994. "Curiously, the initial letter suggests that possible previous non-precleared violations, on a county by county basis, of the apparently precleared Alabama statute [requiring notarization or witnessing of absentee ballots] created a situation whereby present adherence to the statute would have to be precleared." He said the Justice Department did not note any reasons for their determination that the change was free of discriminatory effect. "Apparently, this determination was made quickly and in a conclusory fashion, based upon 'evidence' from sources of which this court is unaware. This court can quickly think of several possible reasons for concluding that the change is not free of discriminatory purpose and effect. First, the change was made in midstream after a preliminary count had been completed and reported to the Secretary of State of Alabama. Such a 'wait and see' approach could clearly suggest discriminatory purpose and effect. Second, the new rule, having been announced after the election, was patently discriminatory as to those potential voters who may have felt that they would have to comply with the seemingly stringent requirements of section 17-10-7 in order to vote an absentee ballot."

He went on to describe what would become for Hooper the reasoning behind his complaint. As for the statutory requirement itself, he said, "The legislative desire to protect the integrity of such ballots is commendable." He said that based on U.S. Supreme Court precedent, the three-judge panel had no choice but to dissolve the TRO. The Supreme Court precedent said that a decision of this sort by the U.S. Attorney General was unreviewable by the district court. The only forum to appeal such a decision was the federal appeals court in Washington, D.C., and Hooper didn't have time to try something there. His final footnote clarified his position, which he apparently thought had been misconstrued: "This court has neither officially approved nor officially disapproved the determination of the Attorney General of the United States nor the order or ruling of any other court, state or federal." However, he used other words that were very unusual for a judge to use in an opinion. He said, "Regardless of whether this judge may be personally repulsed by the circumstances pertinent to this case, this judge's respect for the law as an institution prohibits his abusing his authority even in an attempt to remedy other perceived abuses." In other words, he didn't like was happening at all, but there was nothing he could legally do about it.

We left the federal courthouse in Birmingham quite dejected. We knew that Reese's order would now be reenacted and that the counties would start sending in their votes. I saw a reporter named Matt Smith from the *Montgomery Advertiser* outside the courthouse and told him that the three federal judges did not think that Reese's order agreed with *Williams v. Lide*. He seemed quite surprised and said he would check it out. I told him he could probably check with the judges' office and verify what I said. He said he would check into it. I did not expect to see what I saw in the newspaper the next day. Smith spoke with a justice on the Alabama Supreme Court, Gorman Houston. That discussion lead to an article about Justice Houston and later a letter to the editor of the *Birmingham News* by Justice Houston. But the article in next day's paper, Wednesday, 23 November 1994, made it sound as if the three federal judges had approved of Reese's decision, when that is not what they had done at all. They had simply ruled on the preclearance issue. But Justice Houston also had some things to say publicly about *Williams v. Lide*. He said that the three-point test of *Williams v. Lide* was never approved by the Alabama Supreme Court. The original appellant in that case, Mr. Lide, had won. Apparently, Lide had filed a cross-appeal in the case. But because the supreme court had decided the case on other grounds for Mr. Lide, there was no reason for the supreme court to decide the unwitnessed absentee ballot issue. Anything said on that issue was not law; it was moot, meaningless.

Williams v. Lide was a very high profile case. It ultimately determined whether the Dallas County Commission would be majority black or majority white. Selma is the county seat of Dallas County. According to the votes counted on the night of the election, Reverend Curtis Williams won, receiving 2,269 votes to Lide's 2,265. Lide filed an election contest, alleging several violations of the election laws. For example, he alleged that legal votes for him were wrongfully rejected, that convicted felons voted for Williams, etc. He also alleged that unwitnessed, unnotarized absentee ballots had been counted for Williams. After analyzing the contested ballots, the trial court entered an order for Lide. Of eleven unwitnessed absentee ballots cast for Williams, the trial judge allowed all but two to be counted.

Lide filed a cross appeal. One of his arguments in that cross appeal was that the trial judge should not have allowed any of those unwitnessed absentee ballots to be counted for Williams. However, he specifically conditioned his appeal on the supreme court's ruling somehow changing the result of the trial court's judgment and giving the election to Williams.[3]

Lide simply wanted to cover all his bases. Just in case the Alabama Supreme Court found enough votes to help Williams win the election, Lide wanted to make sure he raised questions about other votes. Because the supreme court affirmed the trial court's judgment in favor of Lide, any statements addressing these absentee ballots admitted by the trial judge became moot. The Alabama Supreme Court upheld the judgment for Lide. A court's comments on a moot issue is not a part of its holding. It is *obiter dicta*, meaning an incidental remark or observation. The holding states the law of the case. *Dicta* is not a statement of law. In this case, the Alabama Supreme Court had stated explicitly that its comments about unwitnessed, unnotarized absentee ballots were about a moot issue: "[T]he condition on which Lide's arguments are predicated has not occurred; therefore, the cross-appeal is to be dismissed as moot."[4] This point may seem obscure to the average layman, but for the judge or lawyer studying a case, it is critical. Justice Houston was attempting to educate the public about what *Williams v. Lide* really held, and it was not what Judge Reese had said that it held.[5]

In addition to that legal point, the opinion does not state that unwitnessed absentee ballots should be counted.[6] So what did Espy do? He obtained an affidavit (sworn before a notary) from Judge John Bush, the trial judge in *Williams v. Lide*, in which Judge Bush swore that the absentee ballots he had allowed to be counted for Williams were unwitnessed ballots. Espy even attached photocopies of the ballots showing that the absentee ballot envelopes were missing any witness or notary signatures. Judge Bush swore: "My factual and legal holdings in that trial [*Williams v. Lide*] were affirmed on appeal by the Supreme Court of Alabama in *Williams v. Lide,* 628 So. 2d 531 (Ala. 1993)." But Bush was incorrect in that statement according to the supreme court's opinion and the public statements of Justice Houston, who had voted in the *Williams v. Lide* case.

Espy had argued to Reese on 17 November 1994:

> Your honor, since there has been some question about exactly maybe what Williams versus Lide said, we have attached for the Court a copy of the trial order of Judge Bush in the *Williams v. Lide* case, along with the exhibits of the actual absentee ballots that he addressed. I know of no more direct testimony that we could bring to this Court than the sworn affidavit of the circuit judge who tried the leading case in this state, along with the actual affidavits that were used and admitted into evidence.[7]

At best, Judge Reese had relied upon another circuit judge's trial opinion as precedent. Another circuit court judge's decision in a case is not binding precedent. Judge Reese issued an amended preliminary injunction on 9 December 1994. In that order, he wrote: "The Trial Court is duty bound, as a soldier upon receipt of an Order from a superior, to follow the law as set out by the Supreme Court, even if it disagrees with the interpretations of the trial court."[8] Hooper's attorneys would later argue in a legal brief that "[f]or the trial judge to attempt such action [ordering the disputed ballots counted], as he says in the 9 December order in the name of being a 'soldier upon receipt of an Order from a superior' is 'Orwellian.' "[9] Either that or just plain stupid. No matter what, Reese's decision was clearly wrong.

The federal judges issued their decision two days before Thanksgiving. On Wednesday, we kept up with the count of the ballot numbers from the counties as these unwitnessed absentee ballots again started to flood in. After counting the votes from forty-one counties, Hooper's lead dropped from 270 to twenty-nine. Those forty-one counties did not include some of the most notorious absentee ballot counties, like Greene County. It didn't look good. The 18 November 1994 *Montgomery Advertiser* reported some of the player's comments. Secretary of State Bennett, Hornsby's Democratic colleague, said, "Hopefully, we can get the [votes] certified tomorrow." The quicker that was done, the less chance Hooper would have to get back into court. Bennett, in his public comments, added that Reese's decision would make it more difficult to weed out fraudulent votes. Joe Whatley's opinion of the case was wrapped up in three words: "That ends it." He spoke too soon.

Notes

1. *Montgomery Advertiser,* p. 1A, November 18, 1994.

2. Reese's written order, which was signed and faxed to the counties on November 18, was not dated November 18. Nor was it dated November 17, the date of his oral order. It was backdated November 16. At the time, we were suspicious but did not understand the rationale for the backdating of his order. However, if the timing of Reese's order with respect to Howard's was important, then it is understandable. Arguably, Reese's order, if it came before Howard's, was not in violation of Howard's order to not tamper with the election materials. However, the issue of the dating of Reese's order never arose, so it was ultimately of no consequence.

3. The Alabama Supreme Court's opinion acknowledged this: "In his brief, Lide states that he intended that his cross-appeal be conditional on this Court's conclusion that one or more of Williams's appellate arguments had merit and resulted in his receiving more legal votes than Lide. Because we affirm the trial court's order [that Lide was the winner of the election], the condition on which Lide's arguments are predicated has not occurred; therefore, the cross-appeal is to be dismissed as moot." *Williams v. Lide,* 628 So. 2d 531, 538 (Ala. 1993).

4. Ibid.

5. We learned later that the democrats threatened to file charges against Justice Houston before the Judicial Inquiry Commission if he revealed this information publicly.

6. "To fulfill these requirements (the *Boardman* factors) from *Wells*, the trial court admitted into evidence only those absentee ballots that were accompanied by an affidavit containing the voter's (1) place of residence, (2) reason for voting absentee, and (3) signature. However, if an absentee voter's affidavit lacked any of those three elements, the trial court permitted the voter to testify at trial to supply the missing elements." *Williams v. Lide*, 628 So. 2d 531, 536 (Ala. 1993). The above is the strongest language in that supreme court opinion supporting Reese's decision.

7. *Odom v. Bennett Trial Transcript*, pp. 329-331.

8. December 9, 1994 Preliminary Injunction, Judge Eugene Reese.

9. Hooper brief to the Eleventh Circuit Federal Court of Appeals, December 29, 1994, p. 42.

Chapter Nine

Alex Howard Weighs In

Wednesday was depressing. It looked as if the unwitnessed absentee ballots would be counted after all, and, if the votes went against Hooper, he would have to challenge Hornsby in the legislature, an expensive and time-consuming venture even if it was successful. No one had ever challenged the winner of a statewide election in the history of Alabama politics. Again, we had to call the Republicans in every county to make sure someone would be present at the counting of these ballots to challenge them and preserve the materials for a potential challenge.

Around midday on Wednesday, 23 November 1994, while unwitnessed absentee ballots were being tabulated across the state and sent into Secretary of State Bennett, we received news that Federal Judge Alex Howard in Mobile had issued an order which he faxed around the state. He reminded everyone that the order he had issued the previous week was still in effect. That order had stated that he had commanded no tampering with any election materials, which included the disputed absentee ballots. For local election officials to count these unwitnessed absentee ballots, they had to open the ballot envelopes and take ballots out. According to Judge Howard, that was tampering. He added that any attempt to open and count unwitnessed absentee ballots was tampering with the uncounted and still-sealed absentee election materials and that any local official who counted them was flirting with being in contempt of a federal judge. He also set a hearing date of 5 December 1994 to determine whether he would make his TRO permanent. Again we had received a reprieve just before it was too late, ironically from the federal courts. But, as Judge Howard would later make clear, this was no garden-variety state election dispute.

On short notice, a rally was set up on the steps of the Judicial Building, at the Supreme Court. The Hooper campaign and Perry Hooper, Jr. did a lot of quick calling around the state. People were outraged at what was happening. With just a few hours notice, we had a group of at least two hundred people in front of the Judicial Building. Judge Hooper made a speech, a rallying cry for a crusade on behalf of integrity in the courts and elections.

"On behalf of the people of Alabama, I stand before you this afternoon to say that justice is not for sale in Alabama. I am proud to say that it is now clear that hundreds of thousands of Democrats and Republicans joined together on 8 November to elect me as chief justice. I am here to say that the people of Alabama will not allow the legal outcome of their election process to be stolen by my opponents, the Alabama Plaintiff Trial Lawyers or the Clinton Justice Department.

"It is truly sad that for the past two weeks, the plaintiff trial lawyers and my opponent have conspired in an effort to use illegally cast absentee ballots to change the outcome of this election. The fact is that after the legal ballots have been counted the majority of the voters of Alabama have elected me to be their chief justice of the Alabama Supreme Court.

"During the past two weeks, the people of Alabama have seen first hand how the plaintiff trial lawyers will go to any extreme in using the Clinton Justice Department and unannounced nighttime court hearings to attempt to unlawfully change the outcome of this election.

"The people standing behind me today are Alabamians from north Alabama to south Alabama and many towns in between. This election is more about them than it is about me. Alabamians are tired of dishonesty in our government and particularly in our state supreme court, and they are not willing to stand idly by and allow this election to be stolen using illegal absentee ballots.

"During the coming days you should be prepared for the plaintiff trial lawyers to continue to find a way to take away the will of the people in this election. But to this point everything they have done has worked against them, and I remain the winner according to the legal votes in this case.

"I urge my fellow Alabamians to continue to fight to insure their election process and court system is not taken away from them. Furthermore, as we enter this special Thanksgiving time, I urge my fellow Alabamians to pray that the honest will of the people will prevail in this matter and that their sacred vote will not be taken away.

"As I said earlier, this campaign is far bigger than Perry Hooper. This campaign is now about the working people of Alabama maintaining their right to elect fellow Alabamians to insure that justice prevails."

Several parties had become involved in this election debacle, and the plot was beginning to form a distinct pattern involving those characters. Circuit Judge Gene Reese sent out faxes and orders when he had the opportunity to try to enforce his order. Secretary of State Jim Bennett did what Alabama Attorney General Jimmy Evans told him to do as long as he could still stand up publicly for honest elections. Jimmy Evans did whatever was needed to help Hornsby's lawyers. The office of U.S. Attorney General Janet Reno volunteered its help when needed. The plaintiff trial lawyers provided the money and volunteers to keep Hornsby in office. Tidbits of information would come back to us about certain people and events surrounding the conspiracy to keep Hooper out of the supreme court. My mother-in-law, a cashier at Morrison's Cafeteria at a mall in Montgomery, happened to meet an employee of the secretary of state's office one day as she went through the cafeteria line. My mother-in-law said that her son-in-law worked for Hooper and asked her what she thought of the Hooper-Hornsby election. The employee of the secretary of state responded: "They're going to steal the election from that man." The executive director of the Alabama Trial Lawyers Association sent a letter to Secretary of State Bennett urging him to include unwitnessed, unnotarized absentee ballots in all vote counting.[1] To his credit, Secretary of State Bennett refused. We also obtained a copy of a letter to Secretary of State Bennett from an attorney in Montgomery named Julian McPhillips. It was dated 17 November 1994 and was a brief explanation of why these illegal absentee ballots should be counted. McPhillips was a one-time associate of Hooper's in private law practice.

Hooper's attorneys quickly filed an amended complaint in Mobile. There was more at stake now than just the preservation of the election materials. Hooper was on the offense now and had to show that Reese's order undermined the election process. He also had to give Hornsby's lawyers sufficient notice to prepare a response. This amended complaint alleged discrimination against the legal voters of Alabama and violation of due process of law under the U.S. Constitution. It is interesting that the complaint had to include as defendants all probate judges (responsible for tabulating the local results), all circuit clerks (responsible for absentee ballots), and all sheriffs (responsible for securing the ballot materials) throughout the state. Our chief complaint was with Reese's ruling, but Hooper had to sue the state officials who were being forced by Reese's ruling to adopt a practice they did not support. Another investigator and I, hired by the Hooper team, were involved in serving the subpoenas on these officials in southeast Alabama, the wiregrass. I decided to spice up this job a little and asked some of these officials informal questions about Reese's ruling. One probate judge who was about to retire after twenty years of service told me that Reese's ruling had destroyed his faith in the judicial system. He had never seen anything as disheartening as what was happening in the chief justice race. I faxed him a copy of Propst's opinion, and he later told me that had somewhat restored his faith. Another probate judge said that the idea of counting unwitnessed absentee ballots was totally new to him. He had kept a notebook of every rule promulgated by the secretary of state or the attorney general, and they were all quite explicit: don't count unwitnessed absentee ballots. He said we were welcome to use that notebook in our case if we wanted to. I thanked him and told him we would get back to him if we needed it. All these officials were Democrats, not Republicans. When I asked a circuit clerk in another county what he thought of Reese's decision, he said that he thought it was "stupid." None of the county officials in south Alabama that I talked to thought Reese's ruling was correct, nor had they counted such ballots in the past. We knew that only a minority of counties actually engaged in fraud, yet we did not know exactly which ones those were. From our short investigation after the election we had a good idea as to the worst offenders, but the formalities of the lawsuit required that we file against every county. The state of Alabama was a defendant, and so was the plaintiff class from *Odom v. Bennett.*

The complaint cited Alabama's history of problems with absentee ballots, especially the problems that were discovered around 8 November 1994. Some of the contentions were: absentee ballots were sent by persons other than those entitled to vote them, absentee ballot managers like the one in Wilcox County did not allow for free and fair counting and challenging of the count, absentee ballots were voted for nursing home residents without their knowledge and understanding, qualified voters were not allowed to vote on election day because someone had already voted absentee, some voters voted twice—once absentee and again at the polls, applications for absentee ballots were submitted and subsequently sent in the name of deceased voters, in some counties absentee ballots accounted for 20% to 30% of the total votes cast even though they normally average 6% to 7% of the total, a substantial number of absentee ballots were mailed to the same address or the same person, "vote brokers" rounded up absentee ballots and were being paid so much per ballot, absentee ballots were lost or mishandled or misused, absentee ballots were delivered to election officials on election day instead of the period before election day, intimidation of minorities, and absentee ballots have traditionally favored Democrats by a wide margin. Those allegations did not even include the issue of Reese's ruling. But these examples of fraud across the state were important to emphasize the need for a check on the integrity of the absentee ballot—the witnessing requirement.

The amended complaint stated that the long-standing practice in Alabama was to reject unwitnessed absentee ballots. That was what the statute specified, that was what an official opinion of the attorney general had specified in 1980, that is what the secretary of state's handbooks of the past had always said, and that is what a 1994 election handbook prepared by the secretary of state said. The understanding of the citizenry and the local voting officials was that unwitnessed absentee ballots were to be rejected. As an Air Force lawyer stationed overseas, that is what we had advised military members to do when their home states required witnesses or a notary. We provided the notary for them to fill out their absentee ballot envelopes. In Judge Reese's court, the representative of the Davis class said that he had a son in the Navy who had not been able to vote in his home state of Alabama because he was overseas and could not obtain a notary or two witnesses. All his son had to do was walk into his ship's legal office, and everything he needed to prepare an absentee ballot was available for him. In fact, because of their habit of moving all over the world and their access to free legal advice, military members are among the best educated on how to vote absentee. Davis' complaint did not ring true to me.

The local officials followed this practice of not counting ballots by excluding them on election day. Their exclusion was the reason Joe Espy filed the case before Reese and on behalf of John Davis in the first place. How could Hornsby's lawyers now come back and claim that there had been a practice of counting them in the past? This practice remained unchanged until the 5:30 P.M. hearing in Reese's courtroom on 17 November 1994, nine days after the 8 November election. The witness/notarization requirement is the easiest and most basic safeguard against absentee ballot fraud. The complaint requested a temporary restraining order to prevent these ballots from being counted. It would be the equivalent of stuffing the ballot box and a violation of due process to now allow such a change in what votes counted. It would also be a violation of the First and Fourteenth Amendments of the U.S. Constitution because it would dilute and debase validly cast votes. It would violate equal protection to grant a privilege to the voters who purportedly cast such ballots and to not extend the same privilege to other voters who sought to vote absentee but did not think their unwitnessed absentee ballot would qualify and, therefore, did not vote. That was the same opinion Judge Propst had voiced in Birmingham. There were many interesting things to expose regarding the voting in the 1994 election, but the bold and revisionist effect of the Reese decision had become the center of the controversy.

Hooper's attorneys filed the amended complaint on Monday, 28 November 1994, following a long Thanksgiving weekend. The next day, we discovered that sometime since Reese's decision Sumter County had counted these absentee ballots. If counted, they would have reduced Hooper's lead to twenty votes. There were still fourteen counties that had not counted them at all. On Wednesday, the secretary of state and Jerry Boggans, Wilcox County probate judge, filed with the Eleventh Circuit Court of Appeals to stay Howard's order. He alleged that he needed to go ahead with the counting and certifying of the results of the election. Of course, he did not claim that when Reese and Phelps held their hearings. On Friday, 2 December 1994, the Eleventh Circuit refused to issue a stay.

The state of Alabama had a problem that went beyond just the chief justice election. Because of the court orders issued, no other election results could be certified, even if the disputed ballots would make no difference in the outcome of the election. That included the results of the elections for U.S. Congress. The state had already passed the deadline for having all the results certified. Of course, the secretary of state could have prevented that by counting and certifying the results in spite of any court orders, but it now appeared that the deadlock would not end quickly. The U.S. Congress has a method for getting around such problems, but that did not solve the problem for the other state offices, like governor, attorney general, treasurer, etc. The Alabama Legislature was set to begin its first session of 1995 in January, the same month when the governor and other constitutional officers would be sworn in. This problem added fire to the controversy and stirred up speculation about the Democrats trying to remain in office beyond their terms if the controversy were not cleared up in time.

The more we learned, the more we knew that Hornsby had no hope of winning an election contest in front of the legislature. Only one county official that I encountered in serving subpoenas said he had counted these type ballots. In Covington County, there was a female probate judge who told me to talk to the assistant circuit clerk. On the night of the election, he had taken the place of the circuit clerk because the circuit clerk was up for election in 1994. The committee that counted absentee ballots had come to him about counting some unwitnessed absentee ballots. He did not think they should be counted. He looked up the statute and showed it to the committee, and they said that they would count them anyway because they knew all the people who had cast unwitnessed ballots and they felt they were genuine. Less than ten ballots were involved in that county. It apparently was not a common practice because the committee had to go to the clerk to ask about it.

The entire dispute hurt Hornsby publicly much more than it hurt Hooper. An article appeared in the *Montgomery Advertiser* that said the chief justice's image had been muddied by his "no-holds-barred" campaign. As the chairman of the University of Alabama political science department said, "[The chief justice] should command the highest respect of the people." In February of 1995 veteran political writer Bob Ingram would reluctantly write that he thought Hornsby's political career, which some had speculated would one day involve a bid for the U.S. Senate or governorship, was over.

On Sunday, 4 December 1994, the *Montgomery Advertiser* made a very persuasive argument regarding the Alabama Supreme Court's opinion in *Williams v. Lide.* It pointed out that even if you were to accept the argument that *Lide* mandates what is called "substantial compliance," the elimination of the witness/notary requirement amounted to little or no compliance, and not substantial compliance. In addition, the *Lide* case said "that irregularities in absentee ballots must not 'adversely affect the sanctity of the ballot and the integrity of the election.' The integrity of the election clearly is affected adversely when absentee ballots are deemed valid with so little actual compliance with the law." The *Advertiser's* editorial cartoon that day was quite humorous. It showed Hooper and Hornsby in a card game. Both had stacks of chips in front of them. Hooper: "I'll see your two state judges and raise you three federal judges."

The *Mobile Register* did its own legal analysis on 4 December. This editorial highlighted the U.S. Justice Department's role in the conflict:

> Weighing in from Washington, an assistant U.S. attorney general said in a letter (we're paraphrasing but not making this up): Many Alabama counties have long ignored the statute's requirements for absentee ballots. Therefore, the loose rule legislated by the Hornsby court and its even looser application by Judge Reese are just dandy for federal purposes. In fact, if Alabama now insists on obeying its own law (which, remember, was already precleared), that will constitute a change in voting procedure and will require federal preclearance.

We later learned that the use of the phrase "many counties" was incorrect, but their analysis of the Justice Department's letter was right on target. They went on to make a prediction:

> It's a safe bet at this point that the Republican candidate for chief justice of the Supreme Court—who has won by every objective rule—will be defeated by two obstacles: the legislative machinations of the Hornsby and Reese courts, and the red tape of the Clinton Justice Department.

The *Mobile Register* is not noted for a conservative bias or favoritism toward Republican candidates for office.

The Alabama Legislature was not officially elected yet. Unlike most elected officials whose terms end in January of the year following an election, unless reelected, legislators' terms end at midnight the night of the election. They could not be paid until they were officially elected. In 1994 their pay was $2,280 per month. Although the legislature itself was not scheduled to meet until January 1995, there was a Legislative Contract Review Committee that met the first Thursday of each month to review contracts written for state agencies. After this committee reviews them, they are sent to the Finance Department. One was scheduled to meet Thursday, 1 December 1994. Only one member showed up, the Chairman Tom Butler. He said that the contracts submitted at that meeting would be held up for forty-five days, just as if someone had objected to the contract at the meeting. He said that state agencies could legally bypass the committee if an emergency "adversely affecting public health, safety, security or the economic welfare of the state required it." State government was beginning to feel the practical effects of the secretary of state's decision to listen to a circuit judge instead of the Alabama Code.

The Democrats tried another tactic. They did not want any type of review in federal court of what had happened in November 1994, nor did they want a review of Reese's order. So the same parties that had sued over the racial make-up of the state appeals courts went to Judge Myron Thompson to ask him to block further lawsuits that would delay certification. The Eleventh Circuit had not yet reversed the settlement that Jimmy Evans had entered into with the plaintiffs in that case. These plaintiffs claimed that because they had settled their lawsuit with the state of Alabama (actually with Jimmy Evans), the case before Judge Howard and any other judge was interfering with the execution of that settlement. The sheriff's office of Jefferson County, represented by the deputy sheriff, and Wilcox County's Jerry Boggan, joined this action by filing motions with Judge Thompson. Judge Thompson rejected the request.

Notice that the same people whom Hooper had accused of trying to stack the state appeals courts and whom many suspected of using vote fraud against those who had been most vocally opposed to stacking the courts were now trying to prevent the federal courts' investigation into the rigging of the election. One of the most notorious counties for absentee ballots problems, Wilcox, was right there with them. Ultimately, these plaintiff trial lawyers wanted complete control over the appeals courts, not a majority on the court. Stacking of the appeals courts with certain judges, the attempted decertification of the seats of Justices Houston and Maddox, and the ability to use illegitimate absentee ballots at will to change the results of elections—the brazenness of it all was enough to take one's breath away.

Judge Hooper's lawyers had collected affidavits from people around the state, black and white, showing that the integrity of the 8 November election had been compromised by the abuse of absentee ballots. Typical examples: Alzheimer patients in nursing homes voting without their family's knowledge, people going to the polls only to find that someone had already voted for them, and the usual dead persons voting. These stories were important to show the need to protect the integrity of the ballot in Alabama. According to *Williams v. Lide,* absentee ballots that do not comply with the law are acceptable if the noncompliance does not affect the integrity of the election. We were, of course, not leaning heavily on Lide as a basis for Hooper's complaint; it was more important to show that a change in the manner of counting votes had occurred after the election.

The Eleventh Circuit Court of Appeals refused the motion by Hornsby's lawyers and the Democrats to order certification of the election to include the illegal ballots. The court said it would wait until after Howard's hearing. Not only did Hornsby's lawyers want to force Hooper to be the one to challenge the election in the legislature, but they knew that if those unopened and unwitnessed absentee ballots were unsealed, there would be little if any evidence for Hooper to use in such a contest. The faster they could get those ballots opened and counted, the less chance we would have of finding the people responsible for casting those ballots. We knew that could happen based on the speed with which the Reese order could be faxed to the counties telling them to count and send in the votes. It was difficult keeping up with those faxes when trying to phone sixty-seven counties.

In the public relations war, Hooper was clearly winning. The more they delayed things, the worse public opinion seemed to turn against Hornsby. The legal arguments and the facts were on Hooper's side. Secretary of State Bennett said that the clerk of the U.S. House of Representatives had given him until 14 December 1994 to certify the results of the congressional elections. As for the state offices, a delay in certification past 16 January 1995 would mean no governor, no attorney general, no legislature, and no chief justice.

On Sunday, 4 December 1995, I traveled with Al Agricola and Bert Jordan to Mobile from Montgomery. I was a potential witness because of my forays into south Alabama. Of particular importance was my eyewitness account of the lack of security at the Wilcox County probate office. After Judge Howard had issued his order to secure the election materials, the Wilcox County election materials were in the same room as the public probate records. The staff of the probate office was around the corner and could not even see whether anyone was tampering with the materials or not. The sheriff was supposed to keep them under lock and key. He was much more zealous in arresting Republican poll watchers because they tried to make the circuit clerk follow the state election rules than he was in safekeeping the results of the election. Bullock County was also a problem. There we discovered that the probate office had been broken into. The election materials were in cardboard boxes in the personal office of the probate judge. We were told that the materials had not been tampered with, but no one could guarantee that. The entire situation was very suspicious.

On the way down, I had to ask Al why didn't Hooper appeal Reese's decision to the Alabama Supreme Court. Was the court that politicized? He simply looked at me and nodded his head. I had wondered about the Supreme Court since the decision in the Guy Hunt case. Hunt was the Republican governor convicted of using his office for economic gain. Yet there was a very strong argument that the statute of limitations had already run before the attorney general charged him. It was highly likely that Jimmy Evans had lost reelection for attorney general because he prosecuted that case.

In Mobile, I made sure I arrived at the federal courthouse early enough to get a good seat. It was packed to overflowing later. What immediately stood out was the number of attorneys for the other side. They had at least ten at their table and a couple more sat in seats behind the table. One represented the city of Mobile, one represented the Davis class from the Reese hearing, one represented a group of probate judges, one represented the probate judge from Wilcox County, and so on. At Hooper's table were Bert Jordan, Al Agricola, Rusty Johnston, and the plaintiffs, Hooper and Larry Roe. Each one of the lawyers on the other side got up to object to the federal court even hearing the case. They claimed it was a question of Alabama law over which the federal courts had no jurisdiction. They didn't even want to get into the question of what had happened in Reese's court and whether it was legitimate or not. Judge Howard said repeatedly "My duty as a federal judge is to make sure that the right of the people of Alabama to vote under the Constitution of the United States is not infringed. And that is a federal, constitutional right over which this court will always have jurisdiction."

Finally, after they had pulled out every argument they could think of, Hooper was able to call his first witnesses. Most of Hooper's witnesses were from Greene County. Their testimony indicated that Alabama had a problem with the integrity of its ballots. The first witness, a black woman named Jessie Mason, was a member of an organization of voters called "Concerned Citizens for a Better Greene County," and they claimed to want honest government and elections. She explained in colorful terms what went on in Greene County. People were threatened that if they did not vote a certain way, then their "check" would be cut off. She did not mean that one of the candidates proposed some type of welfare reform. She meant that the person threatening would somehow get the voter's government benefits cut off if the voter did not vote a certain way. She also told about the suitcase full of 500 absentee ballots that showed up at the post office the day of the election to be delivered to a nonexistent post office box.

Jack Drake, one of the attorneys for the Davis class of absentee voters, cross examined her. He tried to damage her credibility by questioning her objectivity. He asked, "Isn't your organization a republican group?" She said, "No, it's about 50-50 of both parties, but mostly independents." Then he tried to make her allegations look petty with his next question. She responded in her country black accent: "Sir, you've never seen anything like what goes on in Greene County. It's like the wild, wild west." But for the somber mood in federal court and the seriousness of the subject matter, that comment might have brought the house down. Instead it got quite a few chuckles and sent Drake scampering for his chair at the table.

Then we called a woman from Cullman County named Helen Watts. Cullman is in north Alabama. Her seventy-eight-year-old mother was in a nursing home with Alzheimer's disease and was unable to make decisions about voting. This woman learned that someone had gotten an absentee ballot from her mother without her family's knowledge. Then we called Rufus Huffman, the black probate judge from Bullock County, who was defeated for reelection on 8 November. Huffman had been a political representative of black voter registration drives in the sixties and chief election officer for Bullock County for the past eighteen years. His opinion was that requiring a witness/notary requirement for absentee ballots was not racially discriminatory. He explained the numerous problems that Bullock County had had with absentee ballots. He explained the inordinate number of absentee ballots that had been cast in his election for his opponent. Jack Drake knew that the black community frequently used absentee ballots and he wanted Huffman to look like just another politician who had sour grapes over losing the election. If they lost the legal battle, they could use that for public relations purposes, at least with the black community. So, thinking that he had Huffman just where he wanted him, Drake confidently asked, "Your opponent in the election for probate judge was black, wasn't he?" Huffman replied, "No, he was a white man."

Jim Bennett testified. Bert and Al had already deposed Bennett to pin down his story. He admitted there existed irregularities in absentee voting in Alabama, and he also admitted that the practice of the secretary of state's office is and always had been to not count unwitnessed absentee ballots. He was also the source for the statistic that absentee ballots should account for no more than approximately 7-8% of the total vote count for a county. John Grods, an immigrant from a formerly socialist Eastern European country, was a Wilcox County resident who testified that 100 people that were not on the registered voter list had voted on 8 November. Yet, as an official poll watcher appointed in accordance with the law by the Republican party, he was not allowed to challenge any of the ballots. It was ironic and embarrassing that an immigrant who had come to this country hoping to find democratic freedoms would instead find Wilcox County.

The legitimate votes from all the counties had already been tabulated on computer by the accounting firm hired by Bennett. Bennett had said publicly that if there was a ruling in Hooper's favor, he could have the results in hours. If not, he would have to wait for the counties that had not yet sent in their counts of the unwitnessed ballots. However, on the day of the hearing in Howard's court, Bennett said that if the court ruled for Hooper, it would take a day to tabulate the results "unless another court intervenes." There again was that comment by Bennett about court intervention. Of course, there were two other times that courts had ruled in Hornsby's favor—Reese's ruling and the three-judge panel in Birmingham. At those times, Bennett did not wait for another court to intervene; rather there was a rush to get the votes into Montgomery.

Bert and Al were prepared to present more evidence, but after hearing these witnesses' testimony, Judge Howard called the attorneys to the bench and spoke to them out of everyone's hearing. I assume, based on what happened next, that he was telling them there was no need for more testimony. The Democrats had no evidence to present except copies of *Williams v. Lide*. Al made sure Judge Howard had the whole story. So he provided the entire record of the *Lide* case for him to review. We did not know whether this hearing would last a week or an hour. I thought the judge would retire to his chambers to deliberate. He didn't need that much time. As soon as the parties had rested, he stayed at his bench and said that this was a case of changing the rules after the election. He said such a change was "patently unfair" and "abominable." He said it was "contemptible" under the U.S. Constitution, and that if he did not rule, then the people of Alabama would lose faith in the election laws of the state. He granted the preliminary injunction and ordered Bennett to count and certify the election without the illegal absentee ballots.

His ruling was better than we could have expected. I immediately called my wife to tell her. The newspeople interviewed Hooper and the attorneys. I still had an uneasy feeling in my gut that this case was not over yet. Hornsby's public relations started the spin on the ruling. Even while their lawyers plotted the appeal to the Eleventh Circuit, which would delay things indefinitely, Hornsby's spokesman, Michael Tucker, told the media: "We look forward to an early resolution so the election can be certified. Hornsby stands ready to abide by the will of the people when that will is determined." Tucker also misstated the Birmingham three-judge panel's decision by saying that Howard's ruling conflicted with four other judges—Reese and the three federal judges in Birmingham. Of course, that was completely false. The three judges in Birmingham did not disagree with Howard, and the chief justice knew that. Hornsby's machine continued to misrepresent what happened in Birmingham even after Propst's memorandum reminded the attorneys not to.

Bennett's public relations spin began on Tuesday, the day after the hearing. He filed a motion with the Eleventh Circuit asking for clarification. He also filed a motion with Judge Reese asking for clarification. He claimed there was a constitutional crisis because two different courts had ordered him to do opposite things. Judge Reese, a state court judge, had ordered him to count the unwitnessed absentee ballots, while a federal district judge had ordered him not to count them. He said publicly, "You can't put a person in the position of being in contempt no matter what they do." This made no sense. Judge Reese's ruling had just been declared unconstitutional by a federal judge; there was nothing with which Reese could hold Bennett in contempt. When a federal judge calls a state judge's decision contemptible, there is no need for clarification.

Al had to educate the secretary of state on sovereignty— that a federal judge's order trumps a state judge's order. Hooper's lawyers asked Judge Howard to hold Bennett in contempt. Jack stuck his foot in his mouth when the campaign was accused of shopping for a friendly judge and finding one in

Judge Howard. He said, "We had to shop around to find a fair judge. We damn sure couldn't find one in Montgomery County." We did not know what would happen in federal court, even with a Republican appointee like Howard. There may have been a fair judge in Montgomery County, and if Hooper eventually won and became the chief administrator of the Alabama court system, he would have to live with that statement. Jack was understandably frustrated with the situation and had to let off some steam.

On 7 December, the Eleventh Circuit ruled in another case, a Florida case in which the Southern Christian Leadership Conference (SCLC) sued the state of Florida claiming that its at-large elections of circuit judges denied blacks their right to political representation. The SCLC wanted a district method of electing judges, something akin to county commission races. The Eleventh Circuit said that such a change in electing judges would mean "the federal court would be proclaiming that race matters in the administration of justice." The case gave hope for a good resolution in Alabama's appeals court settlement case, as well as another case dealing with circuit judge elections in Alabama.

On that same day, the news media reported that Bennett said he would start the certification process at 10:00 A.M. on Thursday, the next day, and finish by 2:00 P.M., and he fully expected to include the illegal ballots. In the afternoon, he said in a second press release that he would have to let reason rule at some point and not wait forever. So he would begin the certification process as soon as possible under Judge Howard's order and not include the illegal absentee ballots. Then, on the 6:00 P.M. news, he said that he was going to wait for the Eleventh Circuit to rule before he acted. But he said he thought he could be finished with everything by the end of Friday. He said that if the illegal absentee ballots were not included, he could certify within an hour. On Friday, 9 December Bennett had still not certified the results of the election. At approximately 9:00 A.M., Bennett received a telefaxed order from Judge Howard that warned him he'd be in contempt of Howard's order if he did not begin certification by noon. However,

Bennett's delaying tactics paid off. Hornsby's lawyers and the attorney general obtained an order from the Eleventh Circuit that placed a stay on any contempt proceeding.

On 10 December 1994 a letter to the editor appeared in the *Birmingham News* written by Justice Houston. It echoed the things he had said in his comments to the *Montgomery Advertiser*. He stated emphatically that the Alabama Supreme Court had not done away with the need for notarization or witnessing of absentee ballots. "The Supreme Court of Alabama has never held that an absentee ballot is legally sufficient if it does not comply with [§ 17-10-7, Alabama Code of 1975, the section requiring witnesses or a notary for an absentee ballot]."

Two editorials showed me that the press was probably on our side. I also began to sense the initial stages of frustration with the whole ordeal. On the same day that Justice Houston's letter appeared in the *Birmingham News*, their office got a call from someone who said that those who have a habit of stealing votes would know how to fill out the absentee ballot in accordance with the law. So the ballots ordered counted by Reese may have been cast by innocent people who had made a mistake. The editorial said that determining which were legitimate and which were illegitimate could get complicated. "Instead, we do something much more practical. We pass a state law and follow it. There's nothing unclear about state law in this case. It is clear to us what the Legislature intended. Those absentee ballots without two witnesses or a notary seal should be thrown out. Why does this matter continue to be dragged out in the courts?"

An editorial from the *Montgomery Advertiser*, on 11 December 1994, examined the issue of courts interpreting versus making law. It said, "A prime example can be found in the dispute over absentee ballots case in last month's election. The law is quite clear as to what is required for a valid ballot. Among the requirements is the witnessing of the ballot by two persons eighteen years of age or older or by a notary public. Yet a court has held, in essence, that what the law says really doesn't matter, that ballots are valid even if they don't meet the requirements." That isn't interpreting the law. That isn't applying the law. That's making law. That is a court saying that the legislative process that produced that law can be discounted. In other words, the law is what the court says it is.

On 13 December 1994, the Eleventh Circuit set a timetable for the next sixteen days: new briefs submitted by 21 December, reply briefs by 23 December, and oral arguments on 29 December. For now, Hooper was on top after Judge Howard's order of 5 December 1994.

Notes

1. December 5, 1994 District Court Trial Transcript, p. 80.

The Eleventh Circuit
Carefully Steps In

Hornsby's lawyers did appeal, and the Eleventh Circuit set oral arguments in the case for 29 December 1994. That meant that all the elections of 8 November would remain unresolved, and inauguration day, 16 January 1995, was fast approaching. No one in the embryonic James administration seemed to know what to do. Elbert Peters, the chairman of the Alabama Republican party, said that he didn't think the Eleventh Circuit would foil the transition from the Democratic governor to the Republican governor. It seemed, however, that holding on to office beyond the end of their terms might just have been the Democrats' plan. The *Montgomery Advertiser* reported that a spokesman for the supreme court said that Hornsby was continuing to hear cases and that he would continue to oversee the state's court system "through the last day, whether it's January 16th or January 16th six years from now."

Ironically, at the same time this battle for the chief justice seat was going on, the new Republican Congress in Washington was explaining to the country just what their commitment to the Contract with America would accomplish. One of the ten promises was a reform of the punitive damages system with respect to products liability. The goal was a uniform standard with a damages cap, certain burdens of proof, and a "loser-pays" provision. One of the key goals of the legislation was to prevent forum shopping, the attempt to find a state with the greatest potential for a huge judgment and sue a company there for a nationwide class of plaintiffs. As long as there was one state left that allowed exorbitant punitive damages, that left open the possibility for companies to be gouged relentlessly. Another development in 1994 was the lack of certification of elections. Alabama, as well as other states like Arkansas and Pennsylvania, had that problem because of election disputes.

The traditional practice of liberals, usually liberal Democrats, has been to attempt to expand the jurisdiction of federal courts to accomplish a liberal agenda. Hornsby's lawyers, experts in that tradition, filed briefs with the Eleventh Circuit contending that this controversy over absentee ballots was purely a state matter and that the federal courts should not meddle in it. Their argument made them sound like good federalists. Whatley was probably preparing to argue to this same court that the federal courts should be involved in altering the voting system for judges in the state of Alabama, i.e., approve the appellate court packing scheme. Liberal Democrats had historically not only approved of the intervention of federal courts in state matters but had invited them in to do so. A 23 December editorial in the *Montgomery Advertiser* portrayed Whatley's argument like this:

"An attorney for those Democrats who are desperately trying to allow state Supreme Court Chief Justice Sonny Hornsby to cling to power told a federal appeals court that the election dispute 'is not a matter for the federal courts to be meddling in. This is a state law and state court issue.' Gee, isn't it amazing how the definition of meddling changes depending on whose donkey is being gored."

Hooper's attorneys clarified the difference between the meddling by federal courts in other cases and the reason for going to federal court in this particular case. Bert Jordan said, "There's a tradition of federal protection when the wrong rises to a systematic and egregious level and this has reached that level." Hooper's case was a legitimate use of the federal courts— protection of the right to vote—and not a liberal expansion of the courts' jurisdiction. Citing a U.S. Supreme Court case, Hooper's attorneys pointed out that "[I]n acting together in statewide fashion, they [state officials like Judge Reese and Attorney General Evans] possessed the 'unmatched powers' of a legislature enacting a retroactive statute. See [*Landgraf v. USI Film Products*], 114 S.Ct. at 1497."[1]

Hornsby's lawyers also tried to argue to Judge Howard in their written brief that the ballots should be counted because some counties had counted improper ballots. For example, they cited Winston County, where a notary public had witnessed eighty-one ballots. This notary had renewed her term but had not yet signed her bond papers, so legally she was not a notary. Whatley's brief claimed that because that happened in Winston County, then all the unwitnessed absentee ballots in the state should be counted. However, there was no comparison. To all involved in the election in Winston County, from the absentee ballots clerk who counted the ballots to the voter, the ballots appeared to be valid and in compliance with state law. And they were in fact witnessed. There was no purposeful attempt to count clearly unwitnessed ballots. Hooper's attorneys did their own research on Winston County and discovered that six unwitnessed absentee ballots were not counted. That means Winston County's policy was to comply with the law governing the type of ballots at issue in Hooper's case.

John Harbert of the Harbert Corporation helped Hooper during his campaign, and he continued to help after the election with financing and personnel. He specifically financed an ad for the Republican party that ran on Thursday, 22 December 1994. It was a half-page ad, titled "They steal elections they don't like." It ran in the *Birmingham News,* the *Montgomery Advertiser,* the *Huntsville Times,* the *Dothan Eagle,* and the *Mobile Press-Register.* It gave a brief summary of the events behind the controversy, and it had a mail-in portion a reader could cut out and send to the Republican party stating objections to what was happening. We thought we might need the mail-ins in case Hooper had to go to the legislature and challenge the election. We were still very unsure of what the outcome in the courts would be. The mail-in had a box for readers to check saying they thought Hooper should be sworn in as chief justice. I thought the most effective part of the ad was its depiction of what had happened since the election. Hornsby's people and the Democrats didn't like it too much. State Democratic party Chairman Bill Blount said the ad was inappropriate while the dispute was being handled in federal court. The ad accused a small handful of Democratic party bosses and rich plaintiff lawyers of trying to steal the election. The Democrats accused the Republicans of recklessly running the ad and undermining the election process. The controversy over this ad was a tempest in a teapot and lasted as long as it took to write a newspaper article about it. However, Hornsby's lawyers thought enough of it to place an unfavorable comment about it in their brief to the Eleventh Circuit.

They also raised the specter of race in the brief. They said that not counting these ballots would disenfranchise black voters because black voters had cast most of the disputed absentee ballots. The ballots are sealed and kept secure by each county, and race is not even identified on the affidavit envelope and most of Hooper's witnesses testifying of fraud before Judge Howard had been black, undermining this argument, Hooper's lawyers replied in their brief:

> The race issue is a 'red herring.' It is raised to distract this court from the real issue, namely, that state officials are attempting to ignore well-established, published and meaningful election rules, to change the rules of the election after it is over, and to strip Alabama's absentee-balloting system of the only statutory mechanism designed to protect its integrity.

We went with much trepidation to Atlanta on 29 December 1994 to hear the oral arguments before the Eleventh Circuit in a large courtroom, which was packed. Some spectators had to stand in the back. Hooper came with his wife, Marilyn. Hornsby came with his wife. Joe Whatley began the argument for the appellants. His first argument was predictable. He argued that Judge Howard had decided that the courts of the state of Alabama could not determine the law of Alabama. His second point was that not counting these ballots was a denial of due process under the Fourteenth Amendment of the U.S. Constitution. In some counties, the ballots had become separated from the envelopes, and there was no way to restore them to a state where one could tell which were the witnessed absentee ballots and which were not. Therefore, Alabama must continue to count all of them. Third, he said that the availability of state law remedies meant that the Alabama Supreme Court should decide the issue.

One judge asked Whatley where *Williams v. Lide* tells the "chair of the voting committee" of a county to count these particular ballots. Whatley referred to page 537, the three-part test, and page 536, top of the third column, another reference to the three-part test. Then, Judge Tjoflat, the chief judge of the three-judge panel, said, "The State of Alabama sought retroactive preclearance by the Justice Department. Why did it seek preclearance after 8 November 1994 if that was the law before?" Whatley said that the Justice Department saw no change, just that it had been a uniform practice. The lawyers repeated this assertion at every opportunity, but they never presented any proof that the assertion was true. Judge Burch pointed out to Whatley that the secretary of state sends out a handbook, and the local officials look to him for guidance. Of course, in this case, the handbook says to not count the disputed ballots. This question lead to a discussion on the ministerial versus the discretionary power of local voting officials.

As I said before, a ministerial function is one in which the official has no choice; it is mandated by law, whereas a discretionary function requires judgment on the official's part. The judges on the panel seemed to agree that local voting officials had no discretion and had to count only those votes allowed to be counted by law. Judge Tjoflat raised the issue that giving discretion to a local voting official implicated a First Amendment right. If a local voting official exercised too much discretion, he could deny someone's right to express himself through the political process. Whatley claimed that problem was taken care of in the contest procedure. Tjoflat raised another issue— some voters who didn't want to use a notary would have not voted thinking they could not send in an unwitnessed absentee ballot. That would be a violation of due process to change that expectation after the election and say, "Oh, but you could have voted absentee after all and didn't know it." This was the concern Judge Propst raised in Birmingham. Whatley's answer was that the state provides a contest procedure, so there was no due process violation. A contest does not help people who

did not vote. It would affect whether certain ballots were valid
or not, but they have to be in existence for a contest committee
to consider them. Whatley then proposed a strange solution:
have another election for those who didn't vote because they
thought they had to have the ballot witnessed. Tjoflat said
that the First Amendment requires the local election official
to have no discretion; they must follow the law and not open
the ballot if it lacks witnessing.

Judge Edmondson said that the Alabama Supreme Court
was the mechanism for deciding Alabama law, not a circuit
judge. He told Whatley that even if the law was what Whatley
said it was, counting these ballots had not been the practice of
the past. He was going by what the secretary of state had said
in Howard's court, not what Whatley was saying in argument
about past practice. Edmondson pointed out a Rhode Island
case, where a systematic change in the manner of tabulating
votes was considered a violation of due process. It was looking
very good for Hooper, but things seemed to change when Bert
Jordan began arguing. He pointed out that Judge Howard
found that there had been a change in Alabama's practice
based on Reese's order. He also pointed out that there was no
evidence that the practice varied throughout the state. Such
assertions of a widespread practice of counting such ballots
were merely the unsupported statements of the lawyers for the
other side. Then Edmondson said he wasn't sure there was a
federal constitutional issue. He said that if Alabama law allows
this, then there was no federal constitutional issue. He said
that if they waited for the Alabama Supreme Court, they
would do damage to one of the parties; that is, whoever was
the winner would not be sworn in on 16 January.

All the judges began asking questions after Edmondson
had finished. I sensed that some sort of confusion had arisen
among the judges on the panel. Had some of these unwitnessed
absentee ballots been counted and mingled in, without distinction, with the legitimate ballots. Is it too late to separate
them? Do we certify the election as it stands now? Edmondson
asked questions indicating he might understand that many
counties had sent in two tabulations—the original legitimate
count and the later count ordered by Reese. However, that still

did not seem to satisfy them. They wanted to know what other counties had done.

Judge Tjoflat was quite clear in his position. He did not think a circuit court judge like Reese could order a change in state law, particularly in light of ° 17-15-6. But the Alabama Supreme Court could change the law. He stated that if the Alabama Supreme Court upheld the Reese decision, then Hooper would clearly be able to show a change in state law. Then Hooper could return to federal court claiming a violation of the U.S. Constitution.

It was Whatley's turn for rebuttal. He advocated going ahead and counting the unwitnessed absentee ballots and sending the contested absentee ballots to the secretary of state's office. Tjoflat flatly said that wasn't good because Alabama law "changed drastically." But then he asked, "Would any candidate win either way?" Jack was sure that Hornsby would win if the unwitnessed ballots were counted, but how could Hooper prove it unless they were actually counted? We knew Hooper had won if they weren't counted. Edmondson said that a count might moot all state and federal issues. As long as physical security of the materials could stay intact, there would be no problem with counting them just to see the result. Whatley raised the Rooker-Feldman doctrine.[2]

The arguments exceeded the allotted time significantly. The judges were apparently very interested in the issue. They wanted a satisfactory solution. They wanted to solve the dispute without getting involved in a contest and interfering too much with the state's business. They seemed in need of guidance. They asked if Hooper's attorneys could go back into state court and appeal. However, too much time had passed since Reese's decision to file with the Alabama Supreme Court. The judges asked about Alabama's certified question process. They wanted the Alabama Supreme Court to say what the law was. I left with the conviction that they would send a certified question to the Alabama Supreme Court. That's also what the newspaper thought too, in next day's paper. That is also what Sonny Hornsby thought, because when I saw him leave the courtroom, he was all smiles. His lawyers had created enough confusion that the judges had to get help from his colleagues on the Alabama Supreme Court. Hornsby's wife Judy told Marilyn that she knew they could be friends if circumstances were only different. Marilyn later said that all she could think about when Judy talked with her was the Jerry Hamilton commercial accusing her husband of murder.

The Eleventh Circuit released its written opinion on 4 January 1995. It was what I expected; however, there were some bright spots. Two of the three judges agreed with Hooper, affirming Judge Howard's order preserving the election materials, and protecting them from tampering and preventing the secretary of state from certifying any election results that include the contested ballots. It modified Howard's order to allow the certification of all races but the chief justice and treasurer races.

However, the order stated that a federal court should refrain from holding a state election law unconstitutional when a "reasonable alternative course of action exists." No one knew what that alternative was, though. They said the federal courts must show deference to the state decision-makers. They specifically vacated the part of Howard's order that ordered election officials to send purged election results in all races to the secretary of state. Of course, that was a moot point; the counties' original results were already purged. That portion of Howard's order may have been the source of the Eleventh's Circuit's confusion over the mixture of legitimate and illegitimate ballots.

The Eleventh Circuit wrote in its opinion there were two courses of action it could have taken. One, it could leave Hooper to appeal Reese's decision to the Alabama Supreme Court, which was clearly not good for us because it was too late to appeal. Two, it could certify the question to the Alabama Supreme Court, retain jurisdiction, and await that court's answer. They also said, in disagreement with Hornsby's lawyers, that a contest in the legislature was not the adequate method of resolving the federal constitutional issues that were presented. Agreeing with Hooper's lawyers, they said Reese's circuit court was jurisdictionally barred by Alabama Code Section 17-15-6 from entertaining statewide election contests. The unnecessary delay of going through the contest process with the legislature would be too great a delay. The Eleventh Circuit felt that a certified question would resolve the issue to satisfy all concerns—the time concern, the constitutional concern (because the Eleventh Circuit would retain jurisdiction), and the state law concern (because they would have Alabama's highest court's opinion about these particular ballots). It would not resolve as they expected.

Here is the text of the question certified to the Alabama Supreme Court:

> It appears to the United States Court of Appeals for the Eleventh Circuit that this case involves a question of Alabama state law that is determinative of the cause, but unanswered by controlling precedent of the Supreme Court of Alabama:
>
> WHETHER ABSENTEE BALLOTS THAT, ON THE ACCOMPANYING AFFIDAVIT ENVELOPE, FAIL TO HAVE TWO WITNESSES AND LACK PROPER NOTARIZATION (FOR EXAMPLE, BALLOT ENVELOPES THAT HAVE ONLY A SIGNATURE OR ONLY ONE WITNESS, OR ON WHICH THE VOTER AND THE NOTARY HAVE SIGNED THE BALLOT BUT THE NOTARY FAILS TO FILL IN THE 'TITLE OF OFFICIAL') MEET THE REQUIREMENTS OF ALABAMA LAW, SPECIFICALLY ALABAMA CODE SECTION 17-10-7, TO BE LEGAL BALLOTS DUE TO BE COUNTED IN THE NOVEMBER 8, 1994 GENERAL ELECTION.

Judge Edmondson dissented. His dissent echoed his concerns expressed at oral argument. He questioned federal involvement when the court did not know what the outcome of the election was and did not even know whether the alleged wrong-doer, in this case Hornsby, had actually done something wrong to affect the outcome in his favor. He said that it was appropriate to let the contested votes be counted in order to see if they affected the outcome. Then there might arise a controversy for the courts to become involved. He misunderstood one very important point. One of the plaintiffs was not a candidate; he was a voter, Larry Roe, who represented the class of all voters that cast a ballot that complied with Alabama law. The voters were the real victims of this violation of the law. The case was not about an election contest; it was about a rigging of an election after the voting had occurred and during the actual counting of those votes.

One interesting comment by Judge Tjoflat during oral argument came in response to Whatley's concern that if no resolution occurred quickly, there would be a delay in certifying the election of chief justice. Tjoflat said that maybe it would be better if Alabama did without a chief justice while this issue was decided. So the Eleventh Circuit was not concerned about the time it would take to decide the case. That wasn't good for us. Whatley asked if certification could go ahead anyway. Tjoflat flatly replied, "That's out." Before the written order was issued, no one was sure whether all the elections would be held up or not. Fob James, the newly elected governor (at least the informal uncertified results showed him to be the winner), said he would go ahead and take the oath on 16 January anyway. Obviously, it would be quite improper for the losing incumbent candidate to remain in office after being voted out. Some of us began to wonder if maybe that was many Democrats' plan anyway. Maybe they couldn't win an election, but they might at least create enough confusion to delay the whole matter awhile and keep certain of their people in office. That didn't work with all the other elections. But that prediction seemed pretty accurate with respect to Hooper's elections. Hooper's lawyers got to work. For now, Hooper was in waiting mode again. Down but not out.

Notes

1. *Landgraf v. USI Film Products,* 114 S.Ct. 1483 (1994).

2. *District of Columbia Court of Appeals v. Feldman,* 460 U.S. 462, 103 S.Ct. 1303, 75 L.Ed.2d 206 (1983), and *Rooker v. Fidelity Trust Co.,* 263 U.S. 413, 44 S.Ct. 149, 68 L.Ed. 362 (1923),

involved cases questioning whether a federal district court could review a decision by a state's highest court. The U.S. Supreme Court ruled that a federal district court may not review the final decision of the highest court of a jurisdiction, like a state. Only the U.S. Supreme Court could review such a decision. Hornsby's attorneys constantly attempted to interpret Reese's decision as merely agreeing with a decision already reached by the Alabama Supreme Court. So far the federal courts had not bought into that argument.

Chapter Eleven

Waiting for the Alabama Supreme Court

On 1 January 1995, the *Montgomery Advertiser* rated the Hooper-Hornsby controversy one of the top ten stories in Alabama for 1994. They called it the nasty campaign for the office of chief justice and a bitter post-election battle, which threatened the reputation of Alabama's supreme court. They included a selection of quotes from various sources—Justice Houston's comment about mud wrestling and Hooper's comment about getting a dialogue going after Hornsby angrily crashed the Republican candidates' news conference. The *Advertiser* also published an editorial saying that early voting coupled with stricter absentee ballot rules would help prevent some of the distortions of the absentee voting process.

Also on 1 January a new law went into effect, allowing a person to order from the circuit clerk of any county only one absentee ballot application. The law was the brain-child of Secretary of State Jim Bennett.

On 2 January 1995, the *Birmingham News* issued an editorial[1] that fairly represented the status of things after the Eleventh Circuit's decision. It appeared before the publication by Hooper's lawyers of the campaign contribution connection. But it clearly presented the expectations of most people after the comments by the federal judges in Atlanta. It also set the stage well for what was to come next. It was good enough to include in its entirety in an endnote.

The *Birmingham News* set up a test for the Alabama Supreme Court. There were still shenanigans going on in other parts of Alabama government. Attorneys were saying that Governor Jim Folsom would have to stay in office if the election results were not certified. One of Hooper's attorneys, Rusty Johnston, said that the state supreme court could give an answer to the Eleventh Circuit by 16 January, especially considering the chaos that would result if they did not. He made the following statement: "It's really not wise to have people serving in office who were not elected." However, Bob Martin, a spokesman for the supreme court, said that would be impractical. There was talk of having only the races certified that would not be affected by the disputed absentee ballots. The Eleventh Circuit's order required the certification of all races except the chief justice and treasurer races. So that issue became a moot point for all races but those two.

Judge Hooper received a letter from Hornsby after the Eleventh Circuit's oral argument. It contained his proposal for ending the election crisis. He proposed that both parties in the lawsuit agree to allow the unwitnessed absentee ballots to be counted. If the results of that count did not change the outcome, then the litigation could end, and Hooper could enter office sooner than if the parties went ahead and litigated to completion. If the outcome changed, then the litigation could continue as before. He said that he was not a party, which technically was true. He said that Hooper, as a plaintiff, could accomplish this task and that such a plan was in the public interest. Hornsby even held a news conference to announce his proposal. We saw that the real purpose behind this proposal, was to make Hornsby look like a reasonable diplomat who wanted, above all, not to interfere with the orderly process of state government. He also wanted to get out of the mess he had created as soon as possible. He needed some favorable news coverage. He had been criticized by just about every journalist in the state of Alabama, which included almost every newspaper that had endorsed him during his campaign for reelection. Strangely enough, Joe Espy, the lawyer for the Davis class in Reese's court, quickly accepted Hornsby's offer and stated that his clients had no objection to the proposal.

Hooper's answer was short and simple: "No." He considered the whole dispute to be not about who won or lost, but respect for the law. He was not going to agree to any arrangement that showed compromise or disrespect for the law. The media were not impressed. Hornsby's plan had been successful. He made Hooper look like the unreasonable obstruction-ist. That, combined with some earlier superficial media reports that made it look as if Hooper had started the confusion, allowed Hornsby to gain a notch in reputation, temporarily. Hornsby's lawyers continually alleged that Hooper wanted to have an election contest in the courts, instead of the legislature where it belonged. Yet when Hooper tried to point out publicly that it was not about a contest of the election but about following the law and not subverting the legitimate votes, Hornsby made it sound as if the dispute was simply a contest between him and Hooper. Yet Hornsby's lawyers made the most fuss in Reese's court arguing that the case was not an election contest.

The *Mobile Press-Register's* 4 January headline read: "Hooper 'nay holds all hostage in vote suit." The legislature was scheduled to begin on 10 January. The governor and other state officers were to be sworn in on 16 January. All of the hullabaloo about the other elections was rendered moot when the Eleventh Circuit issued its 4 January order, lifting the stay on all the elections except those of the chief justice and the treasurer.

Hornsby's attempt at conciliation and public relations back-fired on him somewhat. It would now be very difficult for him to appear as if he was uninvolved in the plan to have the absentee ballots counted. Now any attempt to veil the dispute behind the rhetoric of "the right of disenfranchised voters to have their vote counted," was frail, at best.

Hooper said, "The ball game's over," meaning that it was too late to count votes that shouldn't be counted. Hornsby's campaign spokesman called Hooper bull-headed. Jack's re-sponse was that the campaign would agree to the certification of the election without unwitnessed absentee ballots and allow the case to continue through the courts. That was the status before the Davis class brought their action in Reese's court. But the Eleventh Circuit had their hands on the case now, and would not allow that.

One rare moment in which Hornsby expressed a lighter side was in a report by the *Advertiser,* which quoted him say-ing, "If there's anybody out there trying to steal votes for me, they're doing a mighty, mighty poor job of it." The true professional vote thieves had chutzpah, craftiness, and the assistance of several state officials. The only problem in this case was that they had a little too much craftiness and, did not realize how bad the public relations backlash would be.

Hooper's attorneys planned to ask three Justices on the Alabama Supreme Court to excuse themselves from the case: Hornsby, of course, but also Justices Cook and Kennedy, who had run for election in 1994. Although Cook and Kennedy's races were not as close as Hornsby's, their vote totals still stood to gain if the additional ballots were counted. Rusty Johnston thought they should recuse themselves, and said so publicly. Bob Esdale, the Clerk for the Alabama Supreme Court, said that if enough Justices stepped aside, the remaining Justices could appoint temporary replacements, or ask the governor to appoint replacements.

The precedent for a special supreme court was not lacking. In 1967, Supreme Court Justice Robert Simpson filed a suit over a car accident in which he was injured and his wife died. Governor Lurleen Wallace, George's wife, appointed five lawyers to act as a special supreme court to hear the case. Sam Heldman, another of Hornsby's stable of lawyers who got involved in the case, said he did not think a special court would be needed. He also said he didn't think that Justices Cook and Kennedy would need to step aside because their races were not close enough to be affected by the contested ballots.

Meanwhile, the tort reform debate continued. One of Hooper's strong supporters was a man named Red Williams, who formerly worked at NASA in Huntsville. He lived just outside Troy, Alabama. He wrote a letter to the editor of the *Montgomery Advertiser* about tort reform and the desperation of the trial lawyers to keep a decent man out of office. Also, on 4 January 1995, when most were too worried about the outcome of the election to think about tort reform, state Representative Steve Flowers wrote a letter to the same editor about a case called *Leahey v. American Legion*. Leahey slipped at an American Legion Post and sued. The main issue on appeal was whether a statute that was passed as part of the

1987 tort reform package was constitutional. That statute had done away with what was called the "collateral source rule." The collateral source rule, a creation of common law, not the legislature, required that a jury not hear whether or not a plaintiff had received reimbursement for injury or loss from another source, e.g., an insurance policy. The 1987 tort reform package had done away with that rule, meaning that a jury could learn whether a plaintiff had already received payment from another source to compensate for a loss. Flowers sponsored the bill and wanted to alert the public that another threat loomed on the horizon against another part of the 1987 tort reform. At the end of January, the U.S. Supreme Court agreed to hear the BMW case, involving the doctor's touched-up paint job on his new car.

The insurance industry also reported on tort reform and the election. James Dill, the Alabama Insurance Commissioner, said that at least six national and regional insurance carriers had stopped selling insurance in the state of Alabama. He said that more withdrawals were being reported weekly. One independent agent in Birmingham said that there were reports that "bad faith" punitive damage awards could affect renewal premiums on *Agent Errors and Omissions* policies, which is insurance for insurance agents. This was also reported in the 2 January *National Underwriters* publication, which reported that insurance companies were doing more than usual to try to prevent lawsuits. An agent for Principal Mutual Life in Mobile said that insurance companies could be harming themselves by engaging in cutthroat-type competition. Such zealous competition not only caused them to rejoice in lawsuits against competitors but also encouraged them to tell clients bad things about other companies in an effort to replace that company's coverage with their own policies.

The plaintiff trial lawyers had gone to the mat for their man, Hornsby. They used Alabama Supreme Court precedent, misapplied it, and found a judge to agree, all in an effort to thwart the democratic process upon which this nation and the state of Alabama had been founded. Insurance companies and other businesses, who were threatened by the plaintiff trial lawyers and who were familiar with their political guerilla warfare, saw the Hooper-Hornsby court battle as a symbol of all that was wrong with the legal system dominated by the plaintiff trial lawyers. They were guilty of ignoring the law to obtain a goal, portraying the opposition as inveterately evil, using the courts and the judges to whom they had given campaign contributions to overcome the democratic process, and cheating that ignored what was best for the majority of the citizens of the state. How ironic that these so-called *Knights of Justice* had attempted to use the court system, which they held up as the most effective means for obtaining truth and justice, to obscure the truth and thwart justice.

Secretary of State Bennett was still babbling about Reese's order as if it held him like a marionette on strings. He said that the Eleventh Circuit's order did not address the Reese order at all. Howard's order had stayed it, and the Eleventh Circuit affirmed most of Howard's order. Nevertheless, Bennett went to Reese's court to obtain his permission to certify all the elections, except the chief justice and treasurer elections. Bennett claimed that, with the existence of Reese's order staying those certifications, until the unwitnessed ballots were counted, he had "somewhat stepped out on a limb." Bennett had stepped out on a limb, not because of Reese's order, but because he had listened to the attorney general's office, still run by Jimmy Evans. His actions and inactions were key in facilitating the election debacle. So he claimed that he was acting courageously in not obeying Reese's order, even after two federal courts had effectively canned it. He said, "They say leaders lead, and that's what I'm attempting to do." Reese removed all anxiety from Bennett's life by "okaying" the order from the Eleventh Circuit the next day.

During the hearing on this matter, Judge Reese could not resist compelling a confession from Al Agricola. He asked him in open court why he had not appealed Reese's 16 November order to the Alabama Supreme Court. Going straight to federal court had thrown a big wrench into the works. Reese said, "Had you not chosen to do that, we might have had an earlier resolution of this." Again, someone tried to lay the blame for the delay of the certification of the elections at the doorstep of Hooper and his lawyers. Al gave a proper, controlled response to Reese's question: "Our client's best interest would not have been protected had we not [gone to federal court to obtain a decision on the federal constitutional questions]."

On 16 January, the inauguration of Alabama's constitutional offices occurred. Seated at the podium with the other constitutional officers was Perry Hooper, Sr. The new governor, Fob James, had invited him to sit on the podium. Also seated with the justices of the supreme court was Sonny Hornsby. Inviting Hooper onto the podium was Governor James' way of being evenhanded while the election was still in limbo. Both candidates for treasurer were also invited. However, none of the four who were involved in the litigation were sworn in. Broaching another contentious issue, a reporter for the *Montgomery Advertiser* asked Hooper if he thought Hornsby should keep working as chief justice. Hooper said, "I think it's clear his term has ended." Hornsby had said in December that he would stay in office and continue to hear cases. He cited a state statute that Supreme Court Justices "shall hold office for terms of six years until their successors are elected and qualified." However, Hooper looked to the Judicial Article in the Alabama Constitution, which says that Justices will serve for a six year term. Hornsby had not yet been elected to the office. In fact, based on the ballots that the state had always counted in the past, Hornsby had lost the election. Three days after the inauguration, attorneys for the plaintiffs in *Odom v. Bennett* appeared before Judge Reese to request summary judgment as to the preliminary injunction.

In its editorial of 25 January 1995, the *Montgomery Advertiser* asked if a constitutional provision that specified the term was six years could be changed by a state statute. It was a good question. One comment from that editorial illustrates how far Hornsby had fallen from grace in the media's eyes: "If Hornsby believed that clear and unequivocal language [as to a six-year term], he would step down until the election dispute is settled. Of course, if Hornsby believed in clear and unequivocal language, there wouldn't be an election dispute in the first place." The dispute lead to Governor James' Finance Director asking for an opinion from the new attorney general as to Hornsby's pay status. The attorney general's opinion on the matter, dated 1 February 1995, concluded: "It is my opinion that, in this peculiar circumstance, the State Comptroller may not legally issue state warrants to pay the salary or expenses of the Chief Justice and Treasurer." He said that the lack of a chief justice was not a constitutional crisis; the supreme court had operated in the past with only seven justices and could operate without a chief justice.

Hornsby responded angrily and threatened to submit the question to the courts if the attorney general did not himself do so by noon of 2 February 1995. During his news conference, he made this statement: "Either I'm the chief justice or I'm not." According to the newspapers and the TV News, Sessions had said that Hornsby and Treasurer George Wallace, Jr., could stay in office "until their authority was successfully 'challenged by litigation.' "[2] This spin misrepresented the attorney general, whose written opinion stated that was not the case at all. Sessions responded to Hornsby by saying he was sorry that Hornsby took it personally. Sessions said that he was simply answering the question posed to him and nothing more. He also said that he had no intention of going to court.

Where did the *Advertiser* get the quote "challenged by litigation?" The article did not say. The words are not in the attorney general's written opinion. The opinion analyzed the statute, the constitution, and Alabama Supreme Court cases dealing with officials holding over in their offices beyond the date of their expired terms. The basis for saying that Hornsby was not entitled to pay was this quote: "Because that analysis (of the Alabama Code, the Alabama Constitution, and the relevant Alabama Supreme Court precedent) ineluctably establishes that the terms of office of the Chief Justice and Treasurer have expired, it is my opinion that the State Comptroller may no longer legally issue state warrants to pay the salaries of Chief Justice Hornsby and Treasurer Wallace." The opinion clearly said that Hornsby was not chief justice, so he should not be paid. Hornsby went on to chastise the attorney general, as if he were a child and Hornsby were a disappointed father: "I am very disappointed in the performance of the attorney general."[3] He also said that the opinion was "irresponsible" and "an example of partisan politics at its worst."

Jeff Sessions was the Republican elected to succeed Jimmy Evans as attorney general. He knew Perry Hooper. In fact, he had been Hooper's campaign manager for the campus of Huntington College in Montgomery when Hooper ran for the U.S. Senate in 1968. On 20 January 1995 he held his first news conference as attorney general. At that conference, he spoke about the absentee ballot controversy. He said, "We ought not to be confusing the public when you have plain law that the Alabama Legislature has passed."[4] He added that it didn't matter whose office was at stake. The question was a legal one that the courts had to resolve even if all of the candidates for the offices of chief justice and treasurer were to agree to dismiss the case. The state of Alabama needed to resolve the issue for the sake of future elections. He also filed an answer with Judge Howard in Mobile, telling Howard that the state of Alabama no longer sided with the plaintiffs in *Odom v. Bennett* on the issue of counting unwitnessed absentee ballots. It was his duty to support the law as it was written, not as it was rewritten by Reese. Jimmy Evans' office sided with those using the courts to usurp the power of the legislature and change the rules after the election. Joe Whatley responded with true class: "So what? We don't care what Jeff Sessions does."[5]

The *Advertiser's* headline made it appear that Sessions' decision on the issue was purely partisan: "AG sides with peers in vote fight." In the article itself, this statement appeared: "Mr. Sessions' Democratic predecessor, Jimmy Evans, chose not to get directly involved in the lawsuit." Jimmy Evans did not oppose the plaintiffs in *Odom v. Bennett*, as it was his duty to do, and he did everything within his power to ensure that this retroactive change in the state's voting laws was rapidly precleared by the U.S. Justice Department. Later, his office advised Secretary of State Bennett to file an appeal of Judge Howard's order in order to prevent the correct counting of the votes in accordance with said order. What did the *Advertiser* consider "direct involvement?" Standing in front of a microphone and holding a news conference? Evans didn't do that; he didn't have to. He was neck deep in the affair on the inside. And he was savvy enough politically to avoid getting caught up in the controversy publicly. In the Jerry Hamilton affair, he had allowed Hooper to take the heat for something for which Evans was responsible. Evans knew when to avoid publicity.

On 2 February 1995 Hornsby filed suit in Montgomery County Circuit Court to have the pay issue settled. Gene Reese was assigned as judge. The attorney general's written opinion stated that the old constitutional provision contained the language "until their successors are elected or appointed, and qualified." The statute upon which Hornsby was relying used similar language. So Hornsby said that his term did not end until his successor was elected and qualified. However, the new judicial article that replaced that language did not use those words. The Supreme Court of Alabama has always said that constitutional provisions should be strictly construed. Yet, some could argue that the judicial article is not "self-executing," but needs legislation to give it practical effect. Therefore, the statute that deals with the terms of judges and upon which Hornsby was relying would also apply. However, that position ignores the fact that the plain language of the judicial article says that the term of the chief justice is only six years. In the case of the treasurer, there is no difference between the language of the statute and the language of the constitution as there is in the case of the chief justice. Even if the "enabling legislation" did apply, that does not mean that the chief justice could hold over in his office.

The second question was this: if the chief justice and treasurer can hold over past the end of their terms, how long can they remain in office? In this case, the attorney general's opinion pointed out that litigation had prevented the certification of the winners in each race, and no one could predict with certainty when the controversy would end. In other words, this legal battle could go on indefinitely. Therefore, the attorney general concluded that case law would have to guide him in determining how long a public official may hold over in the office. The first and earliest case cited was *City Council of Montgomery v. Hughes,*[6] in which the Alabama Supreme Court said that "it was never within the legislative contemplation, that, under this [holdover] clause, an official term could be prolonged beyond a reasonable time for the newly elected officer to qualify."[7] Otherwise, "defeated candidates . . . [might use] vexatious litigation to prolong their official terms."[8] That 1880 case had a ready-made answer for Hornsby's argument that he could hold over, and it was "you can't hold over forever." Case law clearly limited the time the hold over could last.

The opinion also cited other cases in which the Alabama Supreme Court explained that the hold over provision was "never intended to prolong the term of office beyond a reasonable time, after the election, to enable the newly elected officer to qualify." But what was a reasonable time? The attorney general said the time was directly tied to the organizational session of the legislature and the traditional date for the inauguration of constitutional officers. During the legislature's organizational session of ten days was the time for candidates to file contests of statewide elections. In this case, not only had the legislature's organizational session come and gone, but it had been over two weeks since the inauguration. No legitimate contest had been filed with the legislature. The results of the election were still undetermined because of "vexatious litigation." No one knew, for sure, when the outcome would be reached. Therefore, it was the attorney general's opinion that the terms of office of the chief justice and the treasurer had expired. The treasurer, George Wallace, Jr., left office without complaint. He had not even run for reelection, so he had no desire to hang on to his office. Governor James appointed Lucy Baxley, the Democrat who appeared to have won the election. She was the ex-wife of Bill Baxley, the man who was the Democratic nominee for governor in 1986. It did not look as if Jim Martin would win even if Hooper won the court battle over the absentee ballots. George Wallace, Jr.'s gracious exit made Hornsby look pitifully self-centered and petty.

Near the end of January, the U.S. Supreme Court decided to hear an appeal of the *Gore v. BMW of North America* case.[9] Eventually, the U.S. Supreme Court ruled in BMW's favor and remanded the case to the Alabama Supreme Court for a second review. It was the first time in history that the U.S. Supreme Court had ever tampered with a state court's punitive damage award. Even before the decision was announced, it was an excellent example to the public of the out-of-control punitive damage system in Alabama.

The *Montgomery Advertiser,* fortunately, seemed to consider it a duty to report the latest in the tort reform battle by publishing relevant articles. One editorial in the 29 January 1995 edition by a law professor from Pace University discussed damage awards as a hidden tort tax. In addition to that hidden tax, a manufacturer cannot know and comply with the liability rules of all the states of the union. According to the article, a manufacturer of a medical device may be immune from suit in Virginia five years after someone was injured by it, but in New York that manufacturer would still be subject to suit. The expense adds to the cost of these products and aids the competitors of the U.S. in the international market. According to Mr. Madden, the article's author, product liability costs had caused 47% of manufacturers to withdraw products from the market, 39 percent to not introduce new products, and 25% to discontinue new product research. Only the lawyers benefit. A study by the Insurance Services Office in 1992 showed that for every ten dollars paid out by insurance companies, another seven dollars was paid out for legal defense costs, including attorney fees. Mr. Madden supported the product liability bills presented to Congress in 1995. They were an attempt to make the nation's laws on the matter uniform. He explained what these reforms would create: "1) a negligence standard for claims brought against retailers and distributors; 2) fair and intelligible punitive damages standards; 3) an elimination of punitive damages against manufacturers who have secured FDA or FAA approval of their products; and 4) a statute of limitations that preserves the claims of persons unable to discover their injury until years after exposure to the product."[10]

In the same newspaper of 29 January 1995 was a letter to the editor from a local Montgomery attorney named Samford Weiss. It first set up a straw man, which was that Hooper was against "substantial compliance." This was the strategy of

Hornsby's lawyers, also. He argued that Judge Reese had to follow the precedent set by the Alabama Supreme Court. Therefore, Reese had to order that unwitnessed absentee ballots be counted. He included citations to *Williams v. Lide* and *Wells v. Ellis.* It was propaganda for Hornsby. The media and the public refused to accept the premise of the Hornsby camp. That premise was that you can shape the rules to whatever you want them to be as long as you can get a judge to say it's okay. On 5 February 1995, Montgomery attorney Robert Segall wrote a letter to the editor, claiming that Reese, like any other circuit judge in Alabama, had to follow "the law." The law, according to these trial lawyers, apparently was that particular interpretation of Alabama Supreme Court precedent that would help Hornsby.

Investor's Business Daily, a national newspaper similar to the *Wall Street Journal,* also continued the coverage. Its analysis of the tort problem appeared in a 20 January 1995 article entitled "Why have tort costs exploded?" It cited a 1992 study by Tillinghast, which estimated the U.S. tort system cost an average of two and a half times more than that of other industrialized countries. It said that in 1991, Americans paid $132.2 billion in tort costs. Tort costs had risen 11% per year from 1950 until the mid-1980s. However, between 1983 and 1987, tort costs nearly doubled. The study used a broad definition of costs because it included the cost of liability insurance, the amount paid out in settlements (not always easy to track), and the cost of processing claims. The Rand Corporation used a figure of between $29 and $36 billion in 1985. The Tillinghast study, which included insurance costs, arrived at a figure of $87.2 billion for 1985. It did not take into account the benefits of the tort system, like increased safety of certain products. Unprepared for the increase in damage awards in the mid-1980s and after a period of lowering the premiums of policies, insurance companies had to suddenly raise rates. Those raises also increased overall tort costs. The trial lawyers used this crisis in the insurance business to argue that it was the insurance companies' own lack of foresight that created their problems. However, that does not explain why tort costs have remained high after the crisis passed, nor why they rose before that period. Liability insurance premiums increased five times between 1968 and 1978.

Some argued that certain traditional legal defenses used by business and insurance companies began to erode in the 1960s. For example, strict liability (liability even if there is no evidence of negligence on the part of a defendant) has expanded to include the actions of more and more companies. Environmental laws often apply a strict liability standard. Plaintiff lawyers have increasingly sought to add the wealthy to their list of defendants in cases because the wealthy have the "deep pockets." They have the money to actually pay the damage award. A jury is likely to sympathize with the injured plaintiff to the point that it ignores the actual liability of the wealthy defendant, and require that defendant to pay the judgment anyway. Such sympathy by the jury for the injured plaintiff is understandable, but it is not justice. It may be welfare by court decree, but if the wealthy defendant is not guilty of causing the damage, it is not justice.

There are several other theories asserted to explain the increase in these costs. Changes in the federal rules of procedure between 1966 and 1974 made it easier to bring class action lawsuits. In the mid 1990s, having seen the abuses caused by class actions, the federal courts began to roll back the advance of the class action lawsuit. According to the Rand Institute, the likelihood for product liability actions to succeed in the 1960s was 20 to 30%. The percentage of likely success increased to almost 50% in the 1980s. Pain and suffering, a difficult damage upon which to place a dollar amount, amounts to 21% of overall tort costs. A "good" lawyer can use the system to increase those costs exponentially. According to the American Bar Association, punitive damages were awarded in less than 5% of the cases nationwide. Supposedly, this figure means that a problem really does not exist. It is also possible that an increase in government-run insurance systems has added to the costs of litigation. Insulated by such insurance from the need for immediate cash, people do not settle as early and can fight for all that's possible through the court system. The plaintiff trial lawyers would prefer to "fight for all their clients are entitled to."

Meanwhile, the lawsuit by Mississippi Valley Title Insurance against Judge Hooper continued slowly. Judge Crowson, the Republican judge in Shelby County, to whom Chief Justice Hornsby had assigned the case before the November election, after all the judges in Montgomery recused themselves, had dismissed it once already based on the statute of limitations. He told the plaintiff to go back and prepare a complaint that alleged specific dates for the alleged acts of fraud. Mississippi Valley did not, so he dismissed it a second time in January of 1995. Knox Argo, the attorney for Mississippi Valley, asserted that Hooper was not acting as an attorney but as an agent for the company. If that was true, then the statute of limitations would have been much longer. Argo had to appeal the case to the Alabama Court of Civil Appeals.

The newspaper reported a strange procedure occurring while the Alabama Supreme Court prepared an answer to the Eleventh Circuit's certified question. I should first give the reader an introductory understanding of appellate courts. An appellate court does not collect evidence. It is purely a reviewing court. It can remand a case to the trial court for further factual findings, but it does not go out and collect evidence itself. It does not have jurisdiction for that practice, nor is it equipped for such an undertaking. It takes the record of a trial court and the arguments of attorneys and decides the correct result, based on the law. Yet we received surprising news in the middle of January of 1995. The newspaper reported that Wayne Mills, the staff attorney for Chief Justice Hornsby, and Bob Martin, a spokesman for the appellate courts, had obtained affidavits from Carole Smith, the circuit clerk and absentee election manager for Sumter County, and another person. These affidavits purported to be supportive of Hornsby's attorneys' argument about the past practice of certain Alabama counties.

The affidavit was prepared craftily. Instead of explicitly saying that Sumter County had counted unwitnessed absentee ballots in the past, Smith's 12 January 1995 affidavit claimed that Sumter County had counted absentee ballots that "substantially complied" with the Alabama election laws. As I said before, Hooper's attorneys did not argue against the substantial compliance doctrine; they simply argued that unwitnessed absentee ballots did not comply at all with Alabama law. A deposition of Carole Smith, prepared later, showed that she did not understand what these affidavits were for and that she did not understand the fine points of the case with respect to "substantial compliance."[11] Bob Martin had telefaxed a prepared affidavit that Smith signed. It was mailed back to the Administrative Office of Courts.

She was used by those supportive of Hornsby to prepare a vague affidavit. One of the people helping to prepare an affidavit for one of these witnesses was none other than Hornsby's staff attorney. The ethical problems with this action are legion. Even after all that had happened, the Hooper campaign was still shocked by this revelation. In her 13 July 1995 deposition, Smith specifically stated that since 1978, when she began working for the circuit clerk in Sumter County, the "ballot had to be signed, it had to be notarized, or it had to be witnessed,"[12] and she instructed the polling officials the same way.[13]

At the end of January, Hooper's attorneys requested the recusal of any justices who gave campaign contributions to Hornsby. A judge recuses when he decides to not vote or make a decision on a case. A judge must recuse when there exists a conflict of interest, (e.g., a case has a business as a party and the judge owns 50% of that business). The rules of judicial ethics also require recusal if the mere appearance of impropriety would cause the public to mistrust or question the honesty and reliability of the judiciary's judgments.[14]

Hooper's lawyers rightly reasoned that any justice who gave a campaign contribution to Hornsby obviously thought he should be elected instead of Hooper. That affiliation may sway, consciously or unconsciously, that justice's decision in the absentee ballot question.[15] Even if that affiliation did not sway that justice's vote, it certainly could appear to affect the vote, and that also would violate the rules of ethics for judges. However, they could not demand that the justices recuse themselves. It was up to the individual justice to decide whether recusal was necessary. Perhaps, as a direct result of the Hooper-

Hornsby battle, the Alabama Legislature later passed legislation requiring judges' recusal in certain situations. No ethics opinion had ever said that a campaign contribution to a judge required that judge to recuse from a case that included a contributor as a party. In this particular case, Hornsby was technically not a party. Of course, everyone knew that the result could definitely affect the outcome of the election. But technically, the Justices could say that Hornsby was not directly involved in the case. So, for the time being, the choice was with each justice. Justice Gorman Houston had already notified the supreme court clerk that he had given $500 to Hornsby, and he would not participate in answering the question. The others were not so quick to act.

We learned later that there was more to the recusal issue than simply campaign contributions. Justices Reneau Almon, Janie Shores, and Kenneth Ingram gave from $250 to $500 to Hornsby's campaign. However, Justices Terry Butts, Ralph Cook, and Mark Kennedy had received campaign contributions from Hornsby's son, his law firm, or from lawyers involved in the ballot dispute. Ingram's son was a member of Hornsby's old law firm, where Hornsby's son also practiced. Kennedy had received $5,000 from Hornsby's son and $7,000 from Hornsby's attorneys. Ralph Cook received $10,000 from Hornsby's law firm and $5,500 from his lawyers. The *Mobile Register* described the situation as a "web of incestuous relationships more appropriate to cockroaches than to judges."

Only one Justice, Hugh Maddox, had no ties to Hornsby, except that they were colleagues on the supreme court. He had run unopposed for reelection in November of 1994 as a democrat. Hooper's attorneys wanted Governor James to appoint a special court, but James could not do that until enough justices had recused themselves to require a special court. Hooper's attorneys brought up the 1967 case, in which a justice on the supreme court was a party in a civil case that was on appeal to the Alabama Supreme Court. All the Justices recused, and Governor Lurleen Wallace appointed five former Alabama State Bar presidents to hear the case. Hooper's attorneys argued that that case set the precedent for the justices to step aside in a case directly involving a colleague. Joe Whatley said that it was the justices' sworn duty to decide cases, and the Republicans wanted a group of handpicked judges to hear the case. That statement was irrelevant to the question and obviously an attempt at public relations, something Hornsby's lawyers were desperate to turn around. Notice that he used the word that had plagued the Democrats ever since the 1986 gubernatorial election—"handpicked." It was also the term used to describe Jimmy Evans' appeal court settlement scheme. Whatley's statement was incorrect and politically gratuitous, a feeble attempt to tar the Republicans with the same brush the Democrats seemed to use so often.

Justice Butts, newly elected in 1994, specifically asked the Judicial Inquiry Commission for an opinion on whether he should recuse himself from hearing and deciding the question from the Eleventh Circuit. The Judicial Article, which amended the Alabama Constitution in the 1970s, created the Judicial Inquiry Commission for investigating accusations of misconduct on the part of judges. The Judicial Article abolished impeachment of judges, so the legislature had to make up a new apparatus for disciplining judges. The Judicial Inquiry Commission also gave its opinion to judges who needed help in deciding whether to recuse from a case or not. Justice Butts said that he asked the Judicial Inquiry Commission as a "common sense approach in seeking to do the right thing ethically."[16] Judge Hooper had said that even though the trial lawyers had bankrolled Butts' campaign, they shouldn't assume that they could control him. Perhaps this act was a sign of Butts' independence, or purely a political decision to protect himself from an ethical accusation if he participated in the case. He made his request for the opinion the day after Hooper's attorneys asked all the justices to recuse. Justice Butts received $8,750 from Hornsby's son, Clay, and he received $10,255 from Hornsby's attorneys in the absentee ballot case. It takes time for the Commission to answer a question like that. At the time, we did not know how important that timing would be.

Financial disclosure reports were due in the secretary of state's office by 31 January 1995, and the *Montgomery Adver-*

tiser did a story on the campaign expenses of the candidates for supreme court. The total for all candidates for those races was $3.5 million. The Democrats spent $2.8 million of that amount. Hornsby's expenses were $671,000, and he still had $98,000 left over. He used this money to pay for his legal expenses in the post-election litigation. That fact did not become public until 1997. The law firm contributing the most to his campaign was Cunningham & Bounds of Mobile, who contributed $15,000. Hooper spent $286,000 and still owed $750. Justice Kennedy reported raising $503,189 and spending $659,000. Harold See, Kennedy's Republican opponent, spent about $170,000. Justice Cook raised $504,000 and spent $491,000. Mark Montiel, Cook's Republican opponent, raised $80,000 and spent $64,000. Terry Butts raised over a million dollars and spent $968,000. B.J. Russell, Butts' Republican opponent, raised $157,000 and spent about the same amount.

In the 5 February 1995, *Montgomery Advertiser,* Bob Ingram predicted that the November elections meant the end of the political careers of certain political officials. Jimmy Evans, Jim Folsom, Jr., and George Wallace, Jr. were on his "for sure" list. But he added another name, Sonny Hornsby. He said, "I would add another name to that list, one that may surprise you—Sonny Hornsby. No matter what the outcome of the contested race for chief justice, I think Hornsby has suffered irreparable damage, so much so that he can forget any future political ambitions. He had some ambitions. The thought of some day being governor or maybe U.S. senator had crossed his mind more than once." From the moment he knew he lost the election, Hornsby's only hope for political survival was to admit his defeat magnanimously and move on. For some reason, he was unable to do that. Jimmy Evans used the Jerry Hamilton affair to destroy Hooper's chance at becoming U.S. senator; Hornsby destroyed his own chance at becoming U.S. senator by pursuing this ballot litigation against Hooper's victory. Jimmy Evans brought Governor Hunt down by prosecuting him, but that action ended up being critical in bringing Jimmy Evans down. Politics sometimes takes strange turns.

On 4 February 1995 the *Mobile Register* explained the chutzpah of Hornsby so well, that I must reproduce it:

Attorney General Jeff Sessions just issued his nonbinding advisory opinion [on whether Hornsby should be paid]: No. Mr. Hornsby immediately displayed his judicial temperament by spluttering his "disappointment" with the performance of the attorney general, calling the advisory opinion "an example of partisan politics at its worst."

Sweet mother of Moses. Where does Mr. Hornsby get such crust? His own campaign practices have raised reasonable doubts about whether law outranks politics in the Alabama Supreme Court. With his outburst about partisan politics, one wonders whether Mr. Hornsby bothered to read the advisory opinion.

We did, and it is a model of clear writing and impartial reasoning. It rests on the state's constitution, which says that the term of a judge "shall be six years." The Alabama Supreme Court itself recently wrote that the constitution should be "strictly construed," adding that "nothing in the constitution suggests that the framers meant anything more than is said by the words used." So, Mr. Sessions reasoned that, six years having more than passed since the chief justice and treasurer were last elected, their time in office has run out.

He even went an extra furlong, paying due respect to a competing argument that fails. The argument rests on state statutes that say a judge shall serve six years "and until his successor is elected and qualified." Does this mean that Mr. Hornsby may serve until the election dispute is resolved?

No. Regarding such holdover service, the state Supreme Court has spoken: "We regard it as the settled law of this state that the words *until his successor is elected and qualified* were never intended to prolong the term of office beyond a reasonable time." Why not? Because losing candidates might file vexatious litigation to prolong their official terms.

Prolong is the operative word. Litigation over the validity of 2,000 unwitnessed absentee ballots in two courts—

the federal appeals courts in Atlanta, and the Alabama Supreme Court. The latter hasn't received briefs or heard arguments, so this dispute will grind on indefinitely.

Would that be a reasonable time for Mr. Hornsby (and Mr. Wallace) to remain in office? Again, the Supreme Court's own opinions answer the question. In one case, it ruled that the Legislature intended to set a fixed term of office, not one of *indefinite duration.* In a later case, it said that the holdover language was meant to allow a *few days* for a successor to get settled in office.

"Thus, Mr. Sessions' conclusion doesn't depend solely on the constitution. It is supported by the Supreme Court's own rulings on holdover officeholders. How in the name of strict construction, then, does Mr. Hornsby find political partisanship in that?

It beats us, but he does. Now he has filed suit in the friendly venue of Montgomery to stay on the job and on the payroll for as long as it takes to settle the disputed election. Mr. Hornsby's case will be heard by none other than Eugene Reese, the Democratic circuit judge who ruled that the unwitnessed absentee ballots should be counted (which would presumably return Mr. Hornsby to office).

All of which puts one thing beyond doubt. When Sonny Hornsby talks about *partisan politics at its worst,* he knows whereof he speaks.

Bob Ingram pointed out that Hooper would be 70 years old on 8 April 1995. The Alabama Constitution prohibits anyone who is age 70 or older from being elected or appointed to a judgeship. Did that mean that, if Hooper were declared the winner after the litigation extended past 8 April 1995, he would then be ineligible to serve? Ingram said that common sense indicated that since he had been elected in November of the previous year, there should not be a problem. But he thought that someone would make a legal issue out of it anyway, and it would end up in court.

On 12 February 1995, the *Montgomery Advertiser* raised the same concern that Ingram had mentioned. According to the article, neither Hornsby in his pay case before Reese nor the attorneys in the absentee ballot case had seriously raised the issue. However, Hooper knew that they certainly would not want to alert him to the possibility that they might raise it in the future, after Hooper's birthday on 8 April. Everyone agreed that the resolution of the issues in the case would last beyond that date. Hooper's attitude was sanguine. He told the *Advertiser:* "The election was on 8 November and that's the date that's going to count."

On 16 February 1995, the *Montgomery Advertiser* printed an article about some Alabama election history. In 1985, a U.S. attorney attempted to prosecute three blacks in Perry County on charges of voter fraud. On the defense team were J.L. Chestnut, Hornsby's lawyer who tried to prevent the counting of Hooper's 100 votes in Dallas County, Lani Guinier, President Clinton's first choice for U.S. attorney general, and Deval Patrick, who recently stepped down as head of the Civil Rights Division of the Justice Department. The U.S. attorney prosecuting the case was Jeff Sessions. When President Reagan nominated Sessions to a federal judgeship a few years after this vote fraud trial, some black political leaders went to Washington to oppose his nomination, and, with the help of Alabama's senator on the Judiciary Committee, Howell Heflin, they were successful. Now those same leaders were doing everything they could to make sure Sonny Hornsby, the supporter of the appellate court packing scheme, stayed in office. A definite pattern had developed. Blacks, suspected of voter fraud, together with lawyers who would later become high ranking attorneys in Clinton's Justice Department, used the judiciary to accomplish the goal of making sure Democrats stayed in office and voter fraud was not prosecuted. In fact, using the Hooper-Hornsby case as an example, one could argue that their goal was to encourage voter fraud.

On 13 February 1995, Governor James swore in Lucy Baxley as treasurer. George Wallace, Jr. had resigned even though Hornsby's argument about waiting until one's successor was "certified and qualified" also applied to him. Jim

Martins' race with Baxley was close, but it was not close enough for the disputed absentee ballots to make a difference. Baxley won by approximately 1,000 votes without counting the disputed ballots. If they were counted, they were likely to help Baxley, anyway, because she was the Democrat. Once he saw that the result in the absentee ballot case would not help him, Martin attempted to extricate himself from the fray and recommended that Baxley be sworn in. However, he wanted to remain in the Hooper litigation because he was concerned with the integrity of elections in Alabama. This was an admirable decision, because he could possibly have been liable for the costs of litigation, especially if he and Hooper lost. Yet he remained in the case even though he had nothing to gain. Governor James appointed him conservation commissioner.

However, it was George Wallace, Jr. who received most of the praise at this time. The *Advertiser* praised him in a 22 February 1995 editorial, in which it pointed out that he probably had better legal grounds than Hornsby for challenging the attorney general's opinion as to their pay status. The editorial also pointed out that, in spite of heavy political pressure, Wallace had refused to approve two questionable appropriations made by outgoing Governor Folsom. The *Advertiser* said, "Whatever his reasons, Wallace bowed out with a classiness that hasn't been shown by the likes of Hornsby and certainly not by Folsom."

There was more in Wallace to admire. During the time when the Hooper campaign was keeping watch over the secretary of state's office, Bennett was not very pleased with the attention his office was getting. Once, as a campaign worker left the capitol building where Bennett's office was located, Bennett passed him on his way in. The Hooper campaign worker asked something about the scheduling of a court hearing, and Bennett responded with the date but also added a snide comment. He said something to the effect of, "But Hooper's gonna lose." The newspaper also reported that Bennett was unhappy with Wallace because Wallace allowed us to use his office as something of a headquarters, a place where we could go when Bennett's office was unavailable. The treasurer's office is right across the hall from the secretary of

state's office. Wallace's office let the Hooper campaign use his
chairs to sit in the hallway outside Bennett's office. Jack told
the news media that the Hooper family had been friends with
the Wallace family for a long time. Wallace simply let Bennett
know that he would continue to help his friends, the Hoopers.
Later we were not surprised to learn that Wallace decided to
switch from the Democratic to the Republican party.

The Alabama Supreme Court did not order oral argument, even though both sides had asked. Hornsby's lawyers
said that the Eleventh Circuit's question had already been
answered in Lide. Hooper's brief was quite different. It asked
for the entire court to step aside and allow the governor to
appoint a special court. The *Montgomery Advertiser* on 20
February 1995 quoted Bruce McKee, one of Hornsby's lawyers in the appeal:

> In partisan politics like Alabama's, the practicality is
> judges have to raise most of their money from lawyers
> and other judges. . . . The law around the country is
> pretty clear that attorney contributions in a system where
> judges are elected in partisan elections did not require
> recusal.[17]

Attorney contributions, however, were not the only issue
at stake. He left out the other circumstances involved in this
case—contributions by and to judges in a case involving one
of their very own court members, the chief justice. Again, the
Mobile Register had an appropriate response to this excuse:

> In principle, this issue is indistinguishable from judges
> resolving a dispute between two corporations when the
> judges own stock in one of them. Would any judge in
> this state deny that such circumstances would require
> recusal?
>
> Given the latest revelations about the Supreme Court's
> mutual admiration society, it is anyone's guess how
> this farce will play out.[18]

Later the attorney general added his motion seeking all
the justices' recusal except for Justice Maddox. Attorney General Sessions pointed out that Hornsby, Kennedy, Cook, and

Butts received much of their campaign funds from the same sources—plaintiff trial lawyers—and together spent more than $1,000,000 on the same media consultant. The motion stated: "Intentionally or not, the four justices were in this fight together, all for one and one for all."

In their briefs to the Alabama Supreme Court, Hornsby's lawyers made the same arguments they made in federal court. They argued that the voting laws were not meant to be an impediment to the right to vote. The attorney general argued that the lack of witnesses to an absentee ballot undermined the integrity of that ballot. He was using the specific language from Lide and *Wells v. Ellis.* By mid-March, the briefs had been filed, and Hooper's attorneys asked the court to expedite the matter and provide an answer by 29 March. On 9 March, they even asked the Eleventh Circuit to speed things up by placing a 28 March 1995 deadline on the Alabama Supreme Court. It cited as one of its concerns the fact that Judge Hooper would turn 70 years of age on 8 April. Hornsby was still in office, while Hooper, the true winner of the election, awaited the resolution by the courts. The entire state awaited the supreme court's decision.

Notes

1. "Good Call. We shouldn't presume that Alabama's court system is incapable of rendering a fair judgment.

"A federal appeals court in Atlanta is exactly right on two counts:

"The courts of Alabama should be able to make a fair determination of what state law says about absentee ballots and the razor-close race for chief justice of the Alabama Supreme Court.

"And, secondly, that if they can't, then federal courts can step in to make sure the constitutional rights of Alabama voters are protected.

"A three-judge panel in Atlanta last week pointed the court contests between sitting Alabama Supreme Court Justice Sonny Hornsby, a Democrat, and Republican challenger Perry Hooper

Sr. back where they should have been heard all along: in state courts.

"We have seen a number of disturbing things as this brouhaha has progressed: The U.S. Justice Department 'preclearing' a change in voting practices after the election. How do you 'preclear' anything after the fact?

"A Montgomery County circuit judge who used an extremely broad sweep of judicial authority to apply to this case court rulings with no direct bearing before ruling in Hornsby's favor.

"And on both sides, lawyers shopping for the judges they wanted to hear their arguments. Democrats went to Democrats, federal and state. Republicans went to Republican federal judges. [We went to a Republican state judge and a Democrat federal judge too.]

"This is a state matter, not a federal matter. Let's not presume Alabama's court system is so politically tainted it is incapable of rendering a fair judgment.

"It's going to be awkward for our highest court to sit in judgment on this issue. For starters, who should hear the case, and who should recuse themselves?

"Justice Hornsby has already said he would not participate. Obviously, that is correct and commendable. [Why commendable?]

"But what about Justice Mark Kennedy, who was also up for re-election? What about Justice Gorman Houston, who wrote a letter to this newspaper outlining his interpretation of absentee voting law decisions?

"Both should give long, hard thought to the matter.

"Two of the three federal judges in Atlanta said they had grave doubts about the decision issued by Circuit Judge Gene Reese which would have allowed disputed absentee ballots to be included in the vote totals.

"It's not hard to understand why. Alabama law is crystal clear on what it takes to have an absentee ballot counted: two witnesses above the age of 18 or the seal of a notary.

"That is not written in Chinese. It is in plain English.

"It may be that in some counties that has not been followed precisely to the letter in the past. It may be that was done not so much for political shenanigans as to help legitimate voters who just hadn't followed the law.

"But such an approach lends itself to abuse. And when practices lend themselves to abuse, you go back to the letter of the law to stop it.

"In essence, this is an opportunity for Alabama's court system, much derided for being overly swayed by political influences, to save face; to prove that it is not a court made of people who lean toward trial lawyers or insurance companies, Republicans or Democrats, but of people who love the law.

"It can do that with a fair hearing and an expedited judgment.

"The whole state is watching."

2. *Montgomery Advertiser*, p.1, February 2, 1995. The article also stated: "But while they [Hornsby and Wallace, Jr.] shouldn't be paid, Mr. Sessions said, they are entitled to stay in office." That is not what Sessions' written opinion said. I was not present at the news conference, so I do not know what Sessions may have said orally. However, I also do not know what type of spin his political enemies or the media may have placed on what he said.

3. Ibid.

4. *Montgomery Advertiser*, p. 3F, January 21, 1995.

5. *Montgomery Advertiser*, p. 5B, January 25, 1995.

6. 65 Ala. 201 (1880).

7. Ibid., p. 207.

8. Ibid.

9. In 1990, Dr. Ira Gore, a physician in Birmingham, AL, purchased a new $40,000 BMW and, approximately nine months later while getting his car detailed, discovered that the paint job had been touched up as a result of some acid damage that occurred during the boat trip from overseas. BMW had a policy of not notifying the customer of a pre-sales repair, if the repair cost did not exceed 3% of the retail price of the car. They reached that figure based on researching the consumer protection laws around

the country. The former owner of the BMW dealership, from which Dr. Gore purchased the car, testified at trial that the touch-up job decreased the value of the car by $4,000. The jury awarded Dr. Gore $4,000 in compensatory damages and $4,000,000 in punitive damages. The plaintiff attorney told the jury that they should multiply the compensatory award of $4,000 by 1000, the approximate number of this type of car that BMW had sold nationwide. The actual number was 987, but he rounded it off to 1000. He argued this even though BMW's action would have been perfectly legal in any other state. So this Alabama jury decided to punish BMW for its legal actions in other states. The Alabama Supreme Court disagreed with that rationale and reduced the award to $2,000,000. Even then, the punitive award was 500 times the compensatory. There was no rational relationship between the amount to which the award was reduced and the argument of Dr. Gore's lawyer as to how much the punitive damages should be. And there was really no rational relationship between the $4,000 and $2,000,000 that the Alabama Supreme Court upheld. That court simply said that $2,000,000 was not out of line for this type of case. What type of case that was is hard to say because this was the first of its kind in Alabama. In the Spring of 1996, the U.S. Supreme Court decided in favor of BMW saying the award was grossly excessive.

10. *Montgomery Advertiser*, p. 3F, January 29, 1995.

11. July 13, 1995 Deposition of Carole Smith, pp. 14-15:

> "Q. [by Jack Drake]. Okay. Let me ask you about some of the statements made in this affidavit and ask you whether they're correct or not. On the first page, the affidavit says, 'Prior to the November 8 general election, our county followed a practice of counting absentee ballots if they substantially complied with the form affidavit contained in the Alabama Code 1975, Section 17-10-7. We did not require strict compliance with the form affidavit for absentee ballots to be counted as votes and included in the election certification for our county.' That's two sentences. Are those statements or were those statements correct when you signed this affidavit?

> "A. They are correct based on the conversation that Mr. Martin and I had about that specific area.

"Q. Okay.

"A. Substantial compliance is not a term that was known to me prior to this lawsuit. Substantial compliance are words that were in the affidavit that were not offered by me. What I explained to him was that it was the policy of our county if there were certain portions of the affidavit on the back of an absentee ballot that were not filled in or missing, we would certify that ballot as countable. I was referring to the section that calls for a return address, date of birth, political party affiliation, and those kinds of things. But I was specific with him that at no time was a ballot counted that was not signed, notarized, or witnessed."

12. Ibid., p. 23.

13. Ibid., p. 28.

14. See Canon 7A.(1), Alabama's Canons of Judicial Ethics (effective February 1, 1976) in Alabama Rules of Court, West Publishing Co., St. Paul, Minnesota, 1997.

15. "[I]t is imperative that [a judge] conduct himself in a manner at all times to prevent any political considerations, entanglements or influences from ever becoming involved in or from ever appearing to be involved in any judicial decision or in the judicial process." Canon 7 A. (1), Canons of Judicial Ethics.

16. *Montgomery Advertiser*, p. 3B, February 17, 1995.

17. *Montgomery Advertiser*, p. 10A, February 20, 1995.

18. *Mobile Register* (formerly Mobile Press-Register), Editorial page, February 19, 1995.

The High Court Speaks

It seemed as if it had taken forever, but the Alabama Supreme Court answered the certified question relatively quickly. On Tuesday, 14 March 1995, in a vote of four to one, the court ruled that the unwitnessed absentee ballots should be counted. Justices Reneau Almon, Janie Shores, Kenneth Ingram, and Ralph Cook concurred in the opinion. It was a *per curiam* opinion, which meant that no particular justice was identified as the author. Justice Cook wrote a special concurrence that was released the next day. Justice Hugh Maddox, the only justice who had no campaign connections with Hornsby, dissented and wrote an opinion. Hornsby and Houston were, of course, recused. Strangely absent from the vote was any mention of Justices Mark Kennedy or Terry Butts. Butts could claim that he was still awaiting the Judicial Inquiry Commission's opinion. But why had the majority not waited until that opinion had been released so that Justice Butts could make an informed decision whether to participate or not?

There were some other strange things about the opinion. Normally, the Alabama Supreme Court releases its opinions every Friday. Only in unusual circumstances does it ever release an opinion on another day. It released this one on a Tuesday. Why? It had taken almost two and a half months for the release of the opinion. Justice Maddox's opinion also contained an unusual statement near its end. He stated:

> The foregoing opinion was hurriedly prepared because the majority opinion was delivered to my office at 11:00 A.M. on 14 March 1995, and I had to get this dissenting opinion filed by 3:00 P.M. on the same date. I reserve the right to make any corrections that I might

need to make in this dissenting opinion at a later date, and to write additionally should I desire.

Also, only five justices participated. Alabama law specifies that if the number of justices in a case falls below six because of disqualification, then the governor shall appoint a sufficient number of justices to have at least six take part in the decision.[1] However, Justices Butts and Kennedy were not disqualified; they simply didn't vote. So, technically, the number was not reduced below six "by reason of disqualification."

On Friday, three days after the Alabama Supreme Court released its answer to the certified question, the Judicial Inquiry Commission issued its answer to Justice Butts' question. It stated:

> It is the opinion of the Commission, in response to your request, that based upon the decision of the Supreme Court, on 14 March 1995, you are not disqualified. However, it is the recommendation of this Commission that you should recuse yourself from any future participation in the above referenced case.[2]

The commission carefully worded its recommendation and stated that Justice Butts did not have to recuse himself. It even used the majority opinion issued by the Alabama Supreme Court to make its decision on the matter. The majority opinion said that those four justices voting in the case did not see any need to recuse themselves. Therefore, those charged with judging the judges took their cue from those very judges as to what was or was not proper. This is akin to a criminal court letting the defendant tell the court what is or is not a crime. The justices who were deciding whether to recuse themselves told the commission that they did not have to; therefore, the commission, charged with policing those justices agreed. The commission opinion said that Justice Butts' interrelationship with the incumbent chief justice during the campaign, plus "the climate surrounding the 1994 Alabama elections," caused it to make the recommendation that he not participate.

The commission also based its decision on the fact that Justice Butts received $8,750 in campaign contributions from Hornsby's son and Hornsby's law firm and shared campaign consultants with Hornsby. He was a candidate for associate justice and was elected, he appeared on platforms with the incumbent chief justice, he was a member of the same political party, he received campaign contributions from the law firms involved in the absentee ballot fight, and the ruling of the supreme court could affect the vote totals in his own race, even if it would not affect the outcome. Justice Kennedy was in almost the identical situation. Justice Ralph Cook was in a similar, but not identical, situation, yet he chose to participate in the decision. Justices Almon, Shores, and Ingram were scheduled for election in later years and did not have to run for reelection in 1994. That distinguished those three justices from Justice Butts.

The Commission ended its opinion with the words, "The Commission does not suggest that you are actually biased, nor does it question your representation that you are able to render impartial judgment in the case at issue. However, the reasonable person/appearance of impropriety standard in Canon 3C(1), along with other canons, provides a basis for this recommendation."[3] It was signed by Braxton Kittrell, a circuit court judge in Mobile and president of the commission. Though a member of the commission, Justice Mark Kennedy did not participate in the commission's work on the question.

Hornsby claimed that the court had declared what had been the law for the past seventy years. In the 16 March 1995 *Montgomery Advertiser,* he was reported as saying, "Since 1924, it has been the public policy of Alabama that people be encouraged to vote and that if people cast an honest vote that vote will be counted."[4] Not only did his statement expand the phrase "substantial compliance" beyond all recognition, but it also ignored the civil rights struggles of the 1960s. Imagine telling blacks that people who cast an honest vote in the 50s and 60s were always counted in Alabama. Hornsby, the Democrat, also said the question was a state law matter from which the federal courts should abstain. Hooper, the Republican, had demanded that the federal courts step in to protect the voters' federal constitutional rights. Sam Heldman, one of Hornsby's lawyers, alleged that Hooper had looked for a sympathetic Republican judge to rule in his favor. Yet the Demo-

crats and Hornsby were gleeful to have the Alabama Supreme
Court, a group of nine Democrats, hear the case. The answer
was clearly a defeat for Hooper. But it was not discouraging.
First, the result was not totally unexpected. Second, we kept
reminding ourselves that the Eleventh Circuit had retained
jurisdiction. That court would still have the final say. Third,
two federal judges, Propst, a Democrat, and Tjoflat, a Republican, had both stated categorically that they did not think the
Alabama Supreme Court cases, *Lide* and *Wells*, supported
Reese's ruling. We did not think that this answer would change
the minds of the federal judges. But the decision did help by
delaying things even further. Hornsby added some other good
news in his news conferences. He said that he had "absolutely
no plans if I lose to contest this in the Legislature." We were
heartened to hear that, but by that time we were too cynical
to really believe it.

Hornsby claimed that we should count every "honest vote"
and that "you can't count some of the votes and not the others." Only legal, valid votes should count. Attorney General
Sessions said that the plain language of the statute was enough
to decide the case against counting the unwitnessed absentee
ballots. Also, Sessions said that the state's electoral process
faces a "new level of danger" if "substantial compliance" with
the code is met by having an unsigned affidavit act as verification of an absentee ballot. He added his thought about the
recusal of the justices who had campaign finance ties with
Hornsby: "Here we have an election contest in which three of
the judges contributed to the campaign [of Hornsby] and they
are sitting in judgment on this dispute."[5]

Following are some comments from media sources about
the opinion. The *New York Times National* edition stated on
16 March 1995:

> In a decision that may reverse the results of the elec-
> tion of its Chief Justice, the Alabama Supreme Court
> has ruled that some 1,700 contested absentee ballots
> that are likely to favor the Democrat incumbent over
> the Republican challenger should be counted. But Mr.
> Hooper, who had the backing of [sic] state Republican
> Party, said the panel's ruling was not final and still had

to be reviewed by the United States Court of Appeals for the 11th Circuit to see whether it amounted to an unconstitutional change in state election law after the voting last Nov. 8.

The Clarke County paper stated unabashedly:

> We believe the high court is wrong; wrong not only to call for the ballots to be counted but wrong in even considering the argument to start with. Hornsby and the Democrats want questionable absentee ballots counted, believing they would tilt the vote to him. And they probably would because entire graveyards are voted across the Black Belt in favor of Democratic candidates.

On 15 March 1995, the *Montgomery Advertiser* reported the result matter-of-factly: "If a federal court in Atlanta agrees with the state court's ruling, those ballots are expected to boost Chief Justice Sonny Hornsby, a Democrat, to a second term on the state's highest court." It reported that Secretary of State Bennett had decided to wait to act. He said that he would not count any ballots until the Eleventh Circuit issued a formal ruling. If he had counted the disputed ballots, he would have been in contempt of that court. The next day, the *Advertiser* reported in more detail:

> A leading Alabama Democrat was advocating state's rights Wednesday while a leading Alabama Republican was calling for a federal court to overturn the state's highest court. Attorney General Jeff Sessions, a Republican, called the ruling badly flawed and criticized the justices for not recusing themselves from the case.

Hornsby was quoted publicly making the bizarre statement that the court had affirmed the public policy that had existed in Alabama for seventy years.

The *Mobile Register* published a catchy headline for its editorial: "Justices present case of supreme arrogance." Commenting on the court's decision, it stated:

> In so ruling [to count the unwitnessed ballots], the court in effect deleted that part of the state statute on

absentee ballots that says, "Your signature must be witnessed" by a notary or two adults. The court doesn't have a line-item veto. By what authority, then, does it strike language from a statute? In his dissent, Justice Hugh Maddox notes that the court ignored its own "fundamental rule" for interpreting statutes, which is "to give effect to the intent of the Legislature." Under the court's new ruling, however, election fraud would be greatly simplified. *Proxy* votes for nursing home residents, for instance, could be cast merely by forging signatures.

On 19 March 1995, Bob Ingram wrote:

If in fact it was the intent of the court to void this law [requiring witnessing of absentee ballots], that is a cause for genuine concern. I could tell you countless horror stories of how illegal absentee votes were cast in past elections: absentee votes being cast by the long dead, by the unregistered, the under-age, felons and non-residents. In fact it was to curb these illegal practices that the law requiring notarization or witnesses was passed in the first place.

He went on to predict that the Eleventh Circuit would reject the Alabama Supreme Court's answer. The *Advertiser* included anonymous comments by readers who called into its voice mail service. One mentioned that after the Alabama Supreme Court's opinion, a local law school in Montgomery had moved the location of a scheduled speech by Hooper from a room holding up to 500 persons to a room holding up to fifty. Another read: "Them yellow dogs are barking up the wrong tree again. The Democrats are great when it comes to kicking the voting franchise around. In 1986 they told half their constituents that their votes in the primary didn't count. We know the fallout from that."

The official editorial by the *Advertiser* stated that the justices should have stepped aside. It also speculated as to the reason that Justices Butts and Kennedy neither voted nor formally recused themselves from the case. Were the two judges trying to avoid bringing into play an Alabama statute which would seem to give Republican Governor Fob James the power to appoint a special court to hear the case? It went on to quote Alabama Code Section 12-2-14, the statute that calls for the governor to appoint a special court when the number of justices drops below six "because of disqualifications." The *Advertiser* had more to say on the issue a couple of weeks later.[6] Tom Johnson, the editor of the *Montgomery Independent,* a small weekly newspaper, titled his editorial " 'Conscience' defied" and quoted this Chinese proverb: "When you find yourself sinking in a hole, stop digging." I have included his entire opinion at the end of this chapter because of its caustic concision.[7]

The *Tuscaloosa News* called the opinion "troubling" for two reasons: it did not follow the clear language of the election statute, and the Justices did not recuse themselves.

> We dread the idea of the federal courts again deciding an issue that should have been handled on the state level. But more dreadful is the perception that an election can be "won" in such a cozy manner, with contributors and colleagues deciding the fate of a befriended candidate.

On 23 March, an article by two Cumberland Law School professors in the *Birmingham News* claimed that the language of the statute was clear. "[W]e want to focus here only on the question of whether the Supreme Court's decision is correct as a matter of law. It is not." The two professors stated that, fundamentally, a court should seek to determine and give effect to the intent of the legislature when interpreting a statute. "By treating the witness requirement as a mere technicality, rather than as the heart of the statute, the court takes a statute designed to prevent vote fraud and renders it impotent. This reading flouts another rule courts follow in interpreting statutes: do not read the statute in such a way to make it a waste of paper."

Justice Maddox's dissent was twenty-five pages long, and he supplemented it later because he had not had time to finish it the first time. Justice Maddox agreed with the Eleventh Circuit and Judge Propst that *Williams v. Lide* and *Wells v.*

Ellis did not specifically address the question the Eleventh Circuit had asked about the unwitnessed absentee ballots. Justice Maddox concluded the ballots should not be counted because of three principles. First, the statute, Section 17-10-7, required notarization or two witnesses' signature. Second, substantial compliance with Alabama law means that the ballot must comply with essential requirements of Alabama law, one of which was that an absentee ballot be accompanied by an affidavit. An unnotarized or unwitnessed voter signature was not a legal affidavit. Third, in accordance with *Wells v. Ellis*, the ballots should not be counted if the irregularity would adversely affect the sanctity of the ballot and the integrity of the election.

Justice Maddox's writings contained some interesting comments. First, he participated in both the *Wells* case and the *Lide* case. He stated that neither case held that an absentee ballot should be counted if it was not properly witnessed. Second, he said that in Lide, the supreme court "did not adopt a rule that would abrogate the requirement of the law, stated on the absentee form itself that '[the voter's] signature must be witnessed by either: A notary public or other officer authorized to acknowledge oaths or two witnesses 18 years of age or older.'" Such a requirement is not a mere technicality, but is an "'essential requirement' that relates to the sanctity of the ballot itself." He said he had done substantial research and had failed to find any other jurisdiction which did away with the witness requirement for an adequate certification of the voter's signature. The majority opinion neglected to, but Justice Maddox quoted Section 17-10-7 in its entirety.

He also noted the use of the word "shall" in the statute, meaning that the legislature had meant the requirement to be mandatory. For example: "[T]he voter shall complete the affidavit." He took pains to define the word "affidavit," using case law and the dictionary. All of them required a lawfully witnessed oath. An unwitnessed affidavit was simply not an affidavit at all. The word "must" added even greater strength to Justice Maddox's interpretation of the statute: "Note: Your signature must be witnessed by either: A notary public or other official authorized to acknowledge oaths or two witnesses 18 years of age or older." He went on to define the words "must," "swear," "oath," and "affirm." He also noted that in the third oath in the statute, "there is an acknowledgment that false information given 'so as to vote illegally by absentee ballot' is a violation of the criminal law." How could someone be prosecuted for such a crime if they had not sworn falsely in an affidavit? So the majority opinion essentially cast doubt on the ability to apply the punishment of the criminal law prohibiting false absentee ballots. He also agreed with the Eleventh Circuit that it was clear that Judge Reese lacked subject matter jurisdiction over the case in the first place. In his final footnote of the opinion, he stated: "It appears to me that the Eleventh Circuit, even though deferring to this Court to address the question of Alabama law, would not be bound by this Court's interpretation, if this Court's interpretation deprived the plaintiffs of federal constitutional rights."

So what did the majority of the Alabama Supreme Court say? What was its analysis? The majority declared, "Shortly after election day, it was discovered that, within the State of Alabama, ballots not in strict compliance with the statute had been counted in some counties and had not been counted in others." The Alabama Supreme Court reiterated Reese's statement that "[n]o one knows what the result of the election will be when these ballots are counted." The opinion also altered the question from the Eleventh Circuit by adding the following bold words: "Does Alabama law permit or require some, but not all, absentee ballots which are signed by the voter, but not notarized or witnessed, to be counted?" That implied that there was inconsistent counting going on in the state. It was the Democrats' argument, for which they had no supporting evidence.

The opinion then gave its version of the litigation history. The four justices concurring in the majority opinion said that the litigation began when "the Republican candidate for Chief Justice sought an *ex parte* temporary restraining order from Shelby County Circuit Court to secure all election records for an anticipated election contest." That order did nothing to change what was required under state law for the securing of ballot materials anyway. Nor did it hinder or delay the return of the results to the secretary of state. The opinion then described the hearing in Reese's court in Montgomery. It mentioned the hearing before Judge Phelps and said that Phelps had taken testimony at that 6:00 P.M. hearing. I know of no testimony presented to Judge Phelps, only affidavits. It then discussed the hearing before Judge Reese. Strangely, in a footnote, the majority thought it necessary to state that the case was assigned to Judge Reese "by the automated assignment system maintained by the Clerk's office when it was filed." Nowhere does the opinion relate that Hooper filed his action in Mobile on 16 November 1994. Nor does it tell the reader that Judge Howard announced from the bench on the afternoon of 17 November 1994 that he would issue his 18 November TRO. That would have been before Judge Reese issued his TRO.

The opinion stated that the Republican party had obtained the TRO in Shelby County. That was untrue. Perry Hooper had obtained that TRO. It pointed out several times that "attorney Agricola had announced that he would appeal Judge Reese's order" to the state appellate court. It then went on to say that "[h]ad the Republican Party appealed from the order of the Circuit Court of Montgomery County issued in November, 1994, the entire controversy involving the November general election would have been resolved long ago. The people of Alabama would have known the outcome of the election, and the losing candidates, had they chosen to do so, could have contested the elections in the state legislature." Of course, that would most likely have resulted in Hornsby being declared the winner. The opinion neglects to mention that various failures and refusals by county election officials in certain counties to abide by the Shelby County order forced Hooper to go to federal court.

As for the hearing before Judge Howard in Mobile on 5 December 1994, the opinion stated: "there was no evidence that any uncounted vote was tainted in any way. There was no evidence of voter fraud. There was no evidence that any irregularities in any uncounted ballot affected the sanctity of the ballots in any way. There was no evidence that the integrity of the election would be affected by the counting of these ballots." But that was not the key issue in the federal district court in Mobile; the issue was the change in the voting laws that occurred after the election and whether that change violated Hooper's constitutional rights.

In one sentence, the opinion mentioned the Eleventh Circuit's decision to uphold Judge Howard's preliminary injunction but quoted extensively from Judge Edmondson's dissent. There was no showing that either candidate had been prejudiced by Reese's decision. The Alabama Supreme Court said that Howard held that ballots "not in strict compliance with the statute," could not be counted. Actually, Howard's holding was that it violated Hooper's and the voters' constitutional rights to have the election practices of the state changed in midstream.

The majority stated that Judge Propst had written that the case in Mobile should not have proceeded after the three-judge panel in Birmingham withdrew its TRO. Judge Propst wrote: "*Res judicata* should have foreclosed a relitigation in a second federal court." But *res judicata* doesn't apply when there has been no litigation in the first place. The Birmingham federal court had not litigated the issue of the federal constitutional rights of the voters at all. That court had made clear that it was only dealing with the Section 2 and Section 5 issues as to preclearance by the U.S. Justice Department. The opinion states that the three-judge panel issued its opinion on 25 November 1994. The correct date was 22 November 1994. The supreme court's opinion claimed that the Birmingham federal court had ordered the disputed ballots to be counted. That was directly opposite to what Propst wrote in his memorandum opinion. The three-judge panel's order of 22 November 1994 noted that its original TRO was "appropriately entered at the time of entry" because "the order of the Circuit Court of Montgomery County, Alabama clearly brought about and will bring about changes to voting standards, practices or procedures."

The majority opinion cited *Curry v. Baker*, 802 F.2d 1302 (11th Cir. 1986), claiming that the federal courts were improperly intruding into state matters. However, *Curry v. Baker* stated that "patterns of state action that systematically deny equality in voting" are subject to federal court review. The Hooper case was not some "garden variety election dispute that adversely affected individuals;" it was a case of "patent and fundamental unfairness." The federal court in Curry pointed out that a state's procedure for reviewing an election must have failed for the federal courts to get involved.

It also stated that a federal court should not get involved if no "stuffing of the ballot box" had occurred. That is exactly what happened in Hooper's case. Instead of some county election official doing the stuffing, a circuit court judge had done it. In Hooper's case, even if he had opted for legislative contest and succeeded in getting the election overturned, that would not have changed the substantive law created by Judge Reese's ruling and upheld by the Alabama Supreme Court. The legitimization of unwitnessed absentee ballots and the dilution of the valid voters' voting power would have stood as precedent for future elections. Interestingly, the Alabama Supreme Court did not censure Hornsby, who had gone into court to obtain a change in the voting practice of Alabama instead of following the contest route. It did criticize Hooper for not filing a legislative contest.

The majority then discussed cases from other jurisdictions in which the federal courts had declined to intervene. These cases involved vote counting mistakes, voting machine malfunctions, and other minor problems that could easily be corrected by a state's administrative machinery. None approached the level of intentional abuse of the system after an election that Hooper's case did. The opinion also distinguished the cases cited by Hooper's attorneys in which the federal courts did intervene. It spent only one paragraph arguing that there were adequate remedies under state law. It did not explain what remedies a voter could obtain under the circumstances of Reese's order. The ostensible purpose of Reese's order was to "help" voters get their votes counted. But that was not the real problem. If the Alabama Supreme Court agreed with Reese's ruling, the legitimate voter had nowhere to turn.

The opinion equated Hooper with the Republican party by saying that both had the same lawyers and that Hooper was an executive officer of the Republican party. Truthfully, the only overlapping lawyer in the two cases was Agricola. Nevertheless, that is not a basis for saying that two different parties to a case are identical. The court had trouble equating Hornsby's interests with those of the other justices who had contributed to Hornsby's campaign. The majority argued that the *Rooker-Feldman* doctrine applied to keep Hooper from going to federal court. The *Rooker-Feldman* doctrine prevents a federal court from reviewing the decisions of a state's highest court. However, in this case, Judge Reese did not represent the state's highest court. The opinion stated that Hornsby's attorneys had "no notice that the hearing [before Judge Howard] would be on the merits." In fact, Hornsby's attorneys briefed the federal court on the merits of the case, arguing *Curry v. Baker* and the *Rooker-Feldman* doctrine. Facts of the litigation history seemed to become confused in the Alabama Supreme Court's opinion. The opinion also said that Johnston and Druhan represented the plaintiff in the Birmingham action, whereas it was Jordan who represented Ralph Bradford in that case.

The opinion included several pages chastising the Eleventh Circuit for accepting jurisdiction of a "hypothetical claim of deprivation of due process rights as exists in the present case." It then stated that it had "directed the Clerk of the Montgomery County Circuit Court to certify the record in *Odom v. Bennett* to this Court." This is unheard of. No one had appealed the Reese order, nor had there yet been any type of summary judgment in the underlying case that would allow for an appeal of that second stage of the litigation before Reese. When the supreme court certified a copy of that record from the Montgomery County court, Hooper's attorneys had not yet had the chance to cross-examine the plaintiff's witnesses. In fact, that court had not even held a hearing, yet the plaintiffs submitted affidavits (witnessed) that had been obtained by Hornsby's staff attorney and another employee in the supreme court named Bob Martin. These actions by the court were unprecedented. The date of the Alabama Supreme Court's order for the certified record was 13 March 1995. 14

March 1995 was the date of release of the supreme court's answer to the Eleventh Circuit. Later, in a brief to the U.S. Supreme Court, Attorney General Jeff Sessions described the denial of due process to the Hooper and Roe plaintiffs as "breathtaking." The Eleventh Circuit had included part of the record of the Reese hearing in its certified question to the Alabama Supreme Court. The record of the proceedings before Reese were actually less well-developed than the record of the proceedings in federal court, yet the Alabama Supreme Court described the Reese record as a "fully-developed adversary proceeding."

Hornsby's staff attorney and Bob Martin were active in obtaining affidavits for use by the court, even though it is not the job of the appellate court to collect evidence.[8] The majority declared, "It is also undisputed that absentee ballots, legally and materially indistinguishable from those that were counted in some counties, were not counted in other counties." A footnote to that statement read: "Based on her experience with past elections, the Circuit Clerk of Sumter County estimated that approximately 1,000 absentee ballots were cast. In Bullock County, twenty-one signed absentee ballots were rejected because of missing witness signatures." Those figures came from the two affidavits collected by Mills and Martin.

The majority opinion included several pages discussing the importance of the right to vote. It then referred to some Alabama cases that were quite different from the facts in the Hooper case. As for the *Wells* case, the opinion said that "[t]he losing candidates [in that case] argued that the absentee votes did not comply with section 17-10-7 because the accompanying affidavits had one of the following problems: (1) defective signatures, either by the absentee voter or a witness; (2) no dates; or (3) lack of a reason for voting absentee." That statement alone leaves the impression that the Alabama Supreme Court reversed the trial court in that case because it did not count absentee ballots with defective witness signatures. However, that opinion gives no more facts about these ballots in the *Wells* case. More importantly, as Justice Maddox pointed out in his dissent, the supreme court did not even address the validity of the ballots. It simply clarified that Alabama adopted the "substantial compliance" doctrine and returned it to the trial court for a determination as to whether these ballots met that standard.

Williams v. Lide was the next topic, but nowhere did the opinion address Justice Houston's statement about the cross appeal making the issue of the absentee ballots in that case moot. It simply recited that the trial court had allowed several unwitnessed absentee ballots to be counted and that the supreme court had affirmed the trial court. The opinion did not explain whether the absentee ballot affidavits in that case had been witnessed or not. Without any witnessing, the documents could not be called affidavits, yet the supreme court referred to them as such. It turns out that according to an affidavit (signed and witnessed) by the trial judge in *Lide,* several of these documents referred to as affidavits were not witnessed. No statement to that effect was in the opinion. One cannot go beyond the confines of the opinion to set precedent, especially on a matter that was, in fact, moot when the supreme court issued the opinion. The supreme court did not need to review *Lide's* cross-appeal; there was simply no mention of this in the supreme court's opinion.

The opinion then mentioned a few other states, but no cases involving similar facts to the Hooper case. The opinion had several appendices. Appendix A listed the states that had adopted the "substantial compliance" standard and Appendix B listed the states following the "strict compliance" standard.

Appendix C was the majority's justification for not disqualifying themselves. The final sentence read: "Rather, these contributions reflect collegial courtesy expressed in a time before this controversy arose." That appendix was followed by materials attached by Justice Houston justifying his recusal in the case. The opinion stated that Hooper had raised the recusal issue after the briefing schedule was over. However, the record shows that it was raised before any briefs were filed and certainly before the close of the briefing schedule. Deputy Attorney General Pryor argued in his brief to the U.S. Supreme Court: "[I]f this statement is true, then it means that the court drafted its opinion before the attorneys submitted their arguments."

Justice Cook wrote a special concurrence in which he defended the jurisdiction of the circuit court (Reese) to hear a case like this. Justice Maddox released his supplement to his original dissent on 27 March 1995. In it, he disagreed with Justice Cook, noting that section 17-5-6 was a simple and clear law. The cases Cook cited were not even applicable to the Hooper case because they all involved local races that had been through contests before the authorities charged by Alabama law to hear local election contests. The certifying official had refused to obey that authority in those cases, and the circuit courts thereby had ample jurisdiction to hear the cases. A statewide race must go to the state legislature for a contest, not circuit court.

Justice Maddox likened this case to the 1986 election contest between Bill Baxley and Charlie Graddick, the two candidates for the Democratic nomination for governor. In that case, Graddick tried to bypass the authority of the Alabama Democratic Executive Committee by going to circuit court. Yet the Alabama Democratic Executive Committee had the authority under Alabama law to hear a primary contest. In Hooper's case, a proxy voter brought an action in circuit court to have certain absentee ballots counted. The plaintiffs avoided the legislature and, before there were even any certified results, filed an action in circuit court. The Alabama Supreme Court had no trouble in the Graddick case refusing to hear the case. Two of the justices voting with the majority in that case, Almon and Shores, agreed with that result. However, in Hooper's case, they claimed that the circuit court had jurisdiction. Justice Maddox added that he thought recusal was the appropriate route for the justices voting in the majority in Hooper's case. Justice Maddox is a Democrat.

Governor James was often critical of judges' decisions. For example, he called Judge Reese's decision in the equity funding case "the Judge Reese School Takeover Ruling." After the release of the supreme court's answer, Governor James, in an attempt to get judges' elections "out of the political realm," floated a proposal to set up a commission to provide a list of nominees, from which the governor would make appointments to the appellate courts. The commission would be made up of the lieutenant governor, the speaker of the house of representatives, two members chosen by the Alabama State Bar, one chosen by the circuit judges association, and two chosen by the governor. He also proposed nonpartisan elections, in which judges would not run under a party name. But that would not get politics out of the judiciary. Most of the decision-making in such an appointment process would take place out of the sight of the voters, and lawyers would have the power and influence to make the decisions as to who would become judges. The players in Alabama's "legal lottery" would keep control, and the voters would have no say.

Interestingly, about this time I received notice of a class on a subject of law. Lawyers in Alabama must attend continuing legal education courses, and these courses send notices on a regular basis throughout the year. Ironically, I received one from the Notary Law Institute which claimed:

> Notarial acts are too frequently viewed as inconsequential, having little meaning or effect. Notarial acts are acts and functions of law. They do mean something. The civil and criminal consequences of notarial misconduct can be surprisingly severe. Attorneys are bound by the Canons of Ethics to ensure the correct and truthful performance of notarizations under their supervision.

I was glad someone took notarizations seriously. I also thought about sending this particular notice to Chief Justice Hornsby and suggesting he attend the course.

A law student named Lori Tarle later wrote a *Law Review* article critical of the supreme court's decision for the *Cumberland Law School Law Review*.[9] She argued that under any theory of statutory interpretation, whether under the textualism principles of Antonin Scalia, the spirit of the law of William Brennan, legal process theory, or Posner's public choice theory, the Alabama Supreme Court's interpretation of Section 17-10-7 was faulty. Her article pointed out that nowhere in the majority opinion is the text of Section 17-10-7 quoted. She referred to *Williams v. Lide*, in which two voters testified that a man came to their door offering to help them vote by absentee ballot. They gave their names, addresses, and social security numbers to the man, but he never asked how they wanted to vote. They testified that their signatures were not the signatures that were on the ballots in evidence in that case. Such fraud was one reason the legislature required absentee ballots to be witnessed. She concluded by saying that the Alabama Supreme Court took the liberty of choosing what it thought was the statute's primary purpose—protecting and furthering the citizen's right to vote. But that concern of the supreme court's had taken precedence over preventing fraud and the sanctity of the ballot. According to the author, they rewrote the statute, violating the principle of separation of powers in the process.

Other news collateral to the ballot dispute illustrated the political climate of 1995. On the day after the Alabama Supreme Court refused to rehear the question from the Eleventh Circuit, 31 March 1995, a little article about a downtown hamburger joint relocating appeared in the *Montgomery Advertiser*. It said the owners included Montgomery County Circuit Judge Gene Reese and Alabama Supreme Court Justice Mark Kennedy. The contact that judges have with each other is not only in court.

Many who were ignorant of court procedure thought that Hooper's hopes were over after the Alabama Supreme Court released its opinion. The *Mobile Register*, which had reported so much news favorably for Hooper, began a very strange series of articles on 2 April 1995. Eddie Curran wrote the series, and clearly attempted to call into question Hooper's ability to be chief justice. He repeated the unsupported accusations about the Jerry Hamilton case, as well as the faulty media reports of the early 80s. Again, the articles never acknowledged the possibility that anyone could act out of human kindness for another human being; there had to be some angle, some unsavory reason for Hooper to try to help Hamilton. Curran even went to the federal prison in Kansas to interview Hamilton. Hamilton made outrageous accusations against Hooper that every one involved in the case said were unbelievable. He claimed someone else killed DeVaughn.

He claimed that his lawyer, now a federal judge, in an effort to protect Hooper, forced him to confess and plead guilty. His story was filled with contradictions. Everyone who knew him also stated that he was a manipulative con man. The evidence indicated he acted alone in kidnapping and killing DeVaughn. Hamilton had made similar accusations while in prison. He had even sent a letter to Judge Hooper apologizing for those accusations. Not long after this series of articles appeared, and while he was still in prison, Hamilton killed himself.[10] Missy DeVaughn's father said that he was found hanging in his cell. Judge Hooper thought that Hornsby's campaign ads, the recent attention from the media, mental illness, and his conscience combined to prompt his suicide.

Other events proceeded apace in early April 1995. The Eleventh Circuit set 7 April as the deadline for the parties in the absentee ballot case to file briefs with that court in Atlanta. Judge Al Crowson refused to reconsider his dismissal of the Mississippi Valley Title case. Perry Hooper, Jr., Hooper's son and a representative in the Alabama House of Representatives, proposed legislation to prohibit judges from soliciting campaign contributions from lawyers with cases pending in their courts. Another legislator introduced a bill requiring photo identification before allowing someone to vote. The Democrats screamed that such a requirement would cause blacks, who still remembered the days of disenfranchisement of the sixties, to be intimidated into not voting.

The tort reform issue continued to crop up. In late March the *Advertiser* ran an article about a former insurance agent who said lawsuits ruined his life. He was an agent for Prudential in Barbour County, and he retired in 1992. The agent said he had been accused of misrepresenting policies to customers, and even though he never had to pay anything in these lawsuits, he said that his reputation suffered. He claimed that he had done nothing dishonest in selling insurance policies and that Prudential would simply settle without fighting the lawsuits. He said, "All it boils down to is greed. People want to get their hands on some money, and they think it doesn't cost anybody anything and that it doesn't hurt anybody. I'm here to tell you that it does."

The 20 March 1995 edition of *Time* magazine covered the U.S. Congress' attempt at tort reform. But its poster boy for tort reform was Jere Beasley. The article, entitled "Where the Torts Blossom," focused on Beasley's success in Barbour County before Judge Robertson, Beasley's former law partner. Beasley had litigated eighty-eight cases before Robertson, the only circuit judge in Barbour County, since 1993. In 1994 alone juries in Barbour County had awarded plaintiffs represented by Beasley $110 million. The article called Barbour County "Beasley Triangle." The article stated: "Last year juries in Alabama awarded $200 million in punitive damages, some of it in cases where actual loss was minuscule compared with the damages."[11] It quoted George Priest: " 'Lawsuits used to be about restitution. Now Jere Beasley goes into court and not only gets the money back; he gets $25 million in punitive damages. There is no other county in the United States like Barbour County.' "

The article gave another statistic. The median punitive damage award in Alabama at that time was $250,000. That's three times the national average. The article also gave an example. Willie Ed Johnson paid $1,000 extra for an inflated loan from Mercury Finance. Beasley convinced a jury to hit Mercury Finance with a $50 million verdict. Fortunately, the defendants settled that case for $1 million.

Jere Beasley would argue that it isn't the courts and the lawyers that are the problem; it's the lack of proper regulation by the state of Alabama. In an 11 April 1995 *Montgomery Advertiser* article covering his luncheon speech to the Alabama Association of Health Underwriters, he said, "The real crisis is that we don't regulate insurance companies. If not for the court system, many would continue to take advantage of the people." He claimed that if there were more regulations, then there would be no need for him to sue insurance companies and get large punitive damage awards against them. *Voila*, no more tort crisis in Alabama, no more big punitive damage awards. But more regulations would not stop the trial lawyers from suing insurance companies. If there were more regulation of the insurance industry, then Beasley and his kind could argue even more persuasively before a jury. The more rules and regulations, the more the trial lawyers argue that the company was acting intentionally and wantonly. An attorney can always use the existence of a regulation to increase a punitive damage award. Larry Bennett, an underwriters association member and president of a Montgomery health insurance company, said, "There's too much litigation even if we do have weak regulations." He said that in 1994 eight companies he represented left the state. He added that when insurance companies have to pay millions of dollars in settlements and jury awards, the companies will recover that money in larger premiums. Of the ten lawsuits of 1994 that resulted in the highest damage verdicts, five involved insurance companies. The jury verdicts in those case resulted in awards totaling $143.7 million.

The public relations blitz that occurred at this time resulted from the legislature's consideration of new tort reform legislation. The trial lawyers ran ads alleging that an injured person would go without the money to get necessary medical care, even if a company purposely caused that person's injuries. Of course, caps on punitive damages have no effect on compensatory damages, the amount that a jury awards a person to cover medical expenses for an injury. Nor did the trial lawyers' ads explain that intentional and wanton acts were excluded from any cap on punitive damages in the legislation being considered, as well as in the 1987 tort reform legislation that had been gutted by several years of supreme court decisions.

At the same time, the U.S. Senate was considering reforms that would cap punitive damages and reform "joint and several liability." "Joint and several liability" is a damages rule applied to multiple defendants that has developed in the courts. That rule says the degree of fault of a defendant is irrelevant when considering who pays how much for a damage verdict. Plaintiff trial lawyers are often at great pains to make sure that large wealthy companies are included as defendants in lawsuits, no matter their fault or lack thereof. The term that attorneys unabashedly use to refer to this process is "deep pockets." Someone with "deep pockets" can pay millions of dollars to the plaintiff and the attorney.

Courtwatch, a publication of Alabama Voters Against Lawsuit Abuse, in its issue of April 1995 reported that the lawsuits in federal court had increased from 90,000 in 1960 to 250,000 in 1990. In 1990, 100 million lawsuits were filed in state court. In Alabama alone, the number was 275,000. It did not explain what type of lawsuits or what the results of those lawsuits were. *U.S. News and World Report* reported that a "Florida firm called *Went For It* finds the names of accident victims and sells them to lawyers." *Courtwatch* also challenged Hornsby to step down from office. It quoted the *Daily Mountain Eagle* as saying, "That's it; six years, not six years and a few months; not six years and until a successor is elected and qualified. Gone is the language that would allow Hornsby to remain in office until the election dispute is settled. If Hornsby believed that clear and unequivocal language [of Constitutional Amendment 328 dealing with a judge's term of office], he would step down until the election dispute is settled."

On 26 April 1995, having reviewed the Alabama Supreme Court's answer to its certified question and briefs filed by the parties in the case, the Eleventh Circuit caused a further delay to the certification of the winner of the race for chief justice. It sent the case back to Judge Howard's court for a full trial to ascertain the prior practice of the counties of Alabama. The Alabama Supreme Court's opinion had created enough doubt for the Eleventh Circuit to desire to know what had been the past practice of Alabama counties.

Notes

1. "[W]hen by reason of disqualification no one of the judges is competent to sit in a case or the number is reduced below six, the fact shall be certified by the Chief Justice, if he is competent to sit, or, if not, by the judge or judges sitting, or, if no one is competent, by the clerk of the court to the Governor, who shall thereupon appoint members of the bar of the Supreme Court to constitute a special court of seven members for the consideration and determination of such case." Alabama Code 1975, § 12-2-14.

2. March 17, 1995 Letter from Judicial Inquiry Commission to Associate Justice Terry Butts.

3. Ibid.

4. *Montgomery Advertiser,* p. 1A, March 16, 1995.

5. *Montgomery Advertiser,* p. 1A, March 16, 1995.

6. "In some counties, absentee ballot solicitation has become a near science. In Perry County last year, there were almost as many absentee ballots cast in the June primary as there were in Jefferson County, even though Jefferson County has more than 50 times the population. An incredible 31 percent of the Perry County vote was in absentee ballots.

" The possibility for election fraud with such inflated reliance on absentee ballots should be impossible to ignore. If the requirement for two witnesses or a notarization is eliminated by the courts, as Hornsby's minions are seeking, that possibility for fraud will grow by epic proportions." *Montgomery Advertiser,* p. 2F, April 2, 1995.

7. "It was a bum week for the state's highest judicial organism, the Supreme Court, which managed to turn an unavoidable obligation into a wounding muddle. Once again, fumbling to say what is state law regulating absentee ballots, the mountain labored and brought forth a mouse. Its number reduced to four by dissent, recusals and absences, the court's Democratic majority certified to the skeptical 11th Circuit Court of Appeals that, in effect, conditional Chief Justice Sonny Hornsby was reelected to the office over his Republican opponent, Perry Hooper Sr.

"Precisely, the majority said that the absentee voting law, as vasectomized by the court, is stripped of its stern provisions discouraging fraud and permits unseen persons to vote as freely as those who present themselves at the polls. The requirements of witnessing and notarization of an absentee voter's affidavit were, the majority said, unreasonable impediments to voting.

"Supreme Court Justice Hugh Maddox, than whom there is no member more devoted to the earnest, even plodding application of the law, entered a strenuous dissent but was only barely able to do so because the majority, acting through its clerk, brusquely cut him out of the decision-making process and curtly informed him at the last minute to get his dissent written if he planned to submit one.

"Maddox, in an extraordinary note, wrote that his 'opinion was hurriedly prepared because the majority opinion was delivered to my office at 11 a.m. on March 14, 1995, and I had to get this dissenting opinion filed by 3 p.m. on the same date.' A close observer of the court said the clerk, Robert G. Esdale, delivered the high-handed message to Maddox as if Maddox worked for him.

"The worst news for the court came almost simultaneously with the release of its opinion. The judicial inquiry commission, a body established by the Judicial Article to serve as a kind of grand jury and conscience of the judiciary, with the power to 'indict,' informed Justice Terry Butts that, in view of his ties with Chief Justice Hornsby, he would be well-advised to refrain from taking part in any proceedings related to the election contest between Hornsby and Hooper.

"This advice went to Butts because he had requested an opinion, but it clearly applied as well to other members of the court. Justice Houston, while insisting he could be impartial despite making a small contribution to Hornsby's campaign, reluctantly recused himself. Butts did not participate, apparently because of his pending request to the Inquiry Commission. Justice Mark Kennedy's whereabouts were not indicated. Hornsby , of course, recused.

"With five participating justices constituting a quorum, the majority four resisted a Republican request that they stand down, instead declaring it to be settled law in Alabama that recusal is left to the judges' conscience [sic] and that the contributions accepted or given by Justices Cook, Almon, Shores and Ingram—the four who upheld the reconstructed absentee-voting law that favors the reelection of Justice Hornsby—were not a 'disqualifying indication of partiality.'

"The Inquiry Commission, made up of judges, practicing attorneys and one lay person, thought otherwise in the case of Butts, whose circumstances were nearly identical to those of the justices who ruled. A private lawyer called over here last Tuesday, two days before the court acted, to tell this page that the Inquiry

Commission was about to advise as it did. The Supreme, one of whose number, Mark Kennedy, is a member of the commission, must have known as much. Nevertheless, the majority four— contemptuous of Maddox and either ignorant or contemptuous of the Inquiry Commission's feelings—bulled through an opinion that happens to support Hornsby's contention as a party to the contest.

"All that the majority court said is merely advisory in that jurisdiction has been taken by the 11th Circuit Court, which asked the Supreme Court, as a bemused courtesy, to offer its interpretation of the voting laws. Remember that the 11th Circuit had already said flatly that Circuit Judge Gene Reese lacked authority to put his approval on a loosey-goosey interpretation of the law. Now the Supreme Court, which bestrides a judicial system that has seen its prestige and previously unexamined trustworthiness decompose under the battering of court-packing, crude politicking and a general perception of politicization, offers a self-serving response to a federal court that has exhibited no tolerance for nonsense.

"Consider the remarkable and regrettable circumstance that the public cynicism and disdain that used to be directed at governors and legislators have now turned upon the judiciary, commissioned to keep the law pure without fear, favor, or political predilection."

8. In another opinion released by the Alabama Supreme Court on March 17, 1995, less than a week after the answer to the Eleventh Circuit's question, that court had stated: "[T]he certified question procedure does not place this Court in a position of making factual findings. . . . " *Ericson GE Mobile Communications & Electronics, Inc. v. Motorola Communications & electronics, Inc.*

9. Tarle, Lori, Comment: Statutory Interpretation and the Alabama Absentee Ballot Controversy, 26 Cumberland Law Review 197 (1995-96).

10. *Montgomery Advertiser*, p. 1, May 3, 1995.

11. *Time*, p. 38, March 20, 1995.

Back to the Drawing Board

What had happened? Obviously, the Alabama Supreme Court's answer for the Eleventh Circuit was not helpful. We knew it was possible that there would be a significant delay. We were getting used to this two steps forward, one step back type of progress. But why had the Eleventh Circuit sent the case to Mobile for trial? The Democrats and Hornsby had a hypothetical defense. If widespread acceptance throughout Alabama of the disputed ballots had occurred historically, then perhaps the weight of that custom could overcome the explicit language of the statute on witnessing of absentee ballots. People had become accustomed to doing things a certain way, therefore it would be an infringement upon their voting rights to tell them they now had to stop. The press didn't accept that. They argued in their editorials that just because a bunch of counties had disobeyed the law in the past didn't mean that disobedience should be sanctioned. Hooper doubted the sincerity of the other side. We saw no evidence of such a widespread practice. The local officials I spoke to in southern Alabama used words like "ridiculous" and "stupid" to describe Reese's order. We doubted that the Democrats had evidence of such practices. If they did, they would have presented it long ago.

Nevertheless, the Eleventh Circuit was leaving no stone unturned. "The court is particularly concerned with the possible effect of any contested absentee ballots included in initial certifications." You cannot identify who voted absentee once a vote is included in the initial certification by a county. The three-judge panel, Tjoflat, Edmondson (no longer dissenting), and Birch, remanded the case back to Howard's court and asked for findings of fact in seventeen questions. They wanted to know every county's past practice. The questions were quite detailed.[1] The questions included discovering the totals from each county of the votes for Hooper and Hornsby before Reese's order and after, whether the totals of the contested ballots could be separated from the county totals, and whether the counties had counted the disputed ballots in the past.

Some of the questions were disturbing because we thought they had already been answered. The question as to what the voters knew they could do seemed clear. The *Birmingham News* put it well in an editorial on 28 April 1995:

> Think of it this way, however. How many people who voted absentee in Alabama knew the substance of some esoteric court ruling? Moreover, how many of them thought some esoteric, illogical court ruling held more sway than the injunction on the ballot form, in black and white, right in front of their eyes?

Doing away with the popular election of judges would further distance the judges from the people. The editorial went on to say that Hornsby could and should end the litigation immediately, before any more months of legal wrangling delayed the certification of the winner.

In the meantime, lawyers for the state of Alabama appeared in a hearing before Judge Reese in response to Hornsby's lawsuit regarding payment beyond the term for which he was elected. Even though the lawyers for the state of Alabama said they would not bring a legal action to eject Hornsby, they said that he should have stepped down and allowed the governor to appoint a replacement while the absentee ballot case was pending. Bill Pryor, the deputy attorney general in charge of the case for Attorney General Sessions, said, "He [Hornsby] is asking to remain chief justice until the litigation is resolved. That could be years and that is not Alabama law." He also asked Reese to recuse himself because he was the judge who originally ruled in the absentee ballot case.

An interesting story about a Boaz attorney appeared in the *Montgomery Advertiser* on 30 April 1995. The attorney's client, Whitehead, collected $12,000 over a year, in weekly paychecks from a poultry company, without working. Albertville police detective Andy Whitten worked on the case. Whitten was later found with a bullet in his head. The chief investigator in the case, Tommy Cole, claimed that the attorney had conceived the idea of killing the detective to keep his client from going to prison for life as a habitual offender. Cole also said that included in the idea was a plan for "the lawyer [to] sue the poultry company for false prosecution. Witnesses told Mr. Cole the lawsuit could have amounted to more than $4 million." This was another extreme example of a lawyer trying to manipulate the judicial system for profit.

It seemed that the politics of the Hooper-Hornsby case infected everything. We had obtained a copy of a smear sheet on Hooper that had been circulated not long after the election. It mentioned Jerry Hamilton. It mentioned Don Martin. It concluded with nonsense about Hooper not serving in office long even if he won the absentee ballot case. It alleged that, if Hooper won, the Judicial Inquiry Commission would recommend charges against Hooper and force him out of office. It was bogus, and it was meant to eliminate his support in the legislature if he filed a contest of the election. One day, during a House Health Committee meeting, Republican Representative Allen Sanderson asked Alabama Citizen Action director and the co-plaintiff with Davis in the absentee ballot lawsuit in Reese's court: "Does your organization take money from the trial lawyers?" Allegedly Odom had sent a smear sheet to legislators. I don't know if it was the same one that we had seen. It contained copies of the *Mobile Press-Register* series on Hooper. Sanderson went on to angrily tell Odom: "I got this smear sheet on Judge Hooper, and I want you to know I didn't appreciate it."[2]

In May, Hornsby offered his compromise again. He even sent a letter to Judge Howard. " 'Let's count the ballots first,' Chief Justice Hornsby said. 'Only in the event that I win one way and Mr. Hooper wins another way is a trial on the merits necessary in Mobile.' "[3] Hooper's response remained unchanged: "I have been opposed to the counting of illegal ballots since day one. The issue to me seems to be whether or not we will uphold the laws of Alabama that are clearly written on the books." Judge Howard rejected the offer.

In May 1995 Joe Whatley filed a request with the U.S. Supreme Court, asking the court to tell the Eleventh Circuit to butt out of Alabama's matters and declare that Howard's decision of December 1994 was a disenfranchisement of other voters. He now did not want a trial before Judge Howard.

Federal Magistrate William Steele had the duty of managing the discovery process, which is the method for obtaining as much evidence as possible before trial. It was quite a task because it involved sixty-seven Alabama counties. He set a trial date of 19 September. As part of the discovery process, the secretary of state had a Montgomery accounting firm tabulate the totals of the ballots cast in the chief justice and treasurer races. The ballots sat in a vault in the basement of the capitol building. The totals—562,417 votes for Hooper and 562,294 votes for Hornsby—did not agree with the numbers we had obtained from each county's probate office. Our figures showed Hooper ahead by 270 votes. The Secretary of State showed Hooper ahead by only 123 votes.

Hornsby's spokesman, Michael Tucker, said that "based on preliminary figures released today and our own tabulations prior to Judge Howard ordering the (contested) ballots sealed up," Hornsby was ahead by 128 votes. After the secretary of state had provided his figures to Judge Howard, however, he discovered that he did not receive the correct vote totals from Wilcox County. Probate Judge Jerry Boggan said that a clerk in his office had made a mistake in compiling the votes on 8 November 1994. That original compilation showed Hornsby receiving 3,197 votes, when he actually received 3,069 votes. The figure for Hooper was also too low by eleven votes. The reported total for Hooper was 1,153 votes, when he actually received 1,164 votes. That meant that the figures Wilcox County gave to Bennett reduced Hooper's lead by 139 votes. Bennett corrected it and sent the true result in for use by Judge Howard's court. Hooper's lead, after the 139 votes were added, was 262 votes out of 1.12 million votes cast.

That figure could explain a strange discussion I had with Bill Gray, the governor's legal advisor. He and Attorney General Sessions were on the governor's radio talk show one Monday afternoon in March or April of 1995. I called and asked why the governor had not appointed someone, anyone, to replace Hornsby while the litigation continued. Sessions denounced the situation as totally unacceptable and said that he hoped the case would soon be settled. Mr. Gray, however, said that while there was pending litigation, they had to allow the winner of the election to remain in office. His statement was inexcusable in the face of the prior publicity, which clearly showed Hooper had the most votes if you did not count the disputed absentee ballots. Here was a man attempting to remain in a constitutional office, the highest judicial office in the state, and he thought he could don the robes of massive judicial authority and make decisions affecting every Alabamian, even though he had not been elected to the office. Here was the governor's legal advisor publicly saying that he could continue in that charade. A brief editorial comment in the *Montgomery Advertiser* read: "I, like Sonny Hornsby, am a resident of Alabama who was not elected to the Supreme Court or any other state office last November. Therefore, I would like to also be provided with a state vehicle."

In mid-May, the Democrats became angry over an action by Bill Pryor, the deputy attorney general. However, their anger was a smoke screen to cover the problematic testimony of one of their own, former Secretary of State Billy Joe Camp. Pryor, accompanied by Secretary of State Jim Bennett and Montgomery County Circuit Clerk Debra Hacket, both Democrats, went into the clerk's office to find Camp's absentee ballot. Camp had testified, in January 1995, that his absentee ballot was not witnessed and did not have to be witnessed to be counted. However, Pryor found Camp's ballot had two court employees' signatures attached. The Democrats were outraged because they said Pryor was in violation of Judge Howard's order to not tamper with the disputed ballot materials. Pryor did not seek to discover Camp's vote, an action that would have violated federal law. The Democrats complained about Pryor; the evidence he uncovered was too damning to them to go unchallenged.

On 26 May 1995, Judge Hooper received a strange telefax at his office. It came from an Anniston attorney's office and said that the attached document was "faxed by an unknown person to my office yesterday." This attorney added: "I doubt it was intended to come to me. You are probably aware of these efforts, but be advised anyway." Attached was a copy of the absentee ballot envelope issued by the state of Alabama. Handwritten at the top left corner were these words: "This is what's on the absentee ballot envelope. If it is not perfectly filled out then doesn't strictly comply." At the top center of the page were the handwritten words: "Fax—Ala. Trial Lawyers." The next page looked like a list of interrogatories (questions for discovery) for a court proceeding. It said, "We need the following from County." Here are a few samples of the questions on this document:

> 4) Who are the names of other friendly absentee workers in 1994 election and previous elections and phone numbers.

> 5) Alert the circuit clerk that he/she will be receiving interrogatories from the Federal District Court in Mobile in the next 10 days and to check with you before they answer.

> 6) Please offer to represent the current clerk as their personal attorney for answering these interrogatories.

Obviously, this document was intended for an attorney. It was also clearly from an attorney who didn't know the rules of grammar very well. But what did "other friendly absentee workers" mean? Attached to the list of questions was a sample affidavit, similar to what Carole Smith, the Sumter County Circuit Clerk, filled out for Bob Martin. It was phrased to help Hornsby.[4]

Hooper gave a copy to his attorneys, who filed papers with the federal court alleging that the Alabama Trial Lawyers were trying to distort the proceedings. The *Montgomery Advertiser* could not reach Don Gilbert, the executive director of the Alabama Trial Lawyers Association, for comment. Joe Whatley told the *Advertiser:* "This is all coming cold to me."[5] On 30 May 1995, Federal Magistrate Steele and Judge Howard sent a caution out to all the local election officials. They warned them that meddling could occur from persons trying to influence the case.[6] We had learned by then that state Democratic party Chairman Bill Blount had sent the fax out to the probate judges, sheriffs, and circuit clerks in all sixty-seven Alabama counties. That may be true, but it also went to plaintiff trial lawyers around the state. In fact, they were the primary recipients.

On the same day, the *Advertiser* reported that event, it also reported that U.S. Supreme Court Justice Anthony Kennedy had rejected, without comment, Whatley's emergency request for the case to be thrown out of federal court. On 22 June 1995 Judge Howard allowed Secretary of State Jim Bennett to make the 139-vote correction in Hooper's favor based on the Wilcox County corrected results.

The June issue of *Reader's Digest* reported on the case. The title was "Vote Fraud: A National Disgrace." It covered several examples of election fraud around the country. The author, Trevor Armbrister, put his section about the Reese decision under the subheading: " 'Rewriting' election rules." On 23 June 1995 "NBC Evening News" returned to Alabama's chief justice election. It gave a brief interview to Judge Hooper, who called Hornsby "the great pretender," as he gave a summary of the events that had lead to the judicial quagmire and a look at the fraudulent practices regarding absentee ballots in Greene County. It was an excellent short history of the events leading to Alabama having an unelected chief justice in office. During that news segment, Alabama looked something like a third world nation.

By 30 June 1995, all the county officials had responded to the discovery. Hooper's attorneys asked Howard to rule immediately and grant him summary judgment without even going to trial. They could ask for this because the results of discovery showed that every county except one, Washington County, had not regularly counted unwitnessed absentee ballots in the past. Six counties were vague in their answers. Chambers and Coosa counties did not answer either way. Jackson, Lowndes, Tallapoosa, and Wilcox counties said they did not know past practice. The other sixty answered a clear "no." Any counties whose affidavits were defective would have to testify at the trial in September in Mobile.

Four counties revealed that they had counted the disputed ballots in the November 1994 election, but that it was not a regular practice. Covington counted eleven, Randolph five, and Marion nineteen. Add those numbers to the fourteen counted by Washington County for a total of forty-nine unwitnessed absentee ballots counted. These votes were included in the initial certifications by the counties to the secretary of state's office in 1994. That meant that those votes were unidentifiable and, therefore, inseparable from the rest of the votes cast legitimately in the 1994 election. Even if each one of those votes was cast for Hooper (an impossibility considering the particular counties) they would not have affected the outcome one way or another because Hooper's lead was approximately 262.

Hooper's motion stated: "Such a change [from not counting them to counting them as Reese's order required] would amount to 'stuffing' the ballot box. As a matter of law, it would be patently and fundamentally unfair and would violate the first and fourteenth Amendments to the U.S. Constitution." The conclusion, which was written by Glenn Murdock, stated:

> Almost eight months ago, the citizens of Alabama exercised the most basic fundamental civil right in democracy, the right to choose who shall govern them. Their choice for chief justice of their supreme court was Perry Hooper. Today, Mr. Hooper still has not taken office, and the will of Alabama's electorate has thus been thwarted. Federal judicial relief is appropriate and necessary at this time to bring an end to a travesty unlike any other in Alabama's sad history of absentee ballot abuse.

Judge Howard denied the motion.

Joe Whatley made his own request to Judge Howard. He asked that the court order the examination of what was estimated to be 38,000 to over 50,000 absentee ballots, legal and illegal, that were cast in Alabama in 1994. Sam Heldman, one of Hornsby's other attorneys, said, "The only definitive way to find out answers to many questions is to look at the ballots. I think we've been trying to do that for a long time." There was absolutely no evidence to indicate that any of the testimony of the local officials was false or incomplete. An examination of 38,000 absentee ballots would prove nothing; it would only delay the resolution of the case for several more months. In fact, it would be similar to an election contest, the very thing that would indicate that the federal court was meddling too far into the workings of the state's election practices. The Democrats would then have an appealable issue if they could force something like that to happen. Both Judge Howard and the Eleventh Circuit denied the request.

The Democrats still played the public relations spin as best they could. Heldman stated: "The whole reason we're back before Judge Howard is the Eleventh Circuit recognized that Republicans had gone too fast back in December. We weren't afforded our constitutional right to have a fair trial before a judge ruled against us. We're looking forward to getting due process and once we get due process—show we're entitled to win." As Hooper's attorneys wrote in the petition dealing with the faxed Alabama Trial Lawyer's memo, "To speak very plainly and candidly with the court, what is going on here is crystal clear: an attempt is being made to 'alert' potential witnesses in this case ahead of time as to what the 'party line' should be."

On 22 June 1995, a Citizens Conference on Judicial Elections finished its meeting. Former Supreme Court Justice Oscar Adams and former Governor Albert Brewer hosted the event. Everyone came down on the side of ending the popular election of judges. Rod Nachman proposed the Missouri plan in which a nominating commission would choose nominees from which the governor would appoint judges. Bill Gray, the governor's legal advisor, said he favored nonpartisan elections. Birmingham Judge Kenneth Simon also sought a form of nonpartisan election of judges. The goal was to take special interest groups out of the process of electing judges.

The Affirmative Action Appellate Court settlement engineered by Jimmy Evans was at the Eleventh Circuit. Attorney General Sessions opposed the settlement, saying that it "purports to be a Voting Rights Act case designed to create voting powers, then denies the people the right to vote." Sessions said the settlement would have created a "committee of political insiders [who] would select candidates" for the appellate courts. Sessions said "it should have been resisted." Joe Whatley, the attorney for the other side, stated that Sessions was using race to oppose the settlement.

In early July, Attorney General Sessions filed papers in federal court accusing Bob Martin, an employee with the Administrative Office of Courts, and Wayne Mills, Hornsby's staff attorney, of lining up false or misleading statements from county voting officials as evidence in the case. In a motion prepared by Bill Pryor, he stated: "These affidavits were cleverly prepared to hide the truth and prolong the agony of this litigation." Bert Jordan said, "When a case is pending in a court, employees of that court are not supposed to be out gathering evidence. It's staggering to me to consider the implications of the employees of the Supreme Court working for one side in a case like this." Martin and Mills prepared the affidavits for officials from Sumter and Covington counties, and either left out past practices or stated the past practice in a misleading way.

Clay Alspaugh, another of Hornsby's attorneys, attempted to put a positive spin on the statements. He said that citizens had a right to get involved in such disputes. "I didn't see what being a court employee has to do with it." He didn't see what was wrong with a judge's employee helping develop evidence in a case in which the judge is practically a party.

Sessions stated: "Thus, an employee of the chief justice was gathering this misleading and cleverly prepared testimony while the Supreme Court was considering the case." Mills contacted Covington County Circuit Clerk Roger Powell, discussed the absentee ballots with him, and asked him to sign a statement similar to the one Smith signed. Sessions said, "Like Mr. Martin, Mr. Mills participated in the gathering of this evidence while the absentee ballot case was pending in the Alabama court system." In a more recent sworn statement, Powell said that "since 1989, it has been the general practice to not count those ballots where the affidavits were not appropriately witnessed or notarized." In fact, while eleven unwitnessed absentee ballots were counted in Covington County, Powell tried to talk the absentee ballot board into not counting them. He did that by reading § 17-10-7 to them. Sessions said that it was time to end the matter.

Martin and Mills claimed that they were doing their jobs. Their attorney, Bobby Segall, said that court employees assist in cases involving the judicial system. Mills claimed it was his job to protect the integrity of the laws already established.

The *Birmingham News* reported concerning Martin and Mills: "This is outrageous. The stench this case is building around Alabama's overly-politicized judiciary continues to intensify, and it will not soon go away."[7] On the same page as that editorial was a cartoon. The cartoon had three tables on a sidewalk. At each table someone sold T-shirts. The sign at the first said, "O.J. is innocent." The sign at the second said, "McVeigh is a Patriot." The sign at the third said, "Sonny Hornsby is in the Right." The fellow at the McVeigh table is whispering something about the fellow at the Hornsby table (who looks suspiciously like Hornsby) and tells the fellow at the O.J. table: "This guy's killing our credibility." Hornsby had fallen far in the eyes of the media. The 12 May *Dothan Eagle* headlined an editorial with "Give Up, Sonny." In another article later in July, the *Birmingham News* stated: "Hornsby is in a position to announce with effective integrity that no one should be chief justice of Alabama by accepting the counting of absentee ballots that are neither witnessed nor notarized. The counting of such ballots carries an abominable and repulsive stench. By stepping aside, he would make it known that he does not believe it appropriate to preside over Alabama's judiciary under a dark cloud."[8] A 10 August editorial, in the *Montgomery Advertiser* also called for Hornsby to voluntarily step down. It noted that substantial compliance is a valid principle, when someone's address on the ballot envelope is incomplete, but it should never apply to the witness requirement. In conclusion, it proffered the hope that Judge Howard would grant Hooper summary judgment and that Hornsby would at least not drag things out with more appeals. "In the famous words of Joseph Welch in another context, at the McCarthy hearings: 'Have you no sense of decency, Sir, at long last? Have you left no sense of decency?' "

The issue of ballot fraud went to Washington, D.C., where the head of a group called *Citizens for A Better Greene County* testified before a House committee about five men arriving at the post office and pulling 1,100 absentee ballots out of suitcases on election day. One thousand out of 4,300 ballots cast in Greene County were absentee ballots. Former Bullock County Probate Judge Rufus Huffman, who testified in Howard's court in December 1994, told of absentee ballots being sold for five and ten dollars apiece.

Just when we thought we were near the end of the case and that it could not get any more bizarre, these words appeared in an 18 August front page article in the *Montgomery Advertiser:* "Court Case filer dead since '94. Having the dead turn up on voter rolls is not entirely unheard of in Alabama politics. Now, there's a case of the dead filing motions in court—and not in just any court case."[9] John Davis, the man who brought the original case in Reese's court and the name given to the class of voters who did not have their absentee ballots witnessed, died on 20 December 1994. Neither Hooper's attorneys, nor the attorney general, nor the courts knew that Davis was dead until August, eight months after he had died. While he was dead, his attorneys had filed numerous legal papers in his name in the absentee ballot case. Either they knew he was dead and didn't tell anyone, or they did not even know he was dead. The *Wall Street Journal,* in its October 16th article about the case, stated: "Indeed, the struggle has taken on such a life of its own that no one involved realized until this summer that the voter who filed one of the main lawsuits died last year."

Hooper's attorneys discovered that Davis was dead when his attorneys filed a motion containing a footnote mentioning that he had died. He had died on 20 December 1994, fourteen days after Judge Howard's written order. The attorney general's office filed a motion for a hearing on the matter. Hooper's attorneys claimed that because the case was never declared a class action, Davis' death strengthened their claim that the case should be dismissed. However, the federal court allowed the Democrats to find a new defendant. They found a plaintiff by the name of Clarence Hellums of Tuscaloosa to replace Davis. The 20 August *Birmingham News* editorial page included the observation: "If his [Davis'] death were the only question, the case should still go forth. After all, in a lot of Alabama counties being dead doesn't keep you from voting absentee." Hornsby, while admitting that he watched the case closely and communicated regularly with the attorneys for Davis, said he would not become a plaintiff because he cast his vote at the polls on 8 November 1994. Mike Odom, the co-plaintiff in Reese's court, also did not cast an absentee ballot. Hooper left the courthouse saying, "It's been weird since day one. I feel like the people of Alabama are about fed up with the weirdness. It's a callous disregard for your client when you ain't talked to your client in eight months."

Notes

1. "4. In any county in which ballots such as the contested absentee ballots were regularly counted prior to the November 8 election, whether a reasonably absentee voter in that county knew or should have known that such ballots were counted;"

"7. Whether state officials such as the Attorney General of Alabama or the Secretary of State of Alabama have taken consistent positions regarding whether ballots such as the contested absentee ballots are to be counted or excluded and, if so, the form in which such positions were communicated to the average voter or county voting official and the time at which such positions were taken;"

"10. The number of votes initially certified to the Secretary of the State of Alabama from each of Alabama's sixty-seven counties in favor of Sonny Hornsby, the Democratic candidate for Chief Justice of the Supreme Court of Alabama."

2. *Montgomery Advertiser,* "Under the Dome," May 8, 1995.

3. *Montgomery Advertiser,* p. 3B, May 9, 1995.

4. Here is some of its language:

"Prior to the November 8 general election, our county followed a practice of counting absentee ballots if they substantially complied with the form affidavit contained in Ala. Code
§ 17-10-7. We did not require strict compliance with the
form affidavit. We did not always require that there be a
notary or two witnesses before we would count the absentee
ballots and include them in the election certification for our
county. However, in the November 8, 1994 election, the
Republican Party had a representative present at the time the
absentee votes were counted. This representative insisted that
we not count ballots that did not contain a notary or two
witnesses. [My comment: Those evil republicans.] No manual
or election handbook from the Secretary of State had ever
been furnished to me or my office to my knowledge. For the
November 8, 1994 election, we did not count absentee ballots
where the ballot envelope did not have a notarization or two
witnesses. If we had followed our past practice, we would
have counted those ballots and included them in the county
certification submitted to the Secretary of State.

"Prior to the November 8, 1994 election, I have accepted and
counted absentee ballots when the affidavit did not contain
the precinct but I knew the person, where he or she lived and
based on my own knowledge, I could determine the correct
precinct. Many ballots that I have counted in the past were no
different than those which were rejected in the November 8,
1994 election.

"Few people in our county know what is required for an
absentee ballot affidavit. [My comment: Even though the
instructions are written directly on the absentee ballot envelope in black and white.] Those who are very familiar with
the absentee ballot process know that the past practice has
been to accept ballots which substantially comply with the
state absentee ballot law."

It is interesting that the very thing described in this affidavit is
what happened to the Republican representative in Wilcox
County. He tried to contest the unwitnessed absentee ballots
being counted by the absentee ballot manager for Wilcox County,

but she would not allow it. In fact, he was threatened with jail for disrupting the counting process. I started to wonder if all absentee ballot roads lead to Wilcox County?

It is possible that the memo was an attempt to allay any fears that local officials might have had of being criminally prosecuted for disobeying the election laws. As a U.S. Attorney, Jeff Sessions had attempted to prosecute people for election fraud. Such fears were unfounded in this situation, however, because the decision to count unwitnessed absentee ballots would not fall within the confines of criminal activity with respect to an election under Alabama law.

5. *Montgomery Advertiser*, p. 3F, May 27, 1995.

6. Howard's order stated: "It has come to the attention of this court that certain parties who may have an interest in the outcome of this litigation may attempt to approach you regarding the interrogatories which have been sent to you by this Court. The purpose of this instruction is to ensure that nothing interferes with the provision by you of direct and complete answers to this Court's questions."

7. *Birmingham News*, Editorial page, July 9, 1995.

8. *Birmingham News*, p. 6C, July 23, 1995.

9. *Montgomery Advertiser*, p. 1A, August 18, 1995.

The Slam Dunk for Hooper

During the drama of the Hooper-Hornsby case, the tort reform debate raged on. The governor was trying to decide whether to call for a special session of the legislature to address the tort reform issue. In August 1995, the *Montgomery Advertiser* reported: "Court strikes last element of tort reform." It took several years for the Alabama Supreme Court to review many of the aspects of the 1987 tort reform package, and the headline exaggerated as to it being the last element. However, this latest Alabama Supreme Court opinion did strike down one of the last elements of the damages caps of the 1987 legislation. It had left intact the $100,000 cap on verdicts against county governments. In this latest case, the Court struck down the $1 million damage cap with respect to doctors in wrongful death actions. The opinion said the law was a violation of equal protection because it assigned a specific value on the human life of "one isolated class of Alabama citizens, namely, the victims of fatal medical malpractice." It also referred to that favorite refrain of the trial lawyers—the law violated the right to trial by jury.

Hooper's disagreement with the decision was not with the court's concern over the wisdom of the legislation but with their readiness to strike down a validly enacted law of the legislature. It meant that a majority of nine judges could overrule the actions of over 100 elected legislators and the governor. In the meantime, *Business Week* reported that ten insurance companies had pulled out of Alabama. Andrew L. Frey, whom BMW chose to represent it before the U.S. Supreme Court, said, at a news conference in Washington a week after Judge Howard issued his order, "What insurance companies start doing is they pay claims that they believe are fraudulent.

They pay claims that they believe are not covered by the policy. I have one client that has just told their agents in Alabama, pay. Don't deny a claim just because it's fraud." He added: "These are not dishonest, sleazy people. These are honest people running a business. Sure, they're trying to make a profit. A lot of these companies are owned by policy holders. So when you award $15 million in punitive damages to somebody, who's paying for it? All the policy holders." Frey orally argued the case before the U.S. Supreme Court the following week.

In September 1995 a Mobile jury returned a $15 million verdict against Rheem Manufacturing Co. because of a water heater fire that burned a two-year-old. The boy was playing near the water heater when other children spilled gasoline, causing the gas fumes to be ignited by the pilot light. Someone had left an open pail of gasoline on the porch. As the *Montgomery Advertiser* reported it: "The lawsuit contended the pilot light was so close to the ground that it too easily ignited the fumes."[1] The jury awarded $3 million to compensate the family for the child's injuries and $12 million to punish the company for purposely making a water heater that would burn a child.

The *Advertiser* also criticized another case in which a black car dealer sued Ford Motor Company for the failure of his business. The dealer sold Ford cars. His dealership went bankrupt, so he sued Ford and received an $8 million judgment. The crux of the lawsuit was that Ford failed to warn him, when he bought the dealership, that it was more likely to fail because he was black. As the *Advertiser* stated: "Indeed, had Ford told him up front that he was likely to fail because of his race, it might well have been sued then—for discrimination. For treating Foster like any other dealer, by not assuming that he would fail, Ford has been heavily penalized, and ultimately so are consumers who must pay the bill in such cases. Obviously it cannot be in Ford's interest to have dealerships fail, so it is ludicrous to suppose that the company would deliberately engage dealers it didn't think could be successful."[2] The editorial pointed to the perceived problem with the civil justice system in Alabama. "In Alabama, too many judges seemingly shine the shoes and kiss the feet of trial lawyers, who give enormous sums to the judges' campaigns."[3] It quoted Yale Law Professor George Priest as saying that Alabama's punitive damages record was "unparalleled in the history of American jurisprudence."

Hooper defenders appeared. Two filed an action in Montgomery Circuit Court seeking to have Sonny Hornsby declared a "usurper" and Hooper declared the winner of the disputed race. Hooper's son, Perry Hooper, Jr., was one of Judge Hooper's greatest defenders. The *Advertiser* reported that at a bill-signing ceremony on the governor's court reform package at the Capitol in August, Hooper, Jr. exchanged "words" with Democratic Senator Roger Bedford. They supposedly disputed about the bill, but one friend of Hooper's said, perhaps jokingly: "Roger mentioned the name 'Sonny Hornsby' unnecessarily in Perry's presence."[4] At Trinity Presbyterian Church in Montgomery, Perry Hooper, Jr. had earlier exchanged words with Judge Joe Phelps, the judge who had originally issued the temporary restraining order that halted Bennett's counting of the 1994 votes. The Hoopers and Judge Phelps attended the same church at the time of the election dispute.

What was Hooper's attitude about the dispute? He was amazingly sanguine. The *Decatur Daily* interviewed him about the case in July.[5] They quoted him: "You have to be patient. For instance, if you're in a foxhole, you've got to wait for your enemy to do what he's going to do. You've got to be tough on the inside, tough on the outside. I'm a little unusual in this respect. I ran to make a difference—not to be chief justice. I have made a difference no matter what the outcome is." Hooper spoke about how Hornsby's "refusal to surrender his robe" had affected the state's reputation. He then played the NBC news segment that covered the case. He finished his speech with his usual comment on the disputed absentee ballots: "The law is absolutely clear. You're supposed to have these witnesses."

Between 8 and 10 August, the Business Council of Alabama hired the Kitchens Group of Orlando, Florida to randomly interview 600 registered voters in Alabama. The survey had a margin of error of + or — 4.0 percent. In response to the question as to which candidate should be declared the winner, 43% said Hooper, 27% said Hornsby, and 8% said it depended on the absentee ballots. Twenty-three percent said they were unsure. Those statistics were pretty amazing.

In response to the statement, "Republican Perry Hooper should be declared the winner of the race, because he received the most votes in the election," 47 percent said that they strongly agreed and 21% said that they somewhat agreed. That meant 68% of the survey respondents said they agreed Hooper should be declared the winner. People knew there was a dispute in the courts and that it was not as simple as "Who received the most votes?" That 32% who thought either that the courts should finish their review or that Hornsby was correct in wanting the disputed ballots counted. That figure tells me that the media and the bar are wrong about the voters being ignorant of judicial candidates and judicial issues. If they have been ignorant of judicial races in the past, it is because the media did not publicize the candidates or the issues. Unlike the media portrayal, publicity about the courts does not disparage the judicial system, unless you stoop to the tactics used by Sonny Hornsby.

In response to a question about counting the unwitnessed absentee ballots, 37% said they should be counted, 54% said they should not be counted, and the rest were unsure. Ninety percent had no problem agreeing that it was time to settle the issue one way or another.

About a week before the trial in Mobile, the Eleventh Circuit refused to allow the Democrats to check every absentee ballot cast in 1994. Such a massive project was not dispositive of the Eleventh Circuit's question. Such an action would have equated to a ballot-by-ballot election contest, something that would have tended to involve the federal courts in something beyond their jurisdiction. There was the question of whether the Hellums class could replace the Davis class. It had less to do with Davis' death and more with whether Hellums was an adequate representative of the class. Davis had said that he did not know about the absentee ballot requirement and that, therefore, his ignorance should not count

against his vote. Hellums' pleading said that his secretary in-
advertently had not notarized his absentee ballot before mail-
ing it in. That would indicate that either Hellums or his staff
knew of the requirement but forgot to do it.

The first part of the trial before Judge Howard involved
the admission of the affidavits from the local county officials.
Because Hornsby's lawyers challenged several of the affidavits
submitted during discovery, some officials had to come to
court to testify personally. Again, as with the affidavits, the
officials testified uniformly that their county had not regularly
counted unwitnessed, unnotarized absentee ballots in the past.
The following is typical testimony that Judge Howard heard
from each of the county officials who testified:

Q. For twenty years you've done absentee ballots?

A. Yes, sir.

Q. Based on your experience during those twenty years
in Tallapoosa County as an absentee ballot election
official, was it the regular practice to count unwitnessed,
unnotarized absentee ballots?

Q. We've never counted them.

Q. In the November 1994 general election do you have
a judgment as to approximately how many unwitnessed,
unnotarized absentee ballots were excluded initially from
the vote count?

A. A total rejection was thirty-nine, but the ones rejected for not being witnessed or notarized was eleven.

Q. Do you have a particular title in connection with
your work as an absentee election official?

A. For the past eight years I've been chief inspector.

Q. And what duties do you have as chief inspector?

A. I'm to instruct the workers that are working the
absentees and—well, the first thing we do is put them
under oath and then I instruct them as to the rules that
we will follow and the procedures that we will follow
in counting the votes.

Q. Have you ever instructed the absentee workers in your capacity as a chief inspector to count unwitnessed, unnotarized absentee ballots prior to November 1994?

A. No, sir.

Cross-Examination

Q. So you followed whatever instructions were on the ballot itself, the ballot envelope itself?

A. And the Secretary of State's handbook. Evidently the same rules were in both of them.

Q. You say "evidently."

A. Well, I read both of them.[6]

Even Sandra Henderson, the clerk from Wilcox County who would not let the Republican poll watcher challenge any absentee ballots, said that counting the disputed ballots was not a regular practice in or before 1994.[7] The testimony was uniform. None of the counties, except Washington County, had counted such ballots as a regular practice. Each had followed the guidelines laid out in the Secretary of State's *Election Handbook*.

The new class representative, Clarence Hellums, also testified. Remember that in his pleadings to the court, he said that he gave the ballot to his secretary who did not notarize it as he had expected. Here is part of his testimony at trial. He was asked, "Were you aware that your ballot had to be notarized or witnessed for it to be counted?" Hellums replied, "Yes, sir, because it says on there: Signature official. So I would assume—I wasn't aware. I would assume it had to be because that what it says on the form. And it says title official. And always in the past my recollection has been that the lady in the clerk's office signs 'circuit clerk' on there. But your question was whether I have a specific recollection as to this election, and my answer would have to be no."[8] He claimed to have not seen the pleading discussing the inadvertence of his secretary.

Vickie Balough and Brenda Carr, employees in the secretary of state's office, testified that the advice to counties had always been to not count unwitnessed absentee ballots. Jim

Bennett redeemed himself somewhat at the trial before Judge Howard. He testified forthrightly that it was his "understanding that ballots that are not witnessed by two people over the age of eighteen or notarized are not counted prior to the Montgomery County court case [the Reese decision]."[9]

The Marion County Circuit Clerk, Garrard, testified that he normally would screen absentee ballots and send them back to the voter if they were defective. Because he was up for reelection in 1994, he said that nineteen had slipped through and been counted in the original certification. That would hardly demonstrate regular practice; by mistake they were counted. Joy Hill, absentee ballot manager for Elmore County, testified that the regular practice had always been to exclude them.

One circuit clerk became somewhat testy about an affidavit he provided in the case. Fred Posey had been circuit clerk of Autauga County since 1940, with a three-year absence while he was in World War II. His testimony was that his job as circuit clerk was not to exclude certain ballots. His job was to hand the ballots to those who counted absentee ballots, and they decided which ones to exclude. He said that he did not think unwitnessed, unnotarized absentee ballots should be counted because the statute said otherwise. He added that he didn't accept John Bush's interpretation of the absentee ballot statute, nor what the "monkeys" on the Alabama Supreme Court had said in *Williams v. Lide*. On 12 January 1995, the Democrats obtained an affidavit from Posey, in which he said: "In the past, when an absentee ballot was presented to me, I would accept the ballot as long as it was signed, even if it did not have an accompanying notary or witness."[10] The Democrats attempted to use that affidavit to claim that Autauga County had a regular practice of counting unwitnessed absentee ballots, which was diametrically opposed to Posey's deposition testimony on 14 July 1995. Posey's meaning of "accept" was that he would accept the ballots to give to the absentee ballot "tabulators," who would then make the decision not to count ballots that were not in compliance with the law. Posey, a Democrat, did not appreciate the misrepresentation of his position by the democrats.

One of the more prominent witnesses in the case presented some odd testimony in the case. Lieutenant Governor Don Siegelman had been secretary of state from 1979 to 1987 and attorney general from 1987 to 1991. Under his name, the secretary of state's office had published two election handbooks that the county election officials had used to decide which ballots were valid.[11]

He also jointly authored with Attorney General Charlie Graddick a 12 August 1980 memorandum that also said such ballots were not to be counted.[12] The *Montgomery Advertiser* reported the following about his testimony in Mobile: "[T]he judge pointed to a part of Alabama's election handbook that requires absentee ballots to be witnessed, and he characterized Lt. Gov. Siegelman's stand as legal gobbledygook."[13] Siegelman was the Democrats' only witness that they called at the actual trial. They also presented Billy Joe Camp's deposition but did not call him to testify. He was the former secretary of state who said he had not had his ballot witnessed, but when Pryor checked it, he found that it had been witnessed.

Judge Howard asked Siegelman about his interpretation of a statement in the election handbook that unwitnessed absentee ballots are not to be counted: "Aren't you saying it doesn't say what it says?[14] What you said is diametrically opposed to that statement. Why do you say that it doesn't say what it says?" Siegelman specifically denied ever telling an election official to count unwitnessed absentee ballots. He denied ever telling election officials not to follow the handbook's instructions. He testified: "Probably not. But again, I don't even know that I was ever aware of its existence. I probably received a copy. Again, I never—I don't think I ever read it. But it was—but I doubt very seriously if we told them not to rely on it."[15] He said the same thing about the 1986 edition of the handbook. Yet, for eight years, Siegelman was the state's highest official responsible for elections. Did he not take his job seriously enough to study what his own office's handbook instructed county election officials to do with unwitnessed absentee ballots? He said that he didn't even read it. And he testified that if he had been aware of what the handbook said about not counting unwitnessed absentee ballots, he would have instructed election officials to disregard it.[16]

Siegelman, in opposition to the handbook put out by his own office while he was secretary of state, claimed that if an absentee ballot was not properly witnessed, then the absentee ballot manager would check to make sure the voter's name was on the absentee voter list. The absentee ballot election manager would then mark the ballot as a challenged ballot and forward it to the district attorney's office. Nevertheless, Siegelman said the vote would still be counted.

In his "OPINION AND ORDER," Judge Howard wrote about Lt. Gov. Siegelman's testimony regarding the memorandum prepared by him and Graddick and the handbook prepared by Siegelman's office:

> The Court FINDS his testimony to be diametrically opposed to the instructions he issued to election officials while he was Secretary of State and there is no credible evidence he ever communicated his current position to anyone while he was Secretary of State. He failed to provide a rational explanation of his present position and the Court finds his testimony to be unworthy of belief. The memorandum instructs "Circuit Clerks and Registers" not to count ballots that do not comply with Alabama law, that is, ballots which are not signed by the voter, are not witnessed by two witnesses or notarized, and Lieutenant Governor Siegelman's efforts to change the import of such instructions are incredible.

> The Court FINDS Seigelman's [sic] testimony with regard to the Alabama Election Officials' Handbook, prepared by Dr. Mountjoy to be unbelievable.

> Lieutenant Governor Seigleman [sic] testified that he had no recollection of ever having seen any of the three Handbooks [prepared by the Alabama Law Institute]. He testified that his office worked closely with Dr. Mountjoy and Lieutenant Governor Seigleman [sic] "did not trust" the work coming out of the Alabama Law Institute. Lieutenant Governor Seigleman [sic]

testified that had anyone asked him about the Handbooks prepared by the Alabama Law Institute, he would
have instructed them not to rely upon them. However,
he never told any election official not to rely on the
Handbook. Furthermore, Lieutenant Governor
Seigleman [sic] claimed to have no knowledge that the
Alabama Law Institute is a body created by statute "as
an official advisory law revision and law reform agency
of the State of Alabama." Ala. Code § 29-8-1 (1975).
In addition, he was on the governing body of the institute as the Attorney General of Alabama. Id. The
Court FINDS Lieutenant Governor Seigleman's [sic]
testimony with regard to the Alabama Election Handbook bizarre. While the Court recognizes that as an
elected official Governor Siegelman [sic] has been a
part of many organizations that may not have come to
his attention, it stretches credibility to assert that, as
Chief Election Official of the State of Alabama, he
was completely unaware of this publication.[17]

Judge Howard's conclusions, which he put in a written
order dated 29 September 1995 were as follows:

The evidence presented in this case shows that the
rules for counting absentee ballots have been consistently applied by every county, except one, in the State
of Alabama. The practice of the State of Alabama with
regard to absentee ballots contained in affidavit envelopes signed by the voter, but without proper notarization or proper witnessing by two adult witnesses, since
at least 1980, has been to exclude the ballot from the
vote count. The consistent and plain position of the
Secretary of State, the chief election official of the State
of Alabama, is that an absentee ballot must include the
signature of the voter and that signature must be notarized or witnessed by two adult witnesses. The Secretary of State has instructed every voting official in
Alabama to that effect and has provided voters with
the same information. The rule is a "bright-line" rule.
Not one election official told this Court that a ballot
such as the contested ballots would receive treatment
other than to reject the ballot.

The change in the rules has resulted in extreme harm to the citizens of the State of Alabama and to Perry O. Hooper. The voters of Alabama chose Perry Hooper to serve as their next Chief Justice of the Supreme Court. However, through the efforts of those persons who wished to change the results of that election several days after the election had taken place, the voters have been denied their rightfully elected Chief Justice for almost one year. Those who voted for him, as well as Mr. Hooper, have been denied his services and the emoluments that accompany the position. When such harm is wrought by a [sic] offense against the United States Constitution it is incumbent upon a federal court to step in to protect the rights guaranteed to each citizen of this nation. This Court will not shirk its duty.

Judge Howard emphasized in a footnote that any disputed ballots that had slipped in accidentally in some counties were not his concern because his job was to determine Alabama's prior "practice."

Judge Howard denied all of the Hellums class claims. He permanently enjoined Secretary of State Bennett from counting any of the contested ballots cast on 8 November 1994 and ordered Bennett to certify the election for supreme court and treasurer by end of business day, 3 October 1995. He ordered Hooper sworn in as soon after certification as practicable. He ordered him sworn in "*nun pro tunc* 16 January 1995," meaning that he was to be considered chief justice from inauguration day on and entitled to all the compensation and benefits that come with the office.[18] He ordered the same for Lucy Baxley, even though she had already been serving in that office, having been appointed by Governor Fob James. He ordered the Hellums class and the state of Alabama to pay all of the attorney fees.

Judge Reese, upon receiving the order, threw Hornsby's claim for chief justice pay out of court. The trial that was anticipated to last as long as two weeks had lasted three days. The trial was so short because the evidence was so overwhelmingly in Hooper's favor.

Over the weekend, the Democrats obtained a stay of Howard's order from the Eleventh Circuit in Atlanta. Birch and Edmondson no longer sat on the three-judge panel in Atlanta. The three judges that Hooper's and Hornsby's lawyers were to argue before in Atlanta were Judge Gerald Tjoflat, a Carter appointee named Lanier Anderson of Georgia, and a Clinton appointee, a woman named Rosemary Barkett of Florida. We weren't finished yet.

Notes

1. *Montgomery Advertiser*, p. 10A, September 13, 1995.

2. *Montgomery Advertiser*, p. 10A, July 7, 1994.

3. *Montgomery Advertiser*, p. 2F, August 20, 1995.

4. *Montgomery Advertiser*, p. 5A, August 21, 1995.

5. *The Decatur Daily*, p. C1, July 11, 1995.

6. Trial Transcript, pp. 126-27.

The testimony of Wade Acton confirmed Tallapoosa's practice of not counting the disputed ballots: "We followed the book guidelines [Alabama Election Handbook published by the Secretary of State] that they would not be counted." See Trial Transcript, p. 113.

7. Trial Transcript, p. 159.

8. Trial Transcript, p. 196.

9. Trial Transcript, p. 54.

10. Fred Posey Affidavit, January 12, 1995.

11. Forward, Alabama Election Handbook, third ed., 1980, published by the Alabama Law Institute: "The reorganization of this book emanated from a suggestion of Don Siegelman, Alabama Secretary of State, and from interviews with probate judges, ..." The relevant handbook language read: "If, upon examination, the affidavit obviously does not comply with Alabama law; that is, if it is not properly witnessed or notarized, is not signed by the voter, or does not otherwise contain sufficient information to

determine that the person is a qualified elector and is entitled to vote absentee, the ballot should not be counted." Alabama Election Officials' Handbook, produced by Dr. Robert S. Mountjoy, p. 7-6.

12. The language from the joint memorandum stated: "If the ballot does not comply with Alabama law, i.e., it is not properly witnessed or notarized; not signed by the voter, or does not otherwise contain sufficient information to determine that such person is a qualified elector and entitled to vote absentee, the ballot should not be counted. In most other cases, when a ballot is challenged, the ballot should be counted; the affidavit, however, should be marked challenged with the basis of the challenge listed and turned over to the District Attorney for investigation." Memorandum from Attorney General Graddick and Secretary of State Siegelman to "all Circuit Clerks and Registers," August 12, 1980, p. 3.

13. *Montgomery Advertiser,* p. 3B, September 22, 1995.

14. Ibid., See also the trial transcript:

"THE COURT [Judge Howard]: But what you've testified here today is clearly diametrically opposed to his Exhibit 65 which you sent out, along with the Attorney General Graddick, to the voting officials. Now, how are they supposed to know that you mean something entirely different from what you say in the Exhibit 65?" Trial Transcript, p. 543.

15. Trial Transcript, p. 571.

16. Trial Transcript, p. 576.

17. ORDER AND OPINION, Judge Alex Howard, September 29, 1995, pp. 32-35.

18. Interestingly, Hooper's attorneys did not even ask for the past pay and benefits that Howard ordered be given to Hooper. The "nunc pro tunc" language eliminated any concern about Hooper being over 70 years of age at the time of the order. At the time of the inauguration, he was only 69 years of age. Hooper's attorneys had asked Howard to make sure his order considered that potential problem when he issued it.

Back to Atlanta . . .
For the Last Time

On 25 September 1995 the *Birmingham News* printed the question "Wagging the Dog: How long will Alabama Democrats allow the never-ending election to go on?" It argued that the people of Alabama will not blame the plaintiff trial lawyers for the delay in getting the election certified. It said "[t]hey will blame the Democratic Party, whose candidate Hornsby is. That's a party reeling from the emergence of the GOP in the South." It pointed out that Hooper put over forty county officials on the stand to testify, while the Democrats put on one, Siegelman, who ran the most expensive race for lieutenant governor ever and received most of his contributions from lawyers, many of them trial lawyers. The editorial concluded: "This litigation is a farce."

Other newspapers argued the same thing after seeing what the evidence in Mobile revealed. They were frustrated and disgusted before the trial; they were outraged after the trial. An appeal to the Eleventh Circuit meant an additional delay. The people running the show clearly wanted to stretch this out as long as possible. Judge Howard had issued the order on a Friday afternoon. We thought Hooper could be sworn in that day because we thought the counting had been accomplished, and that all we needed was for Secretary of State Bennett to announce the totals for Hooper and Hornsby and certify the winner. But Bennett said it couldn't happen until Monday. Governor James went to Bennett's office to demand an immediate certification. Bennett later argued that his inaction was justified by the Eleventh Circuit's quick ruling to stay Howard's order while the Democrats appealed once again. Bennett said that he "absolutely and resolutely" supported Howard's ruling, but that he would "conduct this certification in the proper and timely manner with no partisan influence from either side."

Hooper still celebrated when he heard about Howard's order. He told the press that the legislature might want to pass a law saying the word "must" means what it says. Statute ° 17-10-7 states that the affidavit must be witnessed or notarized. His response to a question about the dispute tarnishing Alabama's judiciary was: "I think we've had judicial reform"[1] by opening the eyes of the public and electing a Republican to the high court for the first time this century.

The lawyers for both sides returned one last time to Atlanta, on 11 October 1995, to orally argue the case again. The Eleventh Circuit needed to make a decision to either continue a stay of Howard's order, modify the order, or reverse the order. Whatley's argument against Howard's order was more of the same rhetoric he had used before. He claimed that Hooper had not proven the denial of due process to some voters who would have voted if they had known of the relaxed Reese standard for absentee ballots. He claimed that Howard's ruling allowed some voters to disenfranchise others, meaning the unwitnessed ballots did not get counted. He tried to scare the judges by saying the Eleventh Circuit was the only circuit in the country to adopt such a practice. He asked for relief under the Fourteenth Amendment to the U.S. Constitution for his clients. He again argued about different practices in the counties, such as whether or not a county rejected a ballot because the notary did not put a seal on the ballot envelope or the notary's term had expired. Whatley, under questioning from the judges, had to admit that allowing the counting of votes that weren't counted in the past makes an election change.

Bill Pryor, representing the attorney general's office, argued zealously for the rights of the citizens of Alabama to have the person they elected almost a year earlier sworn into office. He argued that the Alabama Supreme Court had been mislead by the cleverly prepared affidavits drummed up by Martin and Mills. Bert Jordan mentioned the fact that they need not prove that anyone relied on the statute and, thereby, didn't file a ballot. It was sufficient that someone could have relied upon it. In this case, there was no small change but a systematic change in the manner of recording votes.

When Whatley claimed that the Alabama Supreme Court had said that some counties had counted the disputed ballots and some had not, Judge Barkett asked, "But wasn't the original allegation filed by the first complainant [Davis] in the Montgomery Circuit Court [Reese] that these votes had not been counted in the past?" All he could say was "yes." Judge Anderson added that it looked as if the incidents in the affidavits filed in the Montgomery Circuit Court in January were mere isolated aberrations from the regular practice anyway.

Most of Whatley's legal argument involved matters the Eleventh Circuit had already decided back in January. The chief concern in September was whether Alabama's prior practice had been consistent or not.

Quickly, on 13 October in fact, the Eleventh Circuit issued its decision. It ruled for Hooper: "First, the district court's findings of fact are not clearly erroneous; rather, its findings are supported overwhelmingly by the evidence." In a footnote, the Eleventh Circuit addressed the discovery issue.[2] The opinion stated that the Hellums class was not denied due process of law because a small number of contested ballots (49) had slipped through.

The Eleventh Circuit noted that it had already taken judicial notice of the issue of the reliance by voters who did not vote, but who would have voted if they had known of the relaxed Reese standard. At trial, the Hellums class did not speak up about the lack of evidence on that issue. Nevertheless, it did not matter because Hooper and the Roe class had included voters who had had their vote diluted by the improper ballots. As for the evidence, "The facts establish [sic] on remand in the district court were stronger in favor of the Roe Class than the prior panel could have expected."

If the Eleventh Circuit directed Howard's court to dismiss this case, it would leave Hooper and the Roe class of voters "without an adequate forum for the vindication of its federal constitutional claims." As for the answer from the Alabama Supreme Court, which the Hellums Class asked the Eleventh Circuit to give effect to, the court stated:

What the Hellums Class ignores is that the Alabama
Supreme Court, in answering our question, construed
an Alabama statute; the court did not, and was not
called upon to, decide the counting of the contested
ballots in the November 8, 1994, general election—in
the face of Ala. Code § 17-10-4 and in the face of a
uniform state-wide practice of excluding such ballots—
infringed the Roe Class' constitutional rights.

In a footnote, the court noted:

As noted *supra*, the Alabama Supreme Court, in answering our certified question, stated that, in the past,
election officials in some counties included in their
vote totals ballots such as those contested in this case.
In making this statement, the Alabama Supreme Court
relied upon some affidavits the Odom plaintiffs [Davis
Class in Reese's court] attached to their motion for
summary judgment in that case. However, these affiants
were not subjected to cross examination in Odom, nor
did the opposing party have an opportunity to oppose
or otherwise contest same. After we remanded the in-
stant case for trial, these affiants were examined under
oath in the district court—whether given in answer to
interrogatories, on deposition, or at trial—was, contrary to their affidavits in Odom, that their counties
never counted absentee ballots such as those at issue
here or that they had no knowledge of how such ballots were treated. Thus, the factual predicate for the
Alabama Supreme Court's observations with respect to
past practice was demonstrated in the district court to
have been erroneous.

The Eleventh Circuit affirmed Howard's order unanimously and *in toto*. On 14 October the *Montgomery Advertiser*
headlined on its first page "Panel: Hooper winner." The *Birmingham News* had a somewhat more cautious first page headline: "Hooper views ruling as 'an end' to battle." Hooper's
comment: "I felt it was very clear all along. We always had the
facts and we always had the law." Even the *Anniston Star*,
which had done its best to cast a good light on Hornsby

during the case, quoted Glenn Murdock: "Everything that I've believed about this case has just been ratified and it has been ratified by a panel that consists of two Democrats and one Republican."

The Democrats said that they were seeking an immediate emergency stay from the U.S. Supreme Court. It looked like it was over, but it wasn't yet. On 14 October U.S. Supreme Court Justice Anthony Kennedy granted the stay. One of Hornsby's attorneys, Sam Heldman, said he thought it was "a very good sign" that the nation's highest court may want to hear the case. Bennett had said that he would be able to certify the vote totals on Monday, 16 October; now that would not be possible.

Whatley had delivered the request to the U.S. Supreme Court at 11:00 A.M. Saturday, 14 October, on behalf of members of the Alabama Democratic party. The standard for determining whether to grant a stay is "irreparable harm." Hooper's attorneys worked frantically to get the cases that the Democrats had neglected to put in their brief to the U.S. Supreme Court in an attempt to lift the stay. In response to Hooper's attorneys, Sam Heldman said, "We would have a fellow sitting on the Alabama Supreme Court making decisions who had no right to be there and had no right to make those decisions. That would be an utterly horrible thing for the whole state. It would be just as bad as someone waltzing into the governor's office and saying 'I'm the governor now.' "[3] I couldn't have said it better myself, but I would have applied it to Hornsby's time on the bench the previous nine months.

Nevertheless, Kennedy issued the order staying Howard's injunction. The 19 October 1995 *Montgomery Independent* commented on Hooper's temperament after the Democrats obtained an emergency stay from Justice Kennedy: "Hooper, especially, would have reason to be catatonic. But through it all, he has maintained remarkable composure, certain of ultimate victory and seemingly impervious to personal anguish from the year-long grind." The editor, Tom Johnson, also reminded his readers that Hornsby had said he would abide by the Eleventh Circuit's decision in the case. Johnson's comment: "Something happened, perhaps a still unfulfilled political death wish or a hijacking of the case by trial lawyers who fear the loss of a friendly Chief Justice."

On Monday, 16 October 1995, Hooper went on Governor James' radio show. On that show, a caller asked Hooper what he thought of caning prison inmates. This was about the time that a young American got caned in Singapore for vandalizing cars. Hooper said, "It's something to be considered." In a *Montgomery Advertiser* editorial cartoon, Hooper is shown sitting at a radio station answering that question, but contemplating Hornsby in his mind.

On 19 October 1995, while preparing his garden for the planting of 500 pink "sweet Williams" behind his house, Hooper learned that the U.S. Supreme Court had lifted the stay, allowing him to be sworn in as chief justice of the Alabama Supreme Court. Hornsby phoned in his congratulations to Hooper that evening. The 20 October 1995 *Montgomery Advertiser* headline read: "Hooper's path finally clears." The article stated that "[t]he 70-year-old former circuit judge said he was inspired by a Bible passage during his nearly year-long wait to take office: *Isaiah 41:30*, which states in part, 'But they that wait upon the Lord shall renew their strength.' " Jim Bennett said, "I look forward to finally bringing these races to their proper conclusion and allowing the voices of Alabama voters to be heard."

The *Advertiser* quoted a politician who opposed Hooper's victory, Mr. Spencer Hogue, one of the "Marion Three," who were prosecuted and ultimately escaped charges of voter fraud in the 1980s, said, "I'm sure most of them who voted absentee in Perry County supported Hornsby. Their intentions should have been allowed, as far as I'm concerned."[4] The *Birmingham News* quoted Hooper's response to a question about Hornsby's lawyers continuing the fight with the U.S. Supreme Court: "I'm trusting the Lord to take care of it. When the Lord opens the door, you can't close it. It's open for me now."[5] As for the democrats' theory about counting unwitnessed absentee ballots, he said, "I've been saying for twelve months, you can't make chicken salad without chicken, and that's what they've been trying to do."

Hornsby, speaking through the Administrative Office of Court's public information officer, said that he wanted there to be a smooth transition for Hooper. He said that he had been doing work at home in recent days. In fact, Hornsby had already moved some of his personal belongings, like pictures, back to his home in Tallahassee.[6] He also told the Associated Press that he asked all court employees to cooperate fully with Hooper "so our courts can deliver fair and equitable judicial services in a timely manner."[7] Joe Whatley, combative to the end, said, "I think these 1,700 people are entitled to have their ballots counted." But he had to admit that the U.S. Supreme Court's decision to lift the stay "indicates that they may not be willing to take the case." Al Agricola said that the vacation of the emergency stay indicated that the chances the U.S. Supreme Court might later unseat Hooper were "less than minuscule."

Glenn Murdock said Hooper's victory was one for "the rule of law." He added: "The Democrat Party bosses attempted to steal this election from all the voters of Alabama. They thought they could hoodwink the public and didn't give the people of Alabama credit for being able to figure out what they were up to." Deputy Attorney General Bill Pryor, who had handled the case for Jeff Sessions, said, "I am very happy for the people of Alabama that this case is finally over and that the plain will of the Alabama Legislature that unwitnessed absentee ballots not be counted has been followed." Governor James blamed the delay on "misconduct, if not corruption" on the part of some judges. He said, "What is happening here begs remedy, it begs discussion, it begs debate and it begs scrutiny by the Legislature."[8] Jeff Sessions later said that "[t]he Alabama Supreme Court got caught with its hand in the cookie jar by the U.S. Supreme Court."[9] He added: "Now, Ingram and the three others who joined him in supporting Hornsby are going to pay the price on election day." Justice Ingram, who would be next up for reelection in 1998, shot back: "I said on several occasions that I was voting on something bigger than Hornsby and Hooper. It went to the right of people who are qualified electors to have their votes counted when they ordered absentee ballots and substantially complied with the laws of Alabama."[10] Sessions, speaking with unusual candor, also said that he thought the Alabama Supreme Court's opinion was an abuse of office designed to assist a friend.

On 20 October 1995, nine months and four days after the inauguration day when he should have been sworn in, Perry O. Hooper, Sr., with his wife Marilyn, his sons, their wives, and their children standing by him, was sworn in as chief justice of the Alabama Supreme Court. As a gesture of respect for the three branches of government, he had the governor swear him in with a representative of the judiciary and the legislature also present. His brood of children, and grandchildren surrounded him, causing Governor James to exclaim: "I've never had to swear in a whole team before."[11] Hooper received a standing ovation from the audience that packed into the Alabama Supreme Court's chambers. The 21 October 1995 *Birmingham News* reported that, as Hooper finished the oath, he spoke the words "so help me God" with a "louder and more powerful voice, pausing briefly after each word as though nailing it down as the most important part of his pledge to the state."[12] In his speech, Hooper said, "You didn't elect somebody who thinks he's smart, but I'm smart enough to know where the power comes from—the Lord." He said that God was in charge and that he found comfort during the legal battle reading the book of Job. He said that he told himself: "Man, Hooper, compared to him, you had it easy." He thanked his wife Marilyn: "She never lost faith. She stuck with it. She didn't waver."[13]

Glenn Murdock also spoke about the fight for honest elections being an ongoing one: "Somehow, dead people are still voting, and nursing home residents are still voting without their knowledge."[14] The *Montgomery Advertiser* editors wrote a scathing editorial in the 23 October 1995 edition. It is worth quoting:

> Hornsby, Trial Lawyers Defiled Court.
>
> Usurper Sonny Hornsby has been tossed out at last. Good riddance. Mark Antony, Oliver Cromwell, and Saddam Hussein had more claim to office than Hornsby.

Hornsby's unconscionable and unseemly attempts to hang on to the office of chief justice of the Alabama Supreme Court failed Friday when election officials certified Republican Perry Hooper Sr. as the winner of the November 1994 election and he was sworn into office.

The certification came one day after the U.S. Supreme Court lifted an emergency stay that had been granted to Hornsby's side in the dispute.

Hornsby has put another nail in the coffin of the state Democratic Party. By dragging this case through venue after venue, by delaying the implementation of the voters' will by almost a full year, Hornsby has reinforced the negative image of state Democrats as the party that tries to sidestep the voters to get its candidates elected.

That image was born in the handpicking of Democratic legislative candidates by the party hierarchy in 1983. It grew uglier when a handful of party leaders set aside the Democratic primary victory of Charlie Graddick for governor in 1986. By clinging to office like a limpet clinging to a slimy rock, Hornsby made the image hideous.

Hornsby also has seriously damaged the image of the trial lawyers with whom he is so closely identified, and that is one result of this fiasco over which we shed no tears.

The reputation of Montgomery Circuit Judge Gene Reese, who started this fiasco by ordering defective ballots counted, also has been sullied. So has the reputation of the Alabama Supreme Court where three of the four justices who supported Reese's position had contributed to Hornsby's campaign.

Himself a former trial lawyer, maybe soon to become one again, Hornsby led the Supreme Court in the dismantling of tort reform measures passed by the Legislature in 1987, thereby making it once again easier for trial lawyers to garner huge judgments in civil lawsuits.

His efforts to scuttle the will of the voters in the 1994 election could be seen as an indication of just how important his hanging onto the chief justice's seat was to trial lawyers. With him gone, it becomes more likely that any tort reform legislation that pro-business forces could pass in the near future would not be quickly undone by the Supreme Court.

Now that Hooper has been sworn in as the winner, it's time to focus on two reforms. The first is the judicial election process—a process that included disgraceful phone soliciting of lawyers by Hornsby himself and equally disgraceful ads by Hornsby and his trial lawyer buddies. The second is reform of Alabama's tort laws, the issue that caused the trial lawyers to dig in their heels. Hornsby's court has presided over a state where punitive damages are awarded 10 times more often than in the average state.

Cleaning house began with the ouster of Hornsby. It should continue with election reform and tort reform.[15]

The *Birmingham News*, with a little more equanimity, advised Hooper to be neither the pro-business chief justice nor the pro-trial lawyer chief justice, something with which Hooper whole-heartedly agreed.

Notes

1. *Montgomery Advertiser*, p.5A, September 30, 1995.

2. "The Hellums class made no showing that it was likely that a significant number of nonconforming envelopes would be uncovered; moreover, the testimony of the election officials before the court, considered as a whole, demonstrated no likelihood that a significant number of nonconforming ballots existed. Finally, we note that John Davis, in the complaint he and Michael Odom filed in *Odom v. Bennett*, alleged that the election officials in all of Alabama's 67 counties were rejecting the contested ballots on the instructions of the Secretary of State."

3. *Birmingham News*, p. A3, October 16, 1995.

4. *Montgomery Advertiser,* p. 3B, October 20, 1995.

5. *Birmingham News,* p. 1, October 20, 1995.

6. *Birmingham News,* p.9A, October 20, 1995.

7. *Montgomery Advertiser,* p. 1, October 21, 1995.

8. *Montgomery Advertiser,* p. 1, October 21, 1995.

9. Ibid., p. 1, October 24, 1995.

10. Ibid., p. 7A.

11. *Montgomery Advertiser,* "Under the Dome," p.5A, October 23, 1995.

12. *Birmingham News,* p. 1, October 21, 1995.

13. Ibid., p. 10A.

14. Ibid.

15. *Montgomery Advertiser,* p. 8A, October 23, 1995.

Chapter Sixteen

Judges and Lawyers

You can find the keys for selecting judges in the law of Moses:

> Take you wise men, and understanding, and known among your tribes, and I will make them rulers over you. And ye answered me, and said, "The thing which thou has spoken is good for us to do." So I took the chief of your tribes, wise men, and known, and made them heads over you, captains over thousands, and captains over hundreds, and captains over fifties, and captains over tens, and officers among your tribes. And I charged your judges at that time, saying, "Hear the causes between your brethren, and judge righteously between every man and his brother, and the stranger that is with him. Ye shall not respect persons in judgment; but ye shall hear the small as well as the great; ye shall not be afraid of the face of man; for the judgment is God's: and the cause that is too hard for you, bring it unto me, and I will hear it."[1]

God also told Moses that the leaders and judges were to be God-fearing.[2]

The word "autonomy" comes from two Greek words, *auto* meaning "self" and *nomos* meaning "law." The only way to overcome autonomy is the law of God. An institution can be autonomous, just like an individual. To rebel against God by ignoring his law and authority is evil, just as direct disobedience of his law is. In fact, ignoring God's law altogether is probably a greater evil, because it means you have rebelled against God's rule entirely. Once you set up a society of autonomous individuals, you have chaos; each individual is a god to himself or herself. The next level of authority, say the police, can restore some order, but what is to keep the police from becoming a law unto themselves? As you can see from the Hornsby-Hooper debacle, the courts can become autonomous also. Without the law of God, a society ultimately has no law.

A judge that fears God will not likely neglect justice and mercy in his judgments. Notice that Moses chose men that were already leaders in the community. What makes a wise and understanding man? Three years of law school? Working at a high-powered law firm? Those activities may produce legal technicians but not necessarily wise men. "The fear of the Lord is the beginning of wisdom."[3] Moses' choosing of the judges did not mean the people had no vote. That would be reading too much into the passage.

If our society has come to the point where only the lawyers can understand the workings of the legal system enough to make competent judges, then the lawyers have themselves to thank for that development. The more complex the system, the more laymen need lawyers. The more laymen need lawyers, the more money lawyers make.

Without God, the individual, or the institution or the society has become a law unto itself. King David said, "Oh how I love thy law; it is my meditation all the day." You cannot avoid a philosophical or religious slant to your thinking. Your mind is not a blank slate. What is the correct standard for judging our thinking? Without God's law, we have nothing by which to judge our thought. We end up calling evil good and good evil.[4]

Are there consequences to obeying God? Are there consequences to a society when its judges disobey God's law and replace it with their own law?

The key to sound jurisprudence is not just following the law. It is following God's law. Any man who does not have the Bible as his interpretative grid does not fear God. He does not need to be a judge. But who chooses the judges? The people? The governor? A committee? In a society that has already cordoned off a particular group of people and favored that group as the only group from which judges may be chosen, the people have lost most of their right to choose. When all others are forbidden from participating in judging, no matter how

God-fearing or wise they may be, then the society has already gone far from the ideal set by Moses. It would be a travesty to further distance that group from the people and limit the choice the voters have with respect to the judges who will rule them.

If the lawyers, the judge-trainees, are already trained at godless, liberal institutions accredited by the American Bar Association (ABA), then removing them even further from the voters will not solve the problem of a politicized judiciary. A politicized judiciary is the natural outgrowth of a society of diverse religions and opinions. You can not prevent political debate in such a society. And it is foolish to attempt to do so. The people can see when their liberties and principles are being eroded by an elite.

The ABA is the leading institution of the lawyer-elite. It threatened to remove accreditation from law schools that allowed the military to recruit law students for the JAG Corps on law school campuses. Why? Because the military thinks that homosexuality is incompatible with military service, a standard that still has a fragile grip on the Biblical heritage this nation once enjoyed. I have included in an endnote some other examples of what elitist legal thinking can do to one's standards and morals.[5] The ABA is the organization that determines what type of law schools we have in this country. I know that the ABA's stand on homosexuality is opposed to the standards of most Alabamians. I think it opposes the values of most Americans.

Hooper was the poster boy for those who want to change the method of selecting judges in Alabama. The best proposal has been the Missouri Plan. According to that plan, a nominating committee would propose a list of names from which the governor would choose an appointee. That appointee would sit as a judge for a few years, setting all sorts of precedent with his votes, then he would face a "retention election." In other words, if after test driving him for a few years, you don't like him (or her), you can reject him.

Those who propose such plans constantly wring their hands about the money and the publicity and the campaigns that depreciate the reputation of the judiciary in the eyes of the public. But the public is not that fragile. They know a dud when they see one, and they know that if they vote for the right person it can reorient the judiciary and restore its reputation. That's what happened in 1994. The people rejected Hornsby and chose Hooper.

The problem is that the media and the legal establishment think you the voters are too ignorant to make such decisions. Yet when the issues of a judicial campaign get a full airing before the public, so that the voters can be educated about the candidates, the media and legal experts complain about how all the debate and controversy are ruining the reputation of the judiciary. But what about covering up the problems in the judiciary? Does that somehow enhance the judiciary's reputation? Does the bar of Alabama believe that Hornsby was a decent fellow, badly maligned by Hooper? Or was the real Hornsby unseen by the public until Hooper, not an appointing committee, smoked him out? Which would have been better for the judiciary, hiding Hornsby's flaws or exposing them?

Future judges, under an appointment plan, will stop seeking the electorate's approval and will simply shift their campaigns to where the power shifts, either to a committee or the governor. The politics will still go on. It will simply be secret, out of the public's eye, where it's "supposed" to be.

Arizona, where the judges are appointed, is a good example of how the shift works regarding issues other than the election of judges. In 1996, an initiative, *Proposition 102*, was on the ballot to require juveniles ages fifteen and over to be prosecuted as adults if charged with murder, rape, or armed robbery. Judges, in particular Arizona Supreme Court Chief Justice Feldman and Maricopa County Presiding Judge Foreman, mounted a massive campaign to oppose the initiative. Chief Justice Feldman called the initiative "frightening."

The state bar, which is supported by the mandatory dues of every lawyer in the state of Arizona, provided $20,000 to the fight against the initiative. Arizona had rules limiting the political activities of sitting judges. In August 1996, when this anti-*Proposition 102* campaign was getting started, the committee of judges who decides how to apply those rules changed them. They said that judges could engage in partisan activities. They could raise money, speak at partisan political events, and lead the campaign against the initiative without fear of being disciplined for violating the rules against judges getting involved in political activity. Fortunately for Arizonans, and in spite of the massive media blitz by the bench and bar, two thirds of Arizonans voted for the initiative.

Even with an appointment system, Arizona could not rid itself of dirty, politicized judicial activity. Don't think that couldn't happen in Alabama, or any other state for that matter.

Even if you have retention elections, someone has to educate you about the judge they oppose. That costs money. How does the judge defend himself or herself from such ads? He isn't really supposed to run a campaign because he was appointed. The trial lawyers will create some sort of front group to oppose pro-tort reform judges. No matter what, if there's money or power involved, it will get politicized. The voter just won't have as much voice as before.

Since the 1996 presidential election and the criticism of certain judges at that time, I have read many legal magazines—the *ABA Journal* and all sorts of legal and judicial publications. In lockstep, they have joined together in a rallying cry for "judicial independence." But do they want judicial independence or judicial autonomy? Public criticism of the legal community and the judiciary has had no effect, not a dent. They have not sat back and evaluated themselves to see if there is a problem. Diverse opinions and religions will create conflict, especially in the legal world where the force of civil government is used to coerce people to do what is "right." Forbidding criticism is not the way to deal with such conflict.

When criticism comes, the legal and judicial communities circle the wagons. They do not consider it the time to see if the values of the judges and lawyers have become so estranged from the rest of society that tyranny is budding. It is time for a public relations blitz. Tell everyone they just don't understand how much good the lawyers are doing. When judges let hardened murderers go with a slap on the wrist, it is because the judge was following the best precedent from the U.S. Supreme Court, protecting the civil liberties of us all, and finding the best way to reincorporate a productive member of society back into the mainstream. The ignorant masses simply need reeducation. Instead of reeducation camps, they send out press releases and editorials and TV ads, telling us what we need to know about how wonderful lawyers and judges are and how critical "judicial independence" is to preserving Western society. It's just like the trial lawyers warning us about impending Armageddon because the right to trial by jury is slipping away when the legislature enacts caps on punitive damages. When an ignorant jury in the rural hinterlands of Alabama awards $50 million dollars to the plaintiff, the jury is considered an amazing and wise method for obtaining truth and justice. But when the electorate decides that lawyers and judges are going too far and want to vote in tort reform, or at least judges who agree with tort reform, then the public simply isn't prepared to make those difficult choices. It's all spin. And it's about money and power.

Lawyers will never agree that it's about money. Rights to a jury trial (and to make a million dollars as a plaintiff) are being attacked by the barbarians at the gate. At one time in this country, lawyers could not charge fees for their work. Some would argue that the only reason for having an organized bar is to restrict entry into the profession for the purpose of keeping legal fees high.[6]

One group of people must not be allowed to view the judicial system as their own playground where their craft and wit can change the rules to help their friends or provide themselves more income or political power. That was what was at stake in the Hooper-Hornsby conflict. Would justice win out? Or would a special interest group foist its own interests on the rest of the state, at the expense of justice and democracy? Thankfully, justice won out in that case. What about next time? What about you? What standard do you live by? What standard do you believe judges should rule by? Does it matter?

Notes

1. King James Bible, Deuteronomy 1:13-17.

2. New King James Bible, Exodus 18:21: "Moreover you shall select from all the people able men, such as fear God, men of truth, hating covetousness; and place such over them to be rulers of thousands, rulers of hundreds, rulers of fifties, and rulers of tens."

3. King James Bible, Proverbs 9:10.

4. New King James Bible, Isaiah 5:20: "Woe to those who call evil good, and good evil; Who put darkness for light, and light for darkness; Who put bitter for sweet, and sweet for bitter!"

5. Here is what a well-known law professor describes as a good way to change society in order to advance homosexual rights: "The standard pattern is judicial recognition of human rights, followed by gradual public recognition that widespread practices are shameful and intolerant. Then comes political victories and long periods, often decades, of fighting over the details." Professor Laurence Tribe, Harvard Law School, quoted in USA Today, Wednesday, September 11, 1996, page 4A.

John Chipman Gray, another Harvard professor of law, said, ". . . [T]he law is made up of rules for decision which courts lay down; that all such rules are Law; that rules for conduct which courts do not apply are not Law; that the fact that the courts apply rules is what makes them Law; that there is no mysterious entity 'The Law' apart from these rules; and that the judges are rather the creators than the discoverers of the Law." In other words, there is no such thing as God's law. It's all man-made— by the judges. He said this at Columbia University in 1909. The process of taking over the law schools has been occurring for a long time.

What happens to people when they go to law school? Something definitely happens. Here is a high profile example. U.S. Supreme Court Justice Anthony Kennedy teaches summer classes in Salzburg, Austria. Here is a paragraph from an article about Justice Kennedy: "The spectacle of a Supreme Court Justice publicly agonizing about the merits of his own decision is unusual in itself, but just the week before I arrived in Salzburg, Justice Kennedy had unburdened himself to his students even more dramatically. The students were especially struck, they told me by his fervor in discussing his decision in the 1992 abortion case, *Planned Parenthood v. Casey*, in which he had changed his position unexpectedly and cast a crucial vote to uphold the core of *Roe v. Wade*. If a member of his family ever became pregnant, Justice Kennedy said, he would do his best to persuade her to keep the child. He would offer to adopt the baby, even to rear it himself, rather than sanction *what he fervently believed was the taking of innocent life*. At this point, students recall, Justice Kennedy's eyes filled with tears and his voice broke. But when it came time to decide the abortion case, Kennedy said, *he couldn't impose his personal views on the nation*." (Emphasis added.) "The Agonizer," Jeffrey Rosen, The New Yorker, Nov. 11, 1996. To show the absolute denial of morality the above story represents, I have taken the liberty to replace some words in Justice Kennedy's talk and put it into a different historical context: "Justice Kennedy said, he would do his best to persuade the concentration camp guards to not send the Jews into the gas chamber." I have no reason to doubt that Justice Kennedy has the sincerest belief that abortion is the taking of a human life. But that is exactly the problem. If he believes that, then *Roe v. Wade* cannot be constitutional. No one has asked him to "impose his personal views on the nation," just a rational interpretation of the law and the constitution that will protect the nation from disastrous decisions like *Roe*. What does he think *Roe* did? It imposed someone's personal view on the nation in a most iniquitous way. But it appears that law school did such a good job of muddling his thinking that he equated a prior decision of the U.S. Supreme Court with supreme truth.

"Frankly, I have heard and read enough negative commentary about lawyers to last me a lifetime; we have colleagues who are working everyday to make this state a better place, and it is high time we talked about it." "Alabama Lawyer," Nov. 1996, President's Page. Of course, lawyers working to make the world a better place is part of the problem. Whose idea of a better place are we talking about? When judges do that, it is called judicial activism. When lawyers do it, it is called making a living. Ironically, the very next paragraph in his article talks about the State Bar supported proposal that Alabama change to an appointment/retention-election system for selecting judges. Yet, the author, Warren Lightfoot, is one of the better lawyers in the state and was recently President of the Alabama State Bar.

When it comes to criticizing judges, the July 1996 "Alabama Lawyer" summed up the comments of N. Lee Cooper, president-elect of the American Bar Association and member of the Alabama State Bar: "[T]he political rhetoric is harmful. President Bill Clinton and Republican presidential candidate Bob Dole are 'irresponsible' to attack the federal judiciary as 'causing' crime, Cooper said. It is imperative that the federal judiciary remain free from political pressure, because only an independent judiciary can preserve constitutional freedoms,. . . ."

One of the biggest news items of this decade is the ethical behavior (or lack thereof) of President Clinton and his wife. People can argue that Clinton's presidency resulted from a popular election. I would like to point out just one thing to you. The Clintons are both lawyers.

"A campaign promise to "be tough on crime" or "to enforce the death penalty" is evidence of bias that should disqualify a candidate from sitting in criminal cases,' Supreme Court Justice John Paul Stevens told an American Bar Association audience in August, ..." *Montgomery Advertiser*, Sunday, December 1, 1996, page 3E.

6. Herbert M. Kritzer, "Rethinking barriers to legal practice," JUDICATURE: The Journal of the American Judicature Society, Vol. 81, No. 3, November-December 1997.

The Aftermath

Perhaps the greatest lesson from this 1994 chief justice election was that monopoly political power can lead to an autonomous mindset. It can lead to lawlessness in the name of law. Hooper checked the judicial power that one party had held for over one hundred years. After most of the controversy had ended, he called himself "some crazy old man" who decided to run for chief justice and who just happened to win. He had taken on the most powerful machine in Alabama politics, the plaintiff trial lawyers, a group that would stop at nothing to defeat its opposition, a group that was well financed beyond measure. People had warned him that the trial lawyers would trash him and his family thoroughly. But Hooper had a mission—to make a statement about Alabama's judiciary. He had a faith—"that all things work together for good to those that love God and are the called according to His purpose."[1] He quoted Sophocles often during this ordeal: "One must wait until the evening to see how splendid the day has been." One man had the courage to oppose a seemingly invincible judicial powerhouse, and God used him to expose that monopoly.

The *Wall Street Journal,* Southeast Edition, 27 December 1995, named Hooper one of its "Winners" in the southeast for 1995. The 25 December 1995 *National Law Journal* named Hooper one of its "Newsmakers" and quoted the following statement by him at his swearing in: "When I got through reading the book of Job, I said, 'Man, Hooper, you had it easy.' "

Rumor had it that before the 1994 election, Hornsby had his eyes set upon a U.S. Senate seat, following in the footsteps of retired U.S. Senator Howell Heflin, who had also served as Alabama's chief justice in the 70s. During this litigation,

Hornsby was almost unanimously vilified in the press and on the streets. On the date Hooper was sworn in, Hornsby was nowhere to be found. He called Hooper the day the Supreme Court denied the *certiorari* petition to congratulate him. Hornsby was not seen for a long time thereafter. He has appeared at a couple of state bar functions, but he has clearly been out of circulation ever since the U.S. Supreme Court lifted the emergency stay. His attorneys could have attempted to petition the U.S. Supreme Court for a full review of the case, but they saw the writing on the wall when that court lifted the stay. It meant that that court did not think that he could succeed on the merits of his arguments. Hornsby did eventually get some good news. In the latter part of 1997, a special court of retired judges, appointed to decide the appeal of Hornsby's complaint for pay, stated that he could be paid for the time he served as chief justice between January 1995 and October 1995, even though he had not been elected to the office.

Here are some interesting statistics about Hooper's victory. He was the first man in eighty-nine years to defeat a standing chief justice, the first challenger to beat any justice in forty-two years, the first Republican justice or chief justice on the Alabama Supreme Court since Reconstruction, and one of only three Republican chief justices in Alabama's history. Other than Hooper, there have been only six chief justices this century. Hornsby also set records. He was one of only two chief justices voted out of office this century.

After the 8 November 1994 election, an Alabama Senator in the Montgomery delegation named Larry Dixon introduced a bill requiring identification of voters by a photo ID at each polling place. Such a procedure would prevent an imposter from voting in someone else's place. The black legislative delegation alleged that such a law would intimidate black voters, especially those old enough to remember the days of Jim Crow and the impediments placed in the way of blacks that made it impossible for them to vote. The Legislative Black Caucus threatened to go to Washington and get Janet Reno to not grant preclearance to any new law of that kind. The bill never passed the legislature.

A problem still existed after Howard's ruling. Reese's order and the U.S. Attorney General's preclearance of that order was still in effect. Howard ruled that it could not have retroactive effect. Now many were concerned that it would facilitate voter fraud by making it easier. An Alabama legislator named Jack Venable offered a bill that would change the language on the absentee ballot. It passed and was signed by Governor James in 1996. The absentee envelope now says in bold capital letters:

> IF YOUR AFFIDAVIT IS NOT SIGNED (OR MARKED), OR IF YOUR AFFIDAVIT IS NOT WITNESSED BY TWO WITNESSES 18 YEARS OF AGE OR OLDER OR A NOTARY PUBLIC OR OTHER OFFICER AUTHORIZED TO AC-KNOWLEDGE OATHS, PRIOR TO BEING DE-LIVERED OR MAILED TO THE ABSENTEE ELECTION MANAGER, YOUR BALLOT WILL NOT BE COUNTED.

Under the most liberal substantial compliance standard, it would be hard for any judge to interpret that language to allow the counting of unwitnessed absentee ballots. The Alabama Legislature also restored a weak version of an impeachment law for judges, something the 1970s judicial article had eliminated.

In October 1996, the Alabama State Bar began an unprecedented investigation into the juries of Barbour County. It subpoenaed 150 people who had been involved in lawsuits in the county. About a month later, Judge William Robertson, Jere Beasley's former law partner, and the only circuit judge in the county, announced that he would retire. He explained that his decision had been made long before this investigation and therefore had nothing to do with the investigation.

Hooper, after becoming chief justice, went on to appoint a Commission to review Judicial Elections and how judicial candidates should conduct them. He presided over the BMW case after the U.S. Supreme Court remanded it back to the Alabama Supreme Court declaring, for the first time in history, that the punitive award in that case violated due process of law. The Alabama Supreme Court's review of that case, as well as others, made it clear that the courts could enact tort reform as well as or better than the legislature. He and Justice Harold See were also instrumental in ensuring that the absentee ballot law was properly interpreted by the courts. In *Taylor v. Cox*, a candidate attempted to have an Alabama Court put a loose interpretation on the requirement that the voter "personally" sign the absentee ballot application. The supreme court reversed. Its approach to voting law had come full circle.

Hornsby and his allies had not only fought a losing legal battle, but their very determination to resist his removal from office at any cost ended up costing them an enormous amount of political capital. It is arguable that they knew they would eventually lose, but they wanted to delay the inevitable as long as possible and allow Hornsby to continue to sit on certain cases "important" to them. But if this was their strategy, it was extremely shortsighted. Neither the people of Alabama nor the courts looked kindly upon their attempt to perpetuate a judicial coup. I don't think they had expected the backlash to be so severe.

Brad Moody, a political analyst at Auburn University at Montgomery, said, "I think the dispute does more damage to the people who are perceived as Sonny Hornsby supporters . . . the Democrats. . . ." He added: "They would have been better off six months ago to say we don't want to drag this out. The vast majority of voters feel this thing should have been settled a long time ago. They are going to blame the pro-trial lawyer judges for extending it." University of Alabama political analyst, William Stewart, said that Hornsby "seemed to fight too hard to stay in office. I think he went on too long. It was obvious for him to win, they were going to have to bend the law." The trial lawyers' reputation was damaged even more than before the 1994 election. Davis Carr, a defense lawyer for business in Mobile, Alabama, made a connection between the tort reform debate and Hornsby: in a comment in the April 1996 *American Spectator:* "Look at the way punitive damage awards shot up between 1987 and 1994. And look how hard it was to get him [Hornsby] out."

There had been concern that if Hooper were declared the winner of the election, Hornsby's participation in certain cases would be suspect. Parties might ask if his vote should count in their case. However, that never became a serious problem. Even while challenging Hornsby's right to serve as chief justice, the governor and the attorney general had conceded early on that they would accept his participation in cases as valid. This concession was one reason why a specially appointed supreme court later ruled in favor of Hornsby receiving pay for the time he served as chief justice even though he had not been elected.

On 17 November 1997, less than a month after Hooper was sworn in, the Alabama Supreme Court released an opinion that dramatically changed the method courts used in awarding punitive damages. The Court held that juries were required to weigh factors that up to that time had been reserved for review by the judge or the appellate courts after the verdict. In addition, the Court held that punitive awards must be split between the plaintiff and the state general fund, after deducting court costs and attorney fees. This was a dramatic change. I know of no other court in the nation that had ever made such a unilateral change. Legislatures had made such changes through the passage of tort reform legislation but not a court. Many expressed concerns that the Alabama Supreme Court was stepping beyond its proper judicial role and legislating, the same charge it had faced previously. The Alabama Supreme Court later reversed itself as to the punitive award split portion of the opinion, but the case still represented a dramatic change in punitive damage awards in the state.

In December 1997, Hooper presided over several dramatic cases that attempted to rein in some of the class action abuse that had been occurring in Alabama. Another 1997 case involved a man who had complained to Liberty National Insurance Company about a policy on paying benefits to insurers it had recently adopted. The company reversed the policy and reimbursed the man. The man sued anyway, and a Birmingham jury awarded him $5.4 million in punitive damages. The trial judge reduced it to $2.7 million. The Alabama Supreme

Court reversed that award because the plaintiff had failed to present substantial evidence of fraud or bad faith by the insurance company. Immediately upon taking office as chief justice, Hooper also acted vigorously to encourage alternative dispute resolution.

He also presided over the *Foremost* fraud case,[2] which was authored by Justice Houston. I have to explain some history for you first. Not long after being elected chief justice, Hornsby had written a special concurrence in the *Southern States Ford* case,[3] in which he advocated the adoption of the "justifiable reliance" standard in fraud cases. Until that time, Alabama had always used the "reasonable reliance" standard. Under the "reasonable reliance" standard, if you, as a reasonable person, could uncover the fraud, there was no liability for the defrauder. Under the "justifiable reliance" standard, the defrauder only prevailed if the false statement was "so patently and obviously false that he [the customer] must have closed his eyes to avoid the discovery of the truth."

The sanctity of the written contract and the importance of showing evidence of fraud are encouraged by the "reasonable reliance" standard. After Hornsby's special concurrence, in *Southern States Ford*, the Alabama Supreme Court followed his lead and adopted the "justifiable reliance" standard in *Hickox v. Stover*, 551 So. 2d 259 (Ala. 1989). After that case, pandemonium reigned. From the cases that were being filed, it appeared as if plaintiffs were purposely going out into the commercial world, buying things, and then lying about a misrepresentation by the salesman. Could the sales contract be used to clear up who was lying and who was telling the truth? Because the contract was in writing, it couldn't lie. Under "justifiable reliance," plaintiffs simply said that they had never read the contract. That was "justifiable." There was no need to investigate the statement by the salesman unless it was "so obviously false that he [the plaintiff] must have closed his eyes to the truth." Under the "reasonable reliance" standard, the contract settled the question. There it was in black and white. A reasonable person would have read the contract before making the purchase. *Foremost* restored the "reasonable reliance" standard that had been followed in Alabama for 140 years before *Hickox*.

Justice See's comments in his special concurrence in *Foremost* summed up the situation well:

> Under this relaxed standard [justifiable reliance], a jury can permit a buyer, who has negotiated and voluntarily agreed to an express contractual obligation, to escape that obligation based on the mere allegation of a misrepresentation. Weighed against the cost of requiring buyers to act as reasonable citizens, the cost of the experiment with "justifiable reliance" has been too high. Unbound by the terms of their contracts, unimpeded by any prospect of summary judgment, and lured by the promise of gain, plaintiffs have choked the courts with a flood of fraud litigation. This serves as an example of the price paid for severing rights from concomitant responsibilities.

His discussion of responsibility sounded similar to a special writing by Hooper in a case reviewed by the Alabama Supreme Court before Justice See was elected to the court. In that case, Hooper had written and shown to the other justices his objection to the justifiable reliance standard, arguing that it seemed to violate the sanctity of contract. Plaintiffs bore no responsibility for their contractual agreements, and it was doing away with the whole concept of a written contract.

Justice Almon stated that he had always disapproved of *Hickox*. He had concurred in that case for another reason. Justice Shores was very candid in her remarks about the supreme court's past actions:

> [The court's] adoption of the more subjective justifiable reliance standard may have allowed careless victims of fraud to reach a jury with their claims. It may also have encouraged victims of fraud to avoid discovering potential fraud when the fraud could have been discovered by checking oral representations against the documents memorializing the transaction. It may even, as has been suggested, have encouraged people to falsely accuse another of misrepresenting the facts, in order to

> bring a lawsuit. It is reprehensible to deliberately mis-
> represent material facts in order to cheat another. It is
> equally reprehensible to lie in order to bring a lawsuit.
> The law can tolerate neither.

She specifically admitted that the court had made a mistake.

After the case ended and Hooper had been sworn in as chief justice, there was the aftermath. Governor Fob James introduced proposed tort reform legislation in the legislature each year after his election in 1994, but without success. The Alabama Senate Judiciary Committee bottled up the reform and never let it out for a vote. The Chairman of the Judiciary Committee, Roger Bedford, had a lawsuit pending against Connecticut Mutual Life Insurance Co. at the time the tort reform legislation was being considered. Bedford had hired Jere Beasley to represent him in the case. Bedford was also Jeff Sessions' democratic opponent in the 1996 U.S. Senate race. After remand of the *BMW* case by the U.S. Supreme Court, the Alabama Supreme Court began to drastically reduce punitive damage awards. *Foremost* removed the drastic effect that "justifiable reliance" had in expanding fraud actions in Alabama. Chief Justice Hooper's opinion was that tort reform had arrived by way of the courts. If the Alabama Legislature had passed tort reform legislation, he probably would have upheld it, but he was glad to see the courts were not waiting for that event to happen.

Hooper's lawyers had fought a critical legal battle for the democratic process. They had taken a case that most lawyers would not have touched with a ten-foot pole, and they had filed an amazing number of emergency appeals in less than a year's time. They found that having a conservative republican administration could be problematic. After Joe Whatley had successfully challenged Alabama's appellate judge election system and Jimmy Evans had worked up the settlement, he and the other lawyers involved went to federal court to have the attorney fees worked out. Because these lawyers had sued the state, the state was required to pay the attorney fees. Whatley asked for $350 per hour. The others asked for comparable amounts. Now, when Bert Jordan and the others wanted to be paid $275 per hour, the State balked. The total tab came to over $1 million. Actually the first one in the administration to complain was Lucy Baxley, the Democratic State Treasurer, whose election was also delayed by the litigation. The state had paid lawyers large fees in the appellate court settlement case and another case that mandated a more even racial balance at two predominately black colleges. As Bert Jordan pointedly said in a 23 November 1995 *Montgomery Advertiser* article: "I don't remember her complaining about these fees being paid then. Why hasn't she complained about it before now?"

Of course, when Hooper's lawyers filed suit in federal court, the democrats were in charge, including Jimmy Evans. Now, the republican governor and attorney general felt wronged that the state should have to pay for what Evans and Hornsby's lawyers had done because upon entry into office, the Attorney General and Governor had almost immediately reversed Evans' policy and sided with Hooper in his fight to not have illegitimate absentee ballots counted. Bill Pryor, the deputy attorney general in charge of the case for the State, said that the attorneys who had drawn out the case—Joe Whatley, Bruce McKee, Sam Heldman, Clay Alspaugh, and Jack Drake—should be partially responsible for Hooper's legal bills. He said, "The real wrongdoers in this case are getting off scot-free." Hooper told the *Advertiser* that his lawyers had no choice but to bill the state: "Because of what was done before Jeff [Sessions] got here we were just left strung up." Governor James made a controversial accusation against the Alabama Supreme Court and Judge Reese. He said that they "tried to take the election away from those who voted." When asked by a caller to his radio show about a lawsuit against the judges for the $1 million in attorney fees, he responded: "When judges promulgate an obvious scheme directly contrary to the statutes and what has been the practice for many years, that's a different matter." He added that it would be reasonable for the judges to pay the attorney fees: "It was a scheme. I don't see why not. It caused me mental anguish."

After the 1994 elections, there occurred a mass exodus

from the Alabama Democratic party to the Alabama Republican party. About thirteen elected officials who were members of the party defected in 1995 alone, followed by ten state judges in Birmingham who all switched on one day in January 1996. Actually this mass conversion began before the Hooper-Hornsby case ended. Many legislators and local county officials switched parties. Justice Houston indicated he would run for reelection to the Alabama Supreme Court in 1998 as a member of the Republican party as a direct result of what he saw as election shenanigans by the Democrats. A Court of Criminal Appeals Judge named "Bucky" McMillan switched to the Republican party in December 1995. Surprisingly, in 1997 Secretary of State Jim Bennett switched from the Democratic party to the Republican. In 1996 four appellate court seats were up for election—two on the Alabama Court of Criminal Appeals, one on the Alabama Court of Civil Appeals, and one on the Alabama Supreme Court. The incumbents on the Court of Civil Appeals and the Supreme Court ran for reelection. The seats on the Court of Criminal Appeals were seats left open by retiring judges. All four Republicans who ran for those seats won. Without question, the massive conversion from Democrat to Republican was largely due to the 1994 Republican victories on the national and the state level. It is possible that if Hooper had lost the absentee ballot fight, no one would have wanted to invest the kind of money necessary to successfully finance a Republican statewide campaign for an appellate court seat. There is no question that, next to the gains by Republicans in federal elections in 1994, Hooper's win in the 1994 chief justice election conflict did more than any other single event in Alabama to drive conservative Democrats into the Republican party and help Republicans win statewide court races. The trial lawyers had been right about one thing. If they failed to defeat Hooper in 1994, the potential for conservative judges to be elected would advance rapidly. After 1994, Democrats began to advocate a change from the election method of choosing judges.

There were other strange events that occurred after the case ended. Judge Joseph Phelps, the judge who initially granted a TRO that stopped the counting of the votes by Bennett, was killed in a one-vehicle accident the year after Hooper's victory. Not long after that, retired Supreme Court Justice "Red" Jones died when he fell off the roof of his boathouse. We were told that Jones wrote the absentee ballot decision even though he was not shown as voting in that case. Justice Jones, though retired, was still writing opinions for the court after his retirement. Joe Espy did not stay as actively involved in the case after it went to federal court. He let someone else do that work. Judge Reese was up for reelection in 1996; to the surprise of many, he was reelected to office. Al Agricola joined the Birmingham firm of Bert Jordan and Glenn Murdock that had lead the litigation on Hooper's behalf, and his Montgomery office became that firm's Montgomery branch. That firm went on to represent Guy Hunt in his successful quest for a pardon from the Alabama Board of Pardons and Parole. Hornsby's executive secretary, Ollie Ingram, went to work for Bill Gray, Governor James' legal advisor, in the early part of October 1995. In 1996, Jeff Sessions ran for Howell Heflin's senate seat and won. Governor James appointed Bill Pryor attorney general to replace Sessions. Pryor was the attorney general's point man in the Hooper case.

What about the four justices who voted to count the absentee ballots? Justices Almon and Shores decided to retire when their terms ended in January, 1999. In 1996, Harold See again ran for a seat on the Alabama Supreme Court against Justice Ingram, one of the four supreme court justices who voted to count the absentee ballots back in 1994. Justice Ingram used the same TV production company used by Hornsby in 1994. Hank Sheinkopf, a New York media consultant, ran the company. PBS did a show about political ads that included an interview with him. He proudly admitted that he ran rabid campaign ads because he thought those about whom he ran the ads were despicable. PBS even showed Hornsby doing some cuts for one of his "feel-good" commercials. Ingram ran several TV ads—one compared Harold See and his views to that of a skunk, complete with video of a skunk; another raised reckless, even false, allegations of adultery and wife battering by Harold See with respect to his first wife. See won by over 88,000 votes, way too many votes for anyone to steal. Hooper's razor thin win in 1994 by 262 votes turned into a landslide win for See in 1996. Governor James appointed Rusty Johnston, one of Hooper's "Patrick Henry" lawyers, to a circuit judge seat in Mobile in 1997. In the latter part of 1997, the Mississippi Valley Title Insurance case against Hooper was rejected by a special supreme court consisting of retired circuit court judges.

Reginald Southall, the independent candidate for County Commission who received over 90% of his votes through absentee ballots, and David Wright, prevented an extended trial and saved the cost of attorney fees by settling the lawsuit filed by Wright. A trial was scheduled for late January 1996, a year into the term for that County Commission seat. The settlement allowed Southall to serve as Wilcox County Commissioner for two years of the four-year term, then Wright would finish out the last two years of that term. In the Democratic Primary of June 1998, Southall ran for County Commission again. He lost and the other two candidates headed for a runoff. He filed a challenge of the election with the Wilcox County Democratic Executive Committee.

Jeff Sessions, the Alabama Attorney General, indicted Sandra Henderson, the absentee ballot manager for Wilcox County who would not allow the republican poll watchers to challenge absentee ballots on 8 November 1994. The indictment charged her with "willfully refusing to perform duties as to absentee voters." After the judge told the prosecutor that he had proven she broke the letter of the law, he acquitted her. The maximum punishment she could have received under Alabama law was a $100 fine.

This indictment came not long after Sessions and federal authorities had begun an investigation into complaints of voting practices. He subpoenaed election records from Perry, Wilcox, Greene and Talladega counties. J.L. Chestnut, the attorney for Hornsby, who had done his best to prevent Hooper from receiving the 100 votes mistakenly left out of the counting in Dallas County, expressed his concerns about the investigation: "Jeff Sessions is back at it again with a racist investigation." The following comment represents his respect for the highest law enforcement officer in the State: "I have no intention of voluntarily complying with anything from Jeff Sessions." He was the one who was concerned that the correction of that 100-vote mistake for Hooper would disfranchise black voters.

Other Greene County residents did not share his viewpoint. The Greene County Circuit Clerk, Johnny Knot, pointed out that all three of those served with arrest warrants in Wilcox County were white. Mrs. Knott said she is a friend of Chestnut's but that she believes an investigation was needed in Greene County to see if fraud really happened. The Greene County Tax Assessor, John Kennard, who is black, said, "I applaud Mr. Sessions and I will do all I can to help him in this investigation. Something needs to be done to end corrupt voting practices in Greene County and maybe this will do it."

Not long after Mrs. Henderson received notice of the indictment in a telephone call from the attorney general's office, Prince Arnold, the black sheriff of Wilcox County, arrested John Grods and issued a warrant for Russell Campbell. He charged them with disorderly conduct on 8 November 1994. John Grods and Birmingham lawyer Russell Campbell were the republican poll watchers who had alleged that Sandra Henderson had not allowed them to properly challenge absentee ballots. Camden lawyer Andrew Cromer commented on the arrest of Grods: "It's retribution, no other way to describe it. John Grods is one of the mildest men you'd ever want to meet. There's no way he could have done the things he is accused of doing." According to the Advertiser, Sheriff Arnold said that Grods and Campbell were nuisances throughout the day when the absentee ballots were being counted.

Russell Campbell had listed in an affidavit fifty reasons why he had challenged the ballots. One of those reasons was that he found sample ballots urging voters to support Democratic candidates stacked on a counter in Sheriff Arnold's office. When he asked the sheriff to remove them, he was told to "get on outta here." Even though Campbell had written authorization to be in the room where the ballots were being counted, he said that Willie Powell, the Circuit Clerk and Henderson's employer, "began yelling and screaming 'get out of here, you've no business being in here, I don't care what kind of paper you have.' "

Other prosecutions were more successful. In August 1997, in Wilcox County, Juanita and Doris Mason, a mother and a daughter, plead guilty to illegal absentee voting, a misdemeanor offense. The prosecutions continued into 1997 and 1998. Both women were sentenced to 12-month suspended prison sentences and ordered to serve two years on probation. The evidence showed that the two women collected information from friends and relatives in the Arlington community. They used the information to fill out affidavits for absentee ballots.

In 1997, Greene County employee Connie Tyree and Greene County Commissioner Frank "Pinto" Smith of Greene County were also convicted of voter fraud. The evidence showed that a briefcase with nearly 100 absentee ballots was brought to the Eutaw Community Center just before the 1994 general election. Tyree, one of Smith's chief election assistants, instructed people to fill out absentee ballots. The *Montgomery Advertiser* reported that none of those filling out the ballots in "assembly line" fashion were the actual voters. The voters whose names were on the ballots found out later that their names had been forged on the ballots. The defense counsel, Collins Pettaway, argued that ignorance of the law was a legitimate excuse in this case. The Montgomery Advertiser reported "Spiver" Whitney Gordon saying in February 1997: "You can prosecute the hell out of us, but we're ready to go to jail without bail, we're going to come back." I assume he was attempting to sound like Martin Luther King, Jr. Minnie Robertson, a black resident of Greene County, said, "If you do something wrong, you should expect to pay the price. They should have thought of what they were doing before they did it."

The Attorney General's Office under Bill Pryor's leadership assisted the U.S. Attorney in prosecuting six others in Greene County in February 1998. Two of those six were quite prominent—Eutaw (Greene County Seat) Councilman "Spiver" Whitney Gordon, a fairly powerful politician in West Alabama, and Greene County Commissioner Garria Spencer. That case was still pending at the time this book was being printed. Supporters of the six went to Washington, D.C. in June 1998 and complained to Attorney General Janet Reno about the prosecutions.

In the 2 June 1998 primary election, the voters of Greene County cast only 147 absentee ballots. That was a drastic reduction from the over 1,400 cast in the primary election of 1994. Instead of voters staying home, even more Greene County residents went to the polls in 1998 than they did in 1994. Absentee ballots were lower in number all across the state in the 1996 elections, everywhere except Perry County. Those who had claimed that prosecuting voter fraud would keep the legitimate voter at home threatened to travel all the way to Washington, D.C. to complain to the president about Louis Freeh handling those prosecutions. They complained that the FBI was using "Gestapo tactics" in their voter fraud investigation. Perhaps the opposite of intimidation of the legitimate voters had occurred. It appears that once the residents of Greene County realized that fraudulent votes would not be tolerated, they felt confident that their vote *would* count.

Everything Hooper had argued during the election was proven after the election. He had continually said that the Alabama Constitution required that "the judicial [department] shall never exercise legislative powers; to the end that it may be a government of laws and not of men." His own case had shown the dangers of the judiciary's attempts to rewrite the law—it threatened the very democratic process itself. Yet, Hooper had triumphed over such a threat and preserved something very important for Alabama.

The lawyers ignored the law to obtain their goal, portrayed their opposition as evil incarnate, used the courts and the judges to whom they had given campaign contributions to overcome the democratic process, and used every trick in their playbook to obtain victory while ignoring what was best for the state of Alabama.

The judges, those entrusted with interpreting the law and providing a consistent precedent, had become politicized. But they had not become politicized in the way opponents of the popular election of judges argue. They did not kowtow to the electorate when they ruled that unwitnessed ballots should be counted. The polls and the newspaper articles and the opinions of the man on the street told those justices to vote to not count those disputed votes. If they were politicized, it was not based on the fact that they would face reelection. They were wedded to a certain philosophical position. Some would argue they were wedded to the big money trial lawyer interests. No matter what the motives, the threat of not being reelected, a threat that was great in this particular case, did not prevent four Alabama Supreme Court Justices from voting in a way that almost guaranteed they would not be reelected. Therefore, one cannot argue that popular election caused that particular decision. Those justices followed their own light in that case. If judges and lawyers have a tendency toward arrogance, it is a natural outgrowth of the entire legal/jurisprudential culture, which often, either knowingly or unknowingly, inculcates an elitist mentality in the judge-trainees of our society, the lawyers.

The line between the liberal and the conservative is vague sometimes. There must be a clear definition, a line that distinguishes between a good judge and a bad judge. I don't know if the terms "liberal" and "conservative" do justice to the problems we face in the judiciary. Faithful judges, judges who will not take a reward, judges who love the law of God and are humble in the face of legislative enactments, are good judges. It will, however, be hard to find such men as long as an "elite" clique, schooled by an educational system dominated by those who believe in judicial autonomy as opposed to judicial independence, is the only pot from which to choose our future judges.

Notes

1. King James Bible, Romans 8:28.

2. Foremost Insurance Company, Grand Rapids, *Michigan v. Parham*, 693 So. 2d 409 (Ala. 1997).

3. *Southern States Ford v. Proctor*, 541 So. 2d 1081, 1087-92 (Ala. 1989).

We welcome comments from our readers. Feel free to write to us at the following address:

Editorial Department
Prescott Press
P.O. Box 53788
Lafayette, LA 70505

More Good Books from Prescott Press

The Eagle's Claw
Christians and the IRS
by Steve Richardson

The Eagle's Claw, based on the author's experience as a CPA defending Christians and Christian organizations from IRS attacks, helps Christians understand the IRS. The IRS makes mistakes, sometimes huge mistakes. Richardson provides appropriate defensive tools to fight back. Some of these attacks were unjustified and some, in his view, were illegal and designed to limit the actions and activities of the Church in our society. In fact, the author states, some of these IRS attacks appear to be motivated by a partisan political agenda.

ISBN 1-56384-128-2

The Slash Brokers
by Jeff S. Barganier

The gruesome but overwhelming evidence is in. The Chinese Communists are secretly involved in the lucrative harvesting of human body parts and fetus consumption.

ISBN 1-56384-150-9

Communism, the Cold War, & the FBI Connection
by Herman O. Bly

One out of four people in the world live under Communist rule. If Americans think they are safe from the "red plague," they'd better think again, says author Herman Bly. He will reveal what he's learned in years of counter-intelligence work, and how our country is being lulled into a false sense of security.

ISBN 1-56384-149-5

===

Dark Cures
Have Doctors Lost Their Ethics?
by Paul deParrie

When traditional ethics were the standard in the field of medicine, one could take comfort in the knowledge that doctors and medical institutions put the health and well-being of the patient above all else. Today, however, pagan ethics have pervaded the professions once properly call "the healing arts, " turning doctors into social engineers and petty gods, and patients into unwitting guinea pigs. The results of this unwise change in direction are horrific and often hard to believe, but also, all too real.

ISBN 1-56384-099-5

Spiritual Warfare
The Invisible Invasion
by Thomas R. Horn

Thomas Horn illustrates through fresh and powerful new insights that while demonic activity has frequently been overlooked, the close collaboration between social architects and ancient evil powers has at times allowed demons to control the machine of world governments, and the moral and social trends of a nation.

ISBN 1-56384-129-0

One Last Call
A Guide for the
Achievement of Lasting Peace
by Donnell L. Harris

One Last Call is a prescription for action to make a better future for ourselves and the generations to come. It is also an invitation to join a serious movement of peace, which will carry us into the 21st century. Now is the time to return order and vitality to our social health. For too long, the social body has been under attack, eaten away by the corrosive cancers of chauvinism, bigotry, prejudice, and hate. You cannot legislate the cure. The new millennium offers a great opportunity for a new start.

ISBN 0-933451-39-3

Make Yourself Ready
Preparing to Meet the King
by Harland Miller

Instead of trying to convince readers that one doctrinal position is more valid than another, *Make Yourself Ready* was written to help Christians prepare for the Second Coming. By analyzing Old Testament events, Miller explains how we can avoid Lucifer's age-old deceptions. Scripturally sound and eminently inspiring, *Make Yourself Ready* will create newfound excitement for the return of the Hope of Heaven and show readers how to become truly ready for Judgment Day.

ISBN 0-933451-36-9

Christian Revolution: Practical Answers to Welfare and Addiction
by Arthur Pratt

In *Christian Revolution: Practical Answers to Welfare and Addiction,* Pratt demonstrates that real social and political change starts with radical honesty about the nature of the problem and how we see it. He has called for Congressional action based on his own scientific evidence of what really works in the treatment of addiction. He affirms a renewed faith in Jesus Christ as the inspiration for such action, seeing the church as a servant of our country, not a mentor.

ISBN 1-56384-143-6